WOMEN OF
BLOOMSBURY

WOMEN OF
BLOOMSBURY

VIRGINIA

VANESSA
—AND—
CARRINGTON

MARY ANN CAWS

ROUTLEDGE
New York • London

First published in 1990
Published in paperback in 1991 by

Routledge
An imprint of Routledge, Chapman and Hall, Inc.
29 West 35 Street
New York, NY 10001

Published in Great Britain by

Routledge
11 New Fetter Lane
London EC4P 4EE

Copyright © 1991 by Routledge, Chapman and Hall, Inc.

Printed in the United States of America

Library of Congress Cataloging in Publication Data
Caws, Mary Ann.
    The women of Bloomsbury / Mary Ann Caws.
      p.   cm.
    Includes bibliographical references.
    ISBN 0-415-90134-0;   ISBN 0-415-90398-X (PB)
    1. Bloomsbury (London, England)—Biography. 2. Women—England—
Bloomsbury (London)—Biography. 3. Woolf, Virginia, 1882–1941.
4. Bell, Vanessa, 1897–1961. 5. Carrington, Dora de Houghton,
1893–1932. 6. Bloomsbury group. 7. Art and literature—England—
History—20th century. 8. Novelists, English—20th century—
Biography. 9. Women artists—England—Biography. 10. London
(England)—Biography. I. Title.
DA685.B65C39 1990
942.1'42—dc20   89-24273
                                                     CIP

British Library Cataloguing in Publication data also available.

for Peg, Patricia, and Sarah Bird; and for my
grandmother, who dared to be an artist

Contents

Acknowledgments

I would like to thank all who encouraged me with this book, its multiple and its triple interweaving; Frances Partridge, for her warm and continuing generosity toward my relations with Carrington and her work—but also for her felt presence, actual, as well as implicit and explicit among these great women of Bloomsbury; Catherine Carrington and the late Noel Carrington, for their gracious reception of me and my questions; George ("Dadie") Rylands, for his welcome, his graciousness, and especially his wit and warmth, all of which brought me closer to Carrington, in person as well as in painting; Quentin Bell, for his generous and helpful exchange of letters with me over a long period, in particular for his comments on Vanessa's and Duncan's art, helping me see another side to their views; Angelica Garnett, for her friendly and neighborly aid; and especially both Quentin Bell and Angelica Garnett for their permission to quote their mother's letters and reproduce her paintings; Henrietta Garnett, for permission to reproduce Duncan Grant's paintings and to quote his letters; Olivier Bell, for her patience; Michael Holroyd, for his counsel and encouragement; the curators of the archives in which, now retrospectively, I seem to have spent a good part of my recent life—Michael Halls of King's College Modern Archives, Adrian Glew of the Tate Gallery Archives, Cathy Henderson of the Humanities Research Center, and Lola Szladits of the Berg Collection of the New York Public Library. All quotations from Virginia Woolf refer to the standard editions of her works published by Harcourt Brace Jovanovich.

I want, in particular, to thank Sally Brown of the British Library, for her willingness to share her interests with me; Sandra Lummis, Joanna Mason, and Clarissa Roche for their generous cooperation; Tony Bradshaw, for his welcome, and his repeated help; Gloria Loomis, for her enthusiasm and effort at some crucial points; Bill Germano, for his faith in this project ahatching, and his suggestions; Diane Gibbons, for her sensitive editing; and the Getty Center for the History of Art and the Humanities for offering me its hospitality and assistance during my tenure as a Getty Scholar in 1989–90.

I am happily indebted to my friends for their continuing support in the many phases of this endeavor, which itself concerns, in large part, an intelligent companionship: to my lifelong friend Sarah Bird Wright, for inviting me to stay in Monk's House, and for her unflaggingness; to Patricia Terry, for being there; to Patrick Cullen, for being here; to Arlyne Landesman, with whom I first spoke about Carrington; to my colleagues and friends near and far for discussing Virginia Woolf with me: Louise De Salvo, Jane Marcus, Brenda Silver, and in particular, Patricia Laurence, for her comments about, and her faith in reciprocity; to my students and friends in the Dartmouth School of Theory and Criticism; to my colleague Nancy Miller, for her lively, cheering, and ongoing ideas, and her editorial acumen; to Baylis Thomas, for his psychological insights, his specific advice, and his wider wisdom; to Noel Perrin, for giving me confidence, about writing and perceiving; to Carolyn Heilbrun, for walking and talking with me, when this project was beginning to take its shape, and for her sustaining friendship. I wish I could thank Roger Fry. I can thank my sister for teaching me only good things about sisters. To all of these, I am especially grateful.

New York, 1990

Cast of Characters

Virginia (Stephen) Woolf (1882–1941): a writer (*To the Lighthouse; The Waves; Three Guineas*) and the sister of Vanessa (Stephen) Bell (1879–1961), daughters of Leslie Stephen (1832–1904) and Julia Duckworth (1846–95); married to Leonard Woolf (1880–1969), a writer (*Downhill all the Way*).

Vanessa Bell (1879–1961): a painter and the sister of Virginia Woolf; married to Clive Bell (1881–1964); Roger Fry (1866–1934) and then Duncan Grant (1885–1975) are her lovers. Her children are Quentin (b. 1910), Julian (1908–1937), and Angelica (Bell) Garnett (b. 1918).

Carrington (Dora Carrington) (1893–1932): a painter and the companion of Lytton Strachey (1880–1932); Mark Gertler (1891–1938), Gerald Brenan (Edward Fitzgerald Brenan, 1894–1986), and Bernard Penrose ("Beakus") are her lovers, and Ralph Partridge (1894–1960) her husband; Ralph later marries Frances Marshall (1900–).

Roger Fry: a critic (*Vision and Design: Transformations*), a painter, and the father (by Helen Coombe Fry) of Pamela (Fry) Diamand (1902–1986); the lover of Vanessa Bell, and then the lover of Helen Anrep (1885–1965).

Clive Bell: a critic (*Art; Since Cézanne*) and the husband of Vanessa Bell; lover of Mary Hutchinson.

Duncan Grant: a painter, and the lover of Lytton Strachey, Maynard Keynes, Adrian Stephen, David ("Bunny") Garnett, George Bergen, and Paul ("Don") Roche; lifelong companion of Vanessa Bell.

Mark Gertler: a painter, fellow student of Dora Carrington at the Slade, one of whose lovers he was.

Gerald Brenan: a writer (*A Life of One's Own*; *Personal Record*), who lived for many years in Yegen, in the mountains of Spain; a lover of Dora Carrington.

Lytton Strachey: a writer (*Queen Victoria: Eminent Victorians*), brother of James Strachey, Freud's English translator, and the lover of Duncan Grant, Roger Senhouse, etc.; Dora Carrington's lifelong companion.

Ralph Partridge: husband of Carrington, and the third member of the Lytton-Carrington-Partridge ménage; subsequently, husband of Frances Partridge, née Marshall.

Frances Marshall: a writer (*A Pacifist's War: Love in Bloomsbury*), and the companion of Ralph Partridge, then his wife.

Bernard ("Beakus") *Penrose*: a sailor, and a lover of Dora Carrington, ten years his senior.

supporting cast: Alix and Julia Strachey, Stephen Tomlin (Tommy), Augustus John and Dorelia ("Dodo") John, Henrietta Bingham, David Garnett, Olive and Annie the cooks, various Bloomsbury characters (such as "the Stracheys and Davidsons and Mortimers," as Vanessa refers to them), and Belle, Carrington's white mare given to her by Lytton in 1926.

Abbreviations

VB Frances Spalding, *Vanessa Bell*. London: Macmillan, 1983.

Vanessa Bell and Virginia Woolf

SA Diane Filby Gillespie, *The Sister's Arts: The Writing and Painting of Virginia Woolf and Vanessa Bell*. Syracuse: Syracuse University Press, 1988.

Gerald Brenan

GB Personal Record: 1920–1972. New York: Knopf, 1975.

Dora Carrington

HB D. C. Patride (sic): Her Book. Unpublished document, British Library.

DG Dora Carrington: Letters and Extracts from Her Journals, ed. David Garnett. Oxford: Oxford University Press, 1972.

CL Gretchen Gerzina. *Carrington: A Life of Dora Carrington*. London: John Murray, 1989; New York: Norton, 1989.

NC Noel Carrington. *Carrington: Paintings, Drawings and Decorations*. Oxford: Oxford Polytechnic Press, 1978.

Roger Fry

RFL Letters of Roger Fry, ed. Denys Sutton. London: Chatto and Windus, 1972. (2 vols.)

RF Frances Spalding, *Roger Fry: Art and Life*. Berkeley: University of California Press, 1980.

Angelica Bell Garnett

DK Deceived with Kindness: A Bloomsbury Childhood. London: Hogarth, 1984.

Duncan Grant

T Douglas Blair Turnbaugh, *Duncan Grant and the Bloomsbury Group: An Illustrated Biography*. Secaucus, N.J.: Lyle Stuart, 1987.

Virginia Woolf

MB Moments of Being: Unpublished Autobiographical Writings. New York and London: Harcourt Brace, 1976.

MFS previously unpublished letters of Virginia Woolf, in *Modern Fiction Studies*, Summer 1984; col. 1, 30, no. 2, pp. 175–202.

NF New Feminist Essays on Virginia Woolf, ed. Jane Marcus. Lincoln: University of Nebraska Press, 1981.

QB Quentin Bell. *Virginia Woolf: A Biography*. London and New York: Harcourt Brace, 1972. (in 2 vols. in Great Britain)

RN Virginia Woolf's Reading Notebooks, ed. Brenda Silver. Princeton: Princeton University Press, 1983.

TCL Virginia Woolf: special issue, *Twentieth Century Literature*, vol. 1, 25, Fall/Winter 1979; especially Brenda Silver, ed., "Anon," and "The Reader."

VWL Letters of Virginia Woolf, ed. Nigel Nicolson and Joanne Trautmann. New York and London: Harcourt Brace, 1975–1980. (6 vols.: 1888–1941)

VWD Journal of Virginia Woolf, ed. Olivier Bell. New York and London: Harcourt Brace, 1977–1984. (5 vols., 1915–1941)

VW Lyndall Gordon, *Virginia Woolf: A Writer's Life.* Oxford: Oxford University Press, 1984.

Bloomsbury, Art

SW Simon Watney. *English Post-Impressionism.* London: Cassell, Studio Vista, 1980.

Unpublished

RF/VB; VB/RF Letters of Roger Fry and Vanessa Bell. (With Fry papers and Charleston papers at Tate Gallery Archives, nos. 8010.8.1–453, Vanessa to Roger; nos. 8010.590–1121, Roger to Vanessa; copy at King's College, Cambridge, in Modern Archives, under Charleston papers: KCL.

VB/VW; VW/VB Letters of Vanessa Bell and Virginia Woolf. (In Woolf Papers, Berg Collection, New York Public Library)

VB/JB Letters of Virginia Woolf to Julian Bell (KCL).

CM/JB Letters of Charles Mauron to Julian Bell (KCL).

DG/VB Letters of Duncan Grant to Vanessa Bell (nos. 8010.5.20–1150, in Tate Gallery Archives, Charleston papers).

LS/DC; DC/LS Letters of Lytton Strachey and Dora Carrington. (In British Library, Strachey collection)

DC/GB; GB/DC Letters of Dora Carrington and Gerald Brenan. (In Harry Ransom Humanities Research Center, University of Texas, Austin).

DC/MG; DC/CN Letters of Dora Carrington, Mark Gertler, and C.A. Nevinson. (Carrington Letters, Humanities Research Center, University of Texas, Austin)

DC/RL; DC/SS Letters of Dora Carrington to Rosamond Lehmann and Sebastian Sprott, King's College, Cambridge.

N.B. When the collection from which the letter comes is obvious, with the recipient and the writer clearly stated, it has not seemed necessary to repeat the appropriate initials in every case (e.g. "In a letter to Lytton of July 25, Carrington says" is plainly from the collection referred to as DC/LS).

All is well. My love, my love.

Carrington, to Lytton
(Some Tuesday in 1917: DC/LS)

Oh but Carrington we have to live and be ourselves.

Virginia to Carrington
March 2, 1932 (VWL: V, 28)

Do you think we have the same pair of eyes, only different spectacles? I rather think I am more nearly attached to you than sisters should be. Why is it I never stop thinking of you . . . ? Lord knows I cant say what it means to me to come into the room and find you sitting there.

Virginia to Vanessa
August 12, 1937 (VWL: VI, 158)

❦ 1 ❦
Personal Criticism:
A Matter of Choice

. . . to suggest, not to conclude.
Virginia, about *Three Guineas,*
October 28, 1938 (MFS, p. 199)

Is it not rare for anyone to encounter another person by
the side of whom she is happy living and working? By whose
side her work itself seems to have some point, and in relation
to whom—in spite of whatever difficulty, jealousy, envy, dis-
accord, boredom, and absences mental and physical there
may be—her life makes more sense than it would seem to
otherwise?

I think so, and it is my conviction along those lines that
has led me to write this tale of three. Three loves and lives
and works, each of which may appear to be in some ways
odd, or to be constructed about an unusual situation, may
appear to be tinged with madness on the one hand, and, on
the other, with an unhappiness not immediately rejected, a
conscious incompleteness not instantly refused, and a kind
of fearful self-disrespect, a drastic undervaluing of the self.
The situations were not always chosen, of course, as in the
case of Virginia (her sexual frigidity, her not having children),
and no less in the other two cases. For one does not choose
one's inclinations, neither the model of bisexuality (as in the
cases of Virginia and Carrington), nor that of falling in love
with someone who cannot fully love one back, for reasons
again of inclination (thus, neither Vanessa nor Carrington,
perhaps, could really have chosen not to have their primary
loves be men who could not fully love them) . . . So it is not so
much the choice I want to look at as the resulting complexity
of situation, and the particular relation to work and living that
must be closely related to that very complexity.

I have tried to understand and evaluate the tempera-

1

ments of these women artists, together with the representa-
tions they made of themselves and the lives they chose to lead:
that is, their self-representations. I have stated my opinion
openly about the decisions they made, and their being worth
the unmistakable pain of the results: I have chosen, in relation to them, not to condemn but rather to cherish.

Above all I intend this to be an example of personal
criticism as I am trying to work that concept through. Personal criticism as I intend it has to do with a willing, knowl-
edgeable, outspoken involvement on the part of the critic
with the subject matter, and an invitation extended to the
potential reader to participate in the interweaving and construction of the ongoing conversation this criticism can be,
even as it remains a text. The experience is open and fluid, as
is the transcription of the implicit conversation. "We are the
music, we are the thing itself," says a character in Virginia
Woolf's *The Waves;* readers, critic, and subject here can echo
that belief, according to which they work.

All three of these women artists were at once witnesses
to the intellectual and artistic Bloomsbury community, and
its creators: they play an essential role in being and creating
quite exactly what they are remarking upon, and in so doing,
reinforce the ideas of flux and blurring of contours that the
continuing reciprocity of my text—this mosaic of interrelated
parts, artistic and personal—wants to address and itself to
participate in. I like to think of this as what personal criticism
aims most urgently at creating and recreating: that very
participation in the subject seen and written about, solicit-
ing, quietly or openly, the reader's own views. I see this as a
three-way concern, and prefer to think of writing *along with,*
rather than writing on, or about . . .

As the art of personal criticism requires a willingness—
an eagerness, even—to be more than a simple observer of a
subject, so the act of personal criticism requires a certain
intensity in the lending of oneself, in the giving of a role to
the past of the artist as to the textual present and the possible
future, to the elements inside and outside the mind, unafraid
as they are of mingling. It is around such an experiential
generosity of community that characters in and out of the
text may find themselves grouped, reading together, seeing

together. Such criticism is the deliberate opposite of a cool science, but is not in disregard of fact; it is composed of an unshakeable belief in involvement and in coherence, in warmth and in relation.

As an advocate of this kind of personal criticism and life-telling, I feel deeply obliged, in my own relation to it and of it—bound both by my project and my most fundamental belief—to make an open statement about my involvement in the issues aroused. Towards our understanding of one well-known writer and two less-known figures, this personal advocacy of freedom and unjudgmental evaluation wants to contribute what it can, based on my own intensity of feeling.

This, it seems to me, is no time for standing aside for a distancing appraisal and a rationalizing overview. The issues are, to some extent, still burning, and the problems of presentation—like those of ambivalence, of creation, and of pain—still acute. Those problems, as it is clear, far outdistance any mere discussion of sexuality and its own problematics—frigidity, homosexuality, bisexuality, and so on. All three women had in the beginning some form of sexual relations with the person or persons they most loved, and then those relations ceased: that is the simple statement of the thing, but it only begins the discussion, and only touches the surface of what is really at issue here—the accusations of society against forms of living that seem intrinsically to call forth sadness, to be already at risk because abnormal in the usual sense, and not strictly categorizable.

To write still more drastically in my own name, I would never have known the radical resistance to the forms of living represented by these women had I not so repeatedly experienced the overt and unbridled scorn of many otherwise apparently open-minded people, on both sides of the Atlantic, when I was called upon to speak about the contents and project of this book. The instance of Virginia Woolf, so well-known, would arouse some discussion, some impassioned partisanship, and a fair amount of snide commentary; nothing at all, however, compared to what awaited me when I spoke—in no matter how measured a way—of the ultimate choices made by Vanessa and by Carrington, each giving up the love (or loves) of men considered normal in their relations to women on behalf of an enduring and all-encompassing love for a man considered the opposite. (How could they, didn't they know? What sort of person would love someone who could not . . . and so on.) The reaction to the bisexuality of Carrington, to the homosexuality of Duncan and of Lytton, and to the choices made by Vanessa and Carrington in their living and working arrangements, so as often to overshadow their own creation, were vivid: a raw nerve seems to be touched on here, and this is exactly the kind of issue in which personal criticism as I conceive of, and try to practice it, must venture with the frankest footstep possible.

I have stated in several places in this book my own point of view about these lives: these choices and these situations, however unusual, seem to me in some sense intimately involved with the creativity of these women. The intricate texture of the resulting interweaving of happiness and misery was in no sense invisible in their creations, was, rather, a deepening factor therein. That they should each have found a way of living so very much their own, and so unlike that of others (and also, in large part, of each other), yet (or therefore) so nurturing to their innate intensity is marvelous enough; that they all should have taken their greatest and most profound joy in such a particular mixture of work and solitude, of creation and love and companionship within the idea of work itself, of work and their own radical alterations of mood in regard to it and to life, should preserve Vanessa and Carrington, specifically, from the accusations of negative mindsets like masochism. For the intensity of their reactions and creations triumphantly surpasses what we can, most of us, expect from our living and our creating.

I have wanted to preserve the first impulse and intimacy of this writing. I mean to salute these women as positive if often perplexing beings and not just as glorious eccentrics; as complex and hardworking creators and not just as the interesting inhabitants of an epoch and a group (however ungroupy) we like so much to read about. I have wanted to present—from closer up than any brand of impersonal criticism would suggest or even allow—with love and warmth and respect toward their lives and works, these women of Bloomsbury, with whom, over these years, I have become so personally involved.

Finding a Language, and Making Do

So they say: "This is what happened"; but they do not say what the person was like to whom it happened.
Virginia Woolf, *A Sketch of the Past* (MB, 65)

How can we best speak of what is extraordinary? We can, first, reduce it to a normal or an abnormal model, so that it can be explained, in simple or more complex fashion, given a profile, a name, a handle: the key word here is "reduce," and the unique may well escape us. Or then, we can celebrate it without trying to understand it, give it the name of genius, or *genius neuroticus* (thus justified): this is surely not reductive, nor is it risky—on the other hand, it is not trying anything at all. Or then again, with more difficulty, and at more risk, we can both salute it and attempt, however modestly and incompletely, to understand it, depict it, and appreciate it as and in itself, and as it is self-represented: this calls upon whatever resources we might have, and may call—more urgently still—for developing some we did not know we had. That is in any case, it seems to me, a risk worth taking.

Problematic as the present project is, I would like at least to try to understand and not to misrepresent: that is indeed the principal motivation behind this telling of a tale. For this interwoven story of three women, with its fragments partially braided and sometimes frayed, wants to be a tale about understanding, which necessarily (if implicitly) includes the self writing as well as those written about. What is tried in telling and in understanding must be that self too: no exemptions.

In this case, and from all sides, explanations come forth, hard or easy, but none completely satisfy. The lives and works, celebrated or not, of these three women seem so very exceptional and similar in their temperamental difference from others that it is tempting to offer or repeat reasons that may prove limiting. For example, in the case of Virginia and Vanessa, their childhood abuse and home atmosphere leading to madness or the repetition of painful conditions; a gloomy father, like Leslie Stephen, or an adored and "imprisoned" one, like Samuel Carrington, fettered to and by a Victorian governess-type wife, as Carrington saw it, hating her mother and passionately attached to her father, for whom, it is generally thought, Lytton then was a substitute; the manic-depressive character disorders of the Stephen family on the one hand and the deaths of Julia, the girls' mother, and of Stella, their stepmother, and Thoby their brother; on the other, Carrington's loss of her brother Teddy and the coldness of her mother, and so on. None of the elements is entirely determining, but many seem to hold out some possibilities of a beginning understanding, providing they are granted sufficient complexity in relation to the unique self-representation of each of these women.

One of the major difficulties in the interpretation of such cases is, I think, that the normative (heterosexual, "sane," "lucid," etc.) standard seems to be the point of reference, and thus explanations of reductive sorts may be offered all the more easily, about the "irregularities" of such cases. They do not seem appropriate to me here, and the understanding I would urge is not in response to such a standard. Precisely, Virginia Woolf bent much of her effort toward the blurring of distinction between what is conceived of as "normal" and not, preferring evolution and flexibility and flux to the static and definitional; her generously and openly interrelational impulse is a sure one:—"I think there ought to be a scrambling together of mediums now" (MFS, 186)—and her tolerance of ambiguity seems to me not just admirable but essential. This is a vexed issue, and touches on the one of pain and of its willing acceptance for what may well be a greater good. That intensity of perception which is often responsible for art is not just in evidence here: it is, in truth, the point of the text I have wanted to participate in and to represent as fully as I can.

These women—two bisexuals, two suicides, two complexly oriented artists, each living with a homosexual—fit, it is true, neither the mold of happy wife, happy mother, happy artist in a happy world—unlikely, as well as boring—nor, happily, that of the sick woman, the neurotic creator whose art in some sense depends upon her anguish. Had the latter been the point of view here, a tempting title would have run: "Women, Art, and Pain," with the accent falling not upon art, where I believe it should, but upon the pain. I want to put it elsewhere, and—insofar as the narrative shape is decided by the teller (thus, these women and, in this case, myself)—that is in my temporary power. I want at once to be true to their self-representations, and to point out—as I do in the acknowledgments—the interweaving of these stories as an at least partial witness to the intellectual, passionate, and creating community of which they were a part. As Virginia Woolf says in relation to the writing, and reading, of female texts, they "continue each other." They were extraordinary indeed, and all the more so, in some telling sense, as they were, again in some sense together, telling a different plot from the expected one. They created, and call on us to do so.

It has been pointed out that women have had a noticeably hard time exercising power, even in the telling of their own tales, and certainly those of others. The power of telling, like the urge for non-reductive understanding, is perhaps not just an acquired talent, but also an acquired taste. What enables us to tell the tales of others and to want to understand them as themselves may often be just our own empathetic projections—that has to be clearly seen. But insofar as each narration can help to reveal another angle of the life, and, indeed of living, it is as worth undertaking as life itself. Even if it is just as often, incomplete in itself: for it can be part of a collective recognition, and that is worth everything. We read these lives together, in both senses.

Clearly, I have had to choose my own angle from which to see these three women here, have had to select, among so many others, the details I found most telling for these stories—those that would tell part of the past and perhaps some part of the future, by implication. That would in some sense bear their own compelling witness, helping to integrate—like some at least partial truth—our own vision of the lives and of the art. That would help us to gather, from these three tales, what is unique and what can be read together. Rather than explaining, rather than interpreting, I would prefer to see this endeavor as explicating or unfolding the possibilities of each subject, to the best of my ability.

Virginia Woolf, like Proust, wrote in part to let each reader read the self; the kind of language she was looking for was already in fragments when she found it, and helped remake it, but not in ruins. Self-writing takes a language that will accept the partial, having the spunk to abjure the holistic, in fiction or in any other form. If it irritates what she calls the "steely intellectuals who treat literature as though it were an ingenious picture puzzle, to be fitted accurately together" (VWD: II, 214) and want to push—in a startling endeavor phrased in no less a startling image—their "little horns manfully into facts," perhaps that marks the moment (even as those facts refuse, just as firmly as fictions) for a response that will call upon all our own courage of refusal of such manfullness. And all our courage of style too, including a willing lightness, which does not rule out gravity.

Of the kind of language she finds, and of its form, she says that its symmetry is made "by means of infinite discords, showing all the traces of the mind's passage through the world," showing, that is, not its harmonious agreement with the concord of tradition, but rather what we might call its ongoing effort. What she wants—and what, at its best, this triple tale would choose for itself—is to "achieve in the end, some kind of whole made of shivering fragments; to me this seems the natural process; the flight of the mind" (quoted in QB, I, 138). The tales may seem singular, but the power of telling is a joining one.

❦ 2 ❦
These Working Women

Art and Relations in Bloomsbury

But looking together united them.
Virginia Woolf,
To the Lighthouse, p. 112

Putting these three women creators together—because of the Bloomsbury connection, but even apart from that connection—represents something of a gamble. Within the general atmosphere of the Bloomsbury space, material and mental, imaginary or not, I have wanted to locate the singular particular figures who make up the backbone of this book. Yet the particular fascination of Virginia Woolf, felt increasingly and by so many, as well as by the two other heroines of this story, threatens to swamp any tale when she is placed alongside others. She is strength incarnate, even in her madness, and no less seductive through it.

That is only the first part of the problem; the second concerns the difficulties of comparing writing work and painting work, to say nothing of the differences between painting and the decorative arts. The third, and perhaps the most difficult to get a grasp on, is the essential difference of the patterns of these three lives and works, perceived and real. Virginia's notoriety and way of relating to Leonard and the world outside and within; Vanessa's early marriage to Clive and care of her children and house, then her relations to Roger and to Duncan and to her art, in all its great variety, with its intermittent successes; and finally, Carrington's care-

9

taker setup with, and adoration of Lytton Strachey, her involvement with others and her complicated relation to her more ambitious painting undertaken privately, and almost never exhibited, and to the decorative and domestic arts on which she spent much of her energy.

The three patterns, so drastically different, entail nevertheless two overriding shared concerns: that of each of these women for their work and the responsibilities concomitant with their great talent, and that of their chronic and anguishingly authentic, if sporadically manifested, doubts as to the latter.

Beyond that, the salient points in common between the three are still worth remarking on, from both the obvious and less obvious angles. Virginia and Carrington both committed suicide, one for the unbearable knowledge of recurrent madness, the other for the loss of the man she loved, however ununderstandable that love might have seemed, and still may seem, to onlookers and readers. Vanessa and Virginia, the rival and loving sisters, shared much, including their observing genius and social self-presentations. Virginia and Carrington were both, to some extent, bisexual, although both had only one documented involvement with another woman. Vanessa and Carrington were both artists of exceptional talent, and both were involved in ménages which cannot fail to seem somewhat unusual, each adoring a homosexual man and married to another man, each living in a ménage à (at least) trois, including that adored and to some extent unattainable being, whom both considered to have more talent than themselves—thus the origin of a kind of anguish that finds its redemption in its relation to art, productive and understanding.

Their work

The crux of the matter, as I see it and describe it in the following pages, is—to put it plainly—their own work. Granted, the title of this chapter has more than a slight tinge of irony about it, since the Bloomsbury group is thought of as at least semi-rich and at least semi-idle. Yet in all these three cases, in spite of the domestic arrangements with a modest amount of help at, for example, Monk's House, Asheham and Charleston, Tidmarsh and Ham Spray, the residences, respectively, of Virginia and Leonard, of Vanessa, Clive, and Duncan, and of Lytton, Carrington, and Ralph in their years together; in spite of all the comings and goings to the Continent and elsewhere; in spite of what may seem a relatively social life, the essence of that actual life was, in fact, the work undertaken and cared about. In all three cases, the question of work and necessity of payment emerges with a frequency that might surprise, given the usual picture of Bloomsbury as such a privileged group that the concerns of ordinary folk were of little importance.

Repeatedly, all three women find themselves relating work and reward: Virginia having to write reviews, for years, when she would rather write novels; Vanessa bothered, in 1911, for instance, that while Roger Fry made 277 pounds by the huge success of his Post-Impressionist show, she could barely pay a bill for 26 pounds, and had somehow to justify the expense of maintaining the Asheham house or then just give it up, an eventuality she felt would be catastrophic. When, on August 12, 1912, she has actually sold a picture, to the Contemporary Art Society, it is really, she claims, by accident, for the representatives really came to choose among Duncan's works. Nothing she will ever do, she laments, will ever make any money, will ever contribute to the expense of the house they all live in. Even writing to Virginia, she asks if she might contribute still a few more woodcuts or other illustrations to a recently written book, just to make a few pence more—modesty, she says, causes her to doubt she could actually make the book more appealing, nevertheless . . . (November 22, 1918). And still, many years later, during another exhibit, she points out that, while Duncan has sold most of his pictures, she has sold only two very small ones, so that her financial future continues rocky (May 7, 1926). Vanessa doubts she will ever touch a penny of her "reputed wealth," and teases (not entirely teasingly) that if Virginia gets launched in France, she will be by far the richer of the two. I will never make any money by my painting, repeats Vanessa in her moments of discouragement.

Carrington, with only a small allowance from her inheritance, and in spite of Lytton's wish to help her on his side, finds herself in the necessity of doing more decorations, more inn signs, more of the saleable and commissioned tinsel and glass paintings than she would like to have to; repeatedly, she is pressed to finish painting a trunk or a room panel or a load of tiles, or do some other decorative task, large or small, because she must, and feels time vanishing for what she considers her real art. (In regard to the latter, Carrington found it difficult that Duncan and Vanessa, not seeing what she meant to do in a picture of the Mill at Tidmarsh, "liked not what I tried for, but for something else . . . . they tend to want you to be like them, and not like yourself—which is really the only thing it's worth anyone's while to be" (DC/LS, July 22, 1920). Her struggle for independence is continuous.

Their relations

These three women, each exemplary, in their ultimate difference, of the woman creator's self-evaluation and inner struggle, and each involved with the ongoing art of Bloomsbury, living in their differing ways, call, with some urgency— at least as I hear them—for a re-reading and a re-viewing on their interrelated as well as their individual terms, of themselves and their work.

In the case of the two artists, Vanessa and Carrington, the problem of women and work was in high evidence. Both had studied, at the Slade, with Henry Tonks, a master teacher and a perfect model of non-encouragement: he says, in a letter apparently without sarcasm, that women: "do what they are told, (and) if they don't you will generally find they are a bit cracked. If they become offensive, it may be a sign of love. They improve rapidly from about 16 to 21, then the genius that you have discovered goes off, they begin to take marriage seriously" (quoted in SA, 201). Neither Vanessa nor Carrington could be said to have done what they were told; the case of Virginia in that regard is surely complicated enough. As for marriage, though all three of them went that path, none of the marriages could be said to be exactly conventional. In the case of the two artists, it was scarcely, to greatly understate the case, what most interested them; none of the three took it more seriously than her work.

Each respected the work of the others; that is essential to point out at the beginning. Virginia invited Carrington to do woodcuts for her stories, such as "The Mark on the Wall," and when Pelican rejected them, she was gravely disappointed. "They added greatly to the charm of the work which will look very blank without them," she said (VWL: II, 368), and used Carrington's illustrations for Leonard's story "Three Jews" and her own "Mark on the Wall" in the first publication of the Hogarth Press, a pamphlet called *Two Stories*. She particularly admired the servant girls with the plates, and her picture of a snail: Carrington's animals have something very engaging and, as it were, personalized about them, and this snail does indeed seem the essence of snailness.

Vanessa too admired Carrington's work, and in particular her woodcuts for Virginia, as she says, although she is aware that Carrington is not skilled at accepting compliments; Lytton, who spends much time at Charleston, is supposed to transmit her admiration, and does so, in a letter to Carrington (July 31, 1917): "She also says 'Tell Carrington if she can bear to have them mentioned, that I liked her woodcuts very much'. . . " If Carrington felt not part of the Bloomsbury circle, and not always welcome, particularly at Charleston (August 7, 1917, to Lytton: "By the way the Vanessa woman has never said anything to me since I wrote & announced my pleasure at coming. I suppose its all right?"), that is surely as much due to what she sometimes perceived as her awkwardness, as to the way in which her solitary nature, often in evidence, contrasts with their habitual delight in a certain togetherness characteristic of Bloomsbury as it created itself.

About Bloomsbury as a concept, Vanessa's amusing description of what life would be like in the south of France when they all cluster about their new discovery is telling, in its relation to their Bloomsbury situation with its closeness: she predicts them all—"the Stracheys and Davidsons and Mortimers" and all the others "bobbing" back and forth and in and out of each other's houses, and their own, wherever they choose to live, in Cassis, or anywhere else in France, in

Italy or even the South Seas. Just as happened with Bloomsbury and Sussex, it will suddenly appear that those are the
places to live in, and everyone, even the Keynes (Maynard
and by this time his wife the ballerina Lydia Lopokova) will
be on the doorstep.

Now Carrington was distant from that way of being, and
from that kind of bantering *tone*, in particular. She was never
part of that "us" or even that "them"—Lytton was, and she
tried to be, on occasion, but most often was not: her journal
and her letters bear evidence to that ineluctable fact. Worst
of all was Carrington's intense pain over the story, repeated
by Ralph, that Leonard and Virginia found it impossible
Lytton should not be bored by her, as it was reinforced by
her own feelings of aloneness and unworthiness, but also by
the collective ambiance that was, in fact, the soul of Bloomsbury. "Bloomsbury itself," says Nigel Nicolson, "was responsible for the legend that Bloomsbury had never existed, that
it was the invention of its enemies. The two people who were
most vocal in denying its reality, Virginia and Leonard, were
the same two who gave the expression widest currency."

Concerning that ambiance, Carrington's description of
Secrets in Bloomsbury is hilarious, and captures, in its high
spirits, something it would be too bad to lose through moder-
ation in recounting:

> Apparently, Clive had told Desmond who told Virginia
> nearly 2 weeks ago, & she had kept it a deadly secret from
> everyone, until Vanessa rang her up and begged her to
> tell nobody as it was vital to keep it secret! It seems to me
> to border on a farce! Vanessa met Ralph Partridge in the
> square last night & said, You must keep it secret. I hope
> Lytton won't tell anyone. I suppose you heard from Vir-
> ginia. Well, now you musn't tell anyone else. They are
> mad. But I think we all get high marks for our secret
> faculties. (n.d., probably between October and November,
> 1920)

Virginia herself liked Carrington greatly; their relation
was a relatively deep one, each recognizing the other's
failings, admiring the other's strong points. They spent time

together on several occasions: "Dinner tonight with Virginia tout seul. Pray for me," writes Carrington to Lytton on December 8, 1916. In spite of Carrington's timidity at going, she was always delighted by, and half in love with, Virginia and her elegance and wit and charm; the feeling was not without return (December 11, 1917, Carrington in a letter to Lytton: "I had a long tête-à-tête with Virginia on Sunday, in which she became distinctly flirtatious, but (needless to remark) I remained calm.") She loathes Virginia's well-known repeating and deforming of tales ("What an asse Virginia is! does she act with or without malice intent?" (sic) January 19, 1918). But when she is hospitalized, the visitor she would most rather see after Lytton is Virginia, as she states more than once. She saves her best marmalade for Virginia, declaring "geniuses should always have the best": her admiration was firm. And when Ralph her husband finally quits helping at the Hogarth Press, she thinks it will be hard indeed for him to find such entertaining and intelligent employers again. When Carrington wonders if that meant the end of their collective friendship, Virginia reassures her that the friendship is, and always will be, intact.

Virginia's liking of Carrington seems to have been an instant one, finding she had more spunk than the men students at the Slade; later, when Ralph was in the picture, Virginia found him simply a pink-fleshed good-looking muscled and useful person to answer bells and fix chicken-coops (and also to supply a little of what "Lytton lacked"), while she considered Carrington was worth "twice his salt." (Carrington herself proved to be a useful guest at Rodmell, says Virginia, "unselfishly insisting either upon cutting the grass or pumping the water" [August 18, 1918; VWL: I, 270]). She seems to have an instant comprehension of the artist in Carrington: a letter of August 1918 to her describes the different colors of the corn turning and how she will be tempted to "I will not say what. Its odd that painting should appeal to your modesty as personal chastity appealed to our mothers. It must be a kind of inversion, I think" (VWL: II, 267). The odd comparison somehow manages to capture a kind of truth about Carrington's quaint and passionately involved attitude, even as she represents the liberated and energetic side of what is to Virginia "you young things."

Since Virginia had, in fact, encouraged Carrington's marriage, when it starts falling apart, with the latter's involvement with Gerald Brenan, and Ralph's frequent betrayals, she partially blames herself: ought we not all to sink together, responsible as we may be for each other's sins? (VW/VB, December 22, 1922). Carrington, whose spiritual balance, says Virginia , has probably been upset by Lytton's influence, is happy one day and miserable the next, while "Ralph flirts," until his informal relation with Frances is consecrated (their "bridal party") with their pact about living together in London and returning to be with Carrington and Lytton on the weekend. Virginia remains on Carrington's side, instinctively again, and plans to give her enough to drink to tide her over that bizarre celebration.

The relation between Vanessa and Carrington is never so close as that between Carrington and Virginia, in spite of their mutual admiration for each other's art: Carrington speaks in her letters to Lytton of Vanessa as of someone much older, and with whom there is not an intimate contact. When Lytton complains of the discomfort at Charleston ("The sordidness of this establishment" with its dead rats, whose odor is cheerfully overlooked by Vanessa engrossed in her work), Carrington is glad he prefers Tidmarsh (where the rurality of the situation is wonderfully described by Virginia, with the ducks and chickens wandering about from room to room); when she sees Vanessa and Duncan in Gordon Square, just back from Cambridge, "looking very lost, walking slowing like a housekeeper with a sad face, and a young butler in his stolen master's clothes seeking a situation," her pen can be as pointed as her tongue, or any pen in Bloomsbury (DC/LS, *passim*).

Vanessa seems to have a far lower opinion of Carrington personally than Virginia (witness a letter of May 20, 1928, VB/VW concerning Lytton's sickness in Paris, over which he got in a panic at Carrington's not talking a word of French, thus "not knowing how she'd procure him any comforts. She has a very bad effect on him, like all these wives, & conversation was perfectly dull. It's very odd. The moment one gets L alone, he wakes up, comparatively at any rate, but in her presence all is depressed & lifeless . . . ")

The sadness of Carrington that Virginia describes on November 2, two years later, finds another manner from Vanessa's. She considers her now with compassion, as she always does, seeing her "slightly shrivelled and to my mind disappointed," "very shabby, small; in her usual stupid petticoat and jacket" (VWL:IV, 233), but loving, and wanting Virginia and Vanessa to come to Ham Spray, since Lytton cares for them so much. (The childlike side of Carrington's being may well be what attaches us to her, so that this petticoat and jacket, simpler perhaps than stupid, stand out as an unconventional marking of her personality so much her own.)

Later, after the deaths of Lytton and Carrington, Virginia will lament the fact they all went so seldom to Ham Spray their home, and that there indeed had been some feeling that Carrington had been acting to screen out his old friends. A too-simple way of putting it, but which seizes nevertheless upon a certain truth, is that she never felt at ease with Bloomsbury as such.

All Together

What a tangled mass of interrelations, and how interwoven—when Virginia speculates on the denseness of the Bloomsbury foliage, branches, and roots, she is at the heart of the matter. Carrington, often anxious over her art and her relations, concerned that she bores Lytton when they go on walks, always dreading that Gerald will turn cold, worried about Bloomsbury gossip (Gerald will tell Virginia who will tell her sister, who will tell Duncan, who will confide in Bunny, and so on, through "Mrs. Dobree and Mr. Penrose and Dadie Rylands and Frances Marshall and Mr. Birrell and then twenty more people each, the noise increasing, enough to drive us all into the sea") (DC/GB, February 10, 1921). Carrington with such a "queer love" for Virginia that she is filled "with emotion when I see her" (September 15, 1923, to Gerald), hating her to be concerned over anything, like the Hogarth Press and Ralph's involvement in it; Carrington in awe of Lytton who tells her about Horace and whatever he has been reading, with whom she reads poetry and plays, even as she despairs of her own character, disgusted with her painting and her grumbling, her slothfulness and cowardice, as she puts it (January 12, 1923, to GB). Rarely exhibiting after her first unselling incident, having to pick up her pictures unsold and never showing her work to Vanessa and Duncan—how can we get to know you if we don't see your paintings, asks Vanessa?—Carrington, fond of Duncan's paintings and enthusiastic over Roger's lectures, wearing Lytton's overcoat cut down (how much this gesture tells of her attitude towards herself, as towards him!): being Lytton, smaller, in this kind of possession the only one possible (had I only been a boy, she says to him, you could have loved me, and I would have made you happy—I wish that had been possible). Carrington longing to huddle in Lytton's clothes even after he is gone.

Vanessa, used to caring for others, maternal and central, so present in Virginia's life, like a fulcrum around which it turns: ". . . and I long—oh why are you the only person I never see enough of?—to see you again" (VW/VB, August 8, 1937). Virginia is overcome with emotion just to find her in the room: just like Roger, she says of herself in relation to her sister. The remark is telling: Vanessa adoring Duncan and her children, with her sorrow over the loss of Julian and her great anxiety about holding on to Duncan, and surviving—as she did—his passions for others, was always Virginia's source of nourishment.

Duncan, always making friends, generous, warm, hard-working, and totally without shame (with a family as colorful and cheerfully unconventional as the Stephens were gloomy), raised partially in the Strachey family, and adored by Lytton for years—even after he lost out to Maynard Keynes's own passion for Duncan—seen by Virginia as always hitching up his trousers, stumbling over the long words in the middle of his sentences, as a sort of queer faun-like creature, blinking his eyes benevolently. Duncan as seen by himself, like his Aunt Hennie, who was thrown out of a cab in Rome as a child: "She behaved oddly for the rest of her life. . . . She used to be sent out for long walks. Sometimes I went with her. We got on very well together. She and I were on the same intellectual level" (T, 19).

Virginia wanting to write a book to explain literature to artists like Vanessa and Duncan, self-suppressing in her writing about Roger Fry, admired and loved, but troubling and frequently troubled. Her view on the relations of the world, art, and the work of words is teasingly but seriously suggested in a letter she writes to her nephew Julian, bringing up a point that is more than difficult to deal with. Speaking of Duncan and Vanessa, she states a drastic political difference between their work and hers: "There they sit, looking at pinks and yellows, and when Europe blazes all they do is to screw up their eyes and complain of a temporary glare in the fore-ground. Unfortunately politics get between one and fiction" (VW/JB, June 20, 1936; KCL; SA 47). As for the pinks and yellows, a possible explanation of the Charleston painters' bright colors might be the glooms of the Hyde Park Gate house of the Stephens as opposed to the colorful Strachey atmosphere, brought in and made visible.

There is, between the sisters, a certain competition for suffering and for a kind of life identified with the artistic. Vanessa's pain is often, as is Carrington's, over the reception of her art (she and Duncan hang two paintings in Maynard's rooms, she says, and he has never even noticed them); whereas Virginia sets out, she herself says, "to prove that being childless I was less normal than she," whereas Vanessa implies that she, Virginia, is settled and unadventurous. Vanessa's nomad or at least venturing soul prefers Paris as a dwelling-place, says Virginia; it is rather as if the motherdom were to be compensated for not just by hard work but also by a certain displacement, to prevent solidity from settling in. Virginia's madness, as her genius, are surely enough to fend off any accusations of settledness on anyone's part, so that the whole competition, not without its sad side, has a definite tinge of humor. It is scarcely necessary to add, I think, that Carrington's way of living puts her, in spite of her domestic talents, as far beyond the pale of normality and settledness as are the two others, and in their company for the intensity of work and living.

Roger bumping out all his front teeth on a bench in Cassis

in the middle of the night (VWL: III, 216), Roger whose French girlfriend, Josette Coatmellec, shoots herself over him, Roger so brilliant and so mesmerizing a lecturer to them all: Carrington, inspired by Roger to read more, look at things again, Vanessa regaining respect for him even in his pain over her preference of Duncan, asking his advice about painting, even though Roger's own painting was weaker than his critical eye. What a difference between Roger's own paintings (compared by Virginia to wallflowers, hanging there unbought) and those of Duncan, at the Paterson and Carfax Gallery on Old Bond Street, as she describes her reactions to them (February 13, 1920; VWD: II, 18). "Meanwhile I say nothing & have nothing to say of Duncan's pictures. They spin in my head like the white wine I'd drunk: so lovely, so delicious, so easy to adore." Roger, above all, enchanted by his correspondence with Virginia and by "the Virginian style" ("I'm not a good letter-writer as you know but you inspire me as no one else does . . . my ideal would be to live in Provence and carry on a copious and constant correspondence with Virginia Woolf," October 24 and October 13, 1921, to VW; RFL: II, 514–15).

Finally, the wittiest among them all, Virginia and Lytton, in a riotously funny exchange recounted by the former at some length, occurring over tea, and having to do with where they would place themselves in literature: Lytton near St. Simon and La Bruyère, asks Virginia? "Oh God, he groaned" and goes on to find himself "a little better than Macaulay," but not his mass, says Virginia who then has to place herself in relation to others: Lytton says she influences him, but she wobbles, she says, and she is rummaging in the bran pie; Lytton has to write history all over, and

> Its all morality—
> & battles, I added.
> And then we walked through the streets together,
>   for I had to buy coffee.
>   (April 29, 1921; VWD: II, 114–16)

How clear the scene, and how living it seems, just right in its recounting and even lyric at the close in its trivality and togetherness; a perfect ending.

This is not, after all, a book about the Bloomsbury group as such, nor is it mainly a book about Roger or Duncan or Leonard or Lytton or Gerald. It is rather about three women creators: the inner depth of their natures and of their work, manifest or not, and the essential and even quintessential struggle I see them involved in, between the two sides of life, between the nurturing and entertaining and loving of others and the nurturing of their own work—the sides, to use the most celebrated case and the most appropriate one here, of Mrs. Ramsay on the one hand, and Lily Briscoe on the other, the nurturing mother and wife and friend of Virginia's *To the Lighthouse* as opposed to the spinster artist on the other. That war of opposites was continually to be waged, particularly in the cases of Vanessa and Carrington and the entertaining lives they led, but also in the case of Virginia, torn between inner and outer. The role of woman, as Mrs. Ramsay perceives it in that novel, is to give coherence and shape to other lives, to inter-relate them. Her effort—and to some extent, her success—is symbolized by the dining room scene, where in the beginning, "Nothing had merged. They all sat separate" (*To the Lighthouse*, 96). Only the candlelight lends some cohesion, at this point, serving as a focus about which the disparate faces can center. It is up to the woman to serve the central and centralizing dish, joining them in an at least temporary group. Yet the toll that cohering personality within the women takes on her is immense, as if in joining the scattered elements, she had put something else of value to and in herself, of which one does not speak, to final waste.

Mrs. Ramsay speaks, and not only for herself:

> But what have I done with my life? thought Mrs. Ramsay . . . She had a feeling of being past everything, through everything, out of everything . . . It's all come to an end, she thought . . . . But this is not a thing, she thought, ladling out soup, that one says. (95)

And then, on the other hand, there sits at the same table Lily the artist, encouraged by, and admiring of Mrs. Ramsay whom she loves. Bored by the conversation, she has, now and at the end of the novel, in the place of all that which seems laid to waste in Mrs. Ramsay's life, her all-consuming, all-redeeming vision:

> She remembered, all of a sudden as if she had found a treasure, that she too had her work. (98)

And, a few pages later, the return of the vision, triumphing over the everyday and the table chatter, over the nurturing of others, by an ineluctable certainty about the self and its evidence:

> ... and she remembered that next morning she would move the tree further towards the middle, and her spirits rose so high at the thought of painting tomorrow that ... (107)

All manner of things could, and do follow from the "that" I leave in that quotation unmodified and incomplete—for this book is, to a large extent, about just "that." These lives can be read—like all our lives—as partial defeat and partial triumph; but I want to leave the reading open, letting the stories and the letters and the journals and the paintings tell their own story. And at the same time I want to invite a triple conversation at this table—between these women and their recreations, their readers, and the readers of this deliberately joining text. As if the conversation, reading, and nurturing were to be mutually nourishing, in the atmosphere of openness.

As a metaphor of this openness, I want to draw a similarity between all three women, having to do with the commencement of a new project as opposed to the completion of an old one. As Quentin Bell points out in relation to Vanessa and Virginia, the starting of a new picture or writing was always for them the greatest moment, because the most potential. The sketch was always more interesting than the finished product. One of Carrington's most complex sketches of mountains, this one near Yegen, in Gerald's part of Spain, has the colors marked: blue grey, pink grey, indigo, green, pink green, and not yet filled in ... like Vanessa's faceless or blurred-face pictures of Virginia, from the side, in the armchair at Asheham, or in the canvas lounge chair facing us, with the details to be completed by the onlooker: those pictures all can be taken as emblematic of their triple longing for intensity and nuance, and yet at the same time, of incompletion and its narrative potential.

Nevertheless, it is their story that has to be heard. In all three creations, the work of portraiture and self-portraiture is intense: Virginia's, in her journals and letters, Vanessa's in several "real" and transfigured self-portraits, and Carrington's in the portrait of the other she loved so much that her loving self is perhaps best seen by means of, and through it, and in the journal she called "Her Book." She leaves us few self-portraits as such: this step beyond personal self-preoccupation and personal anguish can be taken in some quiet sense as a metaphoric key to the plea made here for interconnections, and the pushing necessarily through, and beyond anguish, to art.

Themselves

As these women creators tell the tale of themselves, to each other and themselves too, the sense of secrecy that abounds in these mental expressions and livings-out, the shifts of meaning and views on truth, make a straightforward telling not just almost impossible, but actually inappropriate.

Virginia's own subtlety and the vectoring of the tale she tells finds such nuanced outlet in the letters, journals, and fiction, that we should keep her words to Vita in mind. Repeated as they are, they are significant past their teasing tone: "I must buy some shaded inks—lavenders, pinks, violets—to shade my meaning. I see I gave you many wrong meanings, using only black ink . . . . No, no, I must buy my colored inks . . . But no: I must get my coloured inks" (VWL: VI, 461–62). That should be, like a motto, writ large, and in all sorts of colors, from faint to strong, at the top of any page concerning her—and, in fact, all of the characters in this triple tale.

Vanessa, seemingly more forthright, like Ralph and Roger, learned finally to keep her unhappiness to herself: the loss of Julian in the Spanish Civil War, that obvious and terrible mother's loss, had as its parallel the subtler loss of a part of her physically loving self by her involvement with Duncan, who could care, in the long run, only for the unphysical part of her, but with enormous and enduring affection, if not with the passion she felt for him. The incomplete use of the self . . . surely a painful doom, no matter how unstated.

Carrington and Duncan the Strachey cousin were intensely secretive—Carrington obsessively so—whereas Ralph and Roger seem more forthright, in anguish and pleasure. Lytton's feline sinuosity of mind and being encouraged the private secrecies of the beings he loved and was close to—Duncan, whom he adored, to which devotion his outpourings of enthusiasm in his love letters bear witness, and Carrington, upon whom he grew to depend utterly. The intertwinings of all these relations were aided and abetted by the delight in the secret and the not-quite said, simultaneous with the outspoken deliberate freedom of word. Duncan simply came and went in his world, among his loves—Vanessa and Bunny Garnett among them—without excuses and with the quietest of footfalls. Carrington would, at her best and worst, make any encounter slightly mysterious, inventing and fabricating, giving another cast to the daylight that the "truth" would have been. Her art of fictionalizing is not the least interesting side of her.

Which did not keep her from admiring Virginia precisely for her straight-seeing, saying she "would make an amazing painter" because her visions were so clear (October 14, 1922: VWD: II, 207n.). Exactly Virginia's powers of sight, not just of description, are at work in her assessment of Carrington; in early November, 1924 (VWD: II, 321), she sees Carrington looking as if she had been "recently beaten by Ralph. Is she really rather dull, I asked myself, or merely a sunflower out of the sun?" That view of Carrington—so very different from the times when Virginia found her robust, quirky, and simply torn between Ralph and her love for Lytton, before her marriage—coincides with the one Vanessa has in France quoted above, with Carrington dragging around after Lytton, weighing him down as she sees it. Perhaps the most devastating thing Virginia ever said and saw about Carrington was that her very way of being did not wear well on her, or on others

(January 31, 1921; VWD: II, 88: "Carrington I think grows older, & her doings are of the sort that age").

Carrington had not the social sparkle of Bloomsbury. There is no denying that the most appealing sides of her—the little-girl delight in everything about nature, the turned-in toes, the holding of her head on one side, the self-efface-ment, the way her hands gestured, like a painter, but with a childish enthusiasm also—are not those that would have appealed to Vanessa. Carrington's very secrecy was the oppo-site of what she saw as the Bloomsbury way, of gossiping and controlling, with which she identified even Virginia whom she loved.

Virginia well knew, of course, that the groupiness of it all as seen from outside was a matter of setting apart a "them" from an "us," of exacerbating personal proclivities: Clive in-sists, she writes (April 2, 1919; VWD: II, 261), that Nessa, Roger, Clive, Lytton, and I, are among the most hated people in London, seen as superficial, haughty, and giving ourselves airs. "I admit I hate not to be liked; & one of the drawbacks of Bloomsbury is that it increases my susceptibility to those shades, which are always made visible by Clive." The "them" and the "us" here are bitterly and frequently on her mind; they are no less on Carrington's mind, feeling, as she does, not part of it all.

In some odd way, Carrington seems to long for Virginia to be Mrs. Ramsay for her, to nurture the artist in her, and in some odd way, Virginia did just that. Lily Briscoe, of whom Vanessa, reading *To the Lighthouse* for the first time, said that she must have been a very good artist, speaks, I think, for Carrington also, as she is nurtured by the other whom she loves, admires, and partly fears for exactly her life-sustaining role. In the light of this supposition I am making, Virginia's recounting of Carrington's marriage is all the more telling. May 23, 1921; VWD: II, 119: "So Carrington did make up her mind to become Partridge—no, that is precisely what she is determined not to do; & signs herself aggressively Carrington for ever."

Carrington for ever. An unmarried Lily Briscoe, not need-ing to talk about Mr. Ramsay's boots, but losing Ralph in the long run, perhaps both because of her love for Lytton and her desire for art. Driven into solitude, with her own suffering and what she calls her own unself-supportingness: but indeed they all three suffered from that. Dragging herself and others down, Carrington? Must we see her that way? I think not.

Nor do I think we have to see only the picture of Vanessa turned inward, darkly, toward her own pain, or Virginia sucked into her self-doom. The painting can be made darker still: Virginia's body swept along, Vanessa's plain dark tombstone; but they are at least buried by the man they loved. Carrington's not having the little monument she wanted Stephen Tomlin to design for her (and that she left some money for), not being even near Lytton, whose ashes were scattered over the downs—worse, still, than having no monument, having no known resting place. Where are her ashes?—no one knows. No service over them, and no resting place. Even the relation of the tale pains, told in this way, and this way, of course, it can be told, like any other.

Any life or death story can be told in many ways; telling it here as triple does nothing to decrease the particular difficulties. But in spite of it all, it was not all pitiable, for any of them. "The remarkable impression of sunlight she made," says Julia Strachey of Carrington. Never flat, their lives, never lacking in intensity, and never unremarkable. We do not have to read backward from their endings to guard against ordinariness, for these were women extraordinary: it bears repeating.

Vanessa, more ironic, and more stable. Carrington, more childlike. Virginia, dependent, like Carrington, ironic like Vanessa. But all of them, fortunate that their loves were of such intensity. What worked for one did not for another, and all were—seen from one angle, tragic; and from another, beautiful. These women.

I am making no claim for the ease of these lives, rather, expressing a hope that this recounting of a few interweavings and intensities may contribute to the understanding of some of the multiple complexities that went into the involvement of these three women, their lives and loves and art:

. . . the old burden of the much life and the little art, and

of the portentous dose of the one it takes to make any
show of the other.

Henry James, preface to *The Altar of the Dead*

Geniuses Get Forgiven

Oh yes, this is what matters—one's friends.
Lytton, to Virginia (VWD: II, 126)

Duncan refused the honor of being a Commander of the
Order of the British Empire in 1950, as a protest against the
social order. Virginia Woolf refused many honors, including
giving the Clark lectures at Cambridge in 1931, being a Companion of Honour, 1935, and honorary degrees from Manches-
ter and Liverpool, in 1933 and 1939 ("I said No thanks; I dont
believe in Honours," VWL: V, 396), even as she wondered, to
Rose Macaulay, if there could be only Grand Old Men of
literature, and thought she would "prepare to be the Grand
Old Woman of English letters." Vanessa sat enthroned in
Duncan's portrait of her (now at the Tate), in her majestic
cape and severe Victorianness, looking out from her formality, and sits there still, at the bottom of the staircase, impos-
ingly.

Carrington had nothing to refuse, except, occasionally,
herself, and always, to others, the sight of her pictures: thus
Vanessa's serious statement, phrased like a light question,
about the difficulty of knowing her, if she was always to hide
her work. And so, in a kind of vicious circle, it was continually
a "them" as opposed to a Carrington self-enclosed in her
otherness, whose pictures were turned to the wall, put away
in her studio, while she entertained elsewhere. We think of
Vanessa painting alongside Duncan, even when in pain,
Vanessa of whom Angelica so wonderfully says that she
would be happy with black coffee and her paints anywhere
and on any desert island; of Virginia finding Leonard "in his
stall" next to her, Virginia in her steel-rimmed glasses and
overalls writing in her studio, intense with all the fire of
passion on her morning's work she would then type more
coolly in the afternoon; and how do we think of Carrington?

I see her on her white horse Belle racing over the downs,

or making jam and decorating with her fine sense of color, or painting a cook and a cat on a window, or—in that most amazingly recounted story about her sailor Beakus, called *A Danish Grave*,—looking from outside in through the window where the others all are, all of them. Or ferreting away Gerald's letters, under the little bookcase on the window sill, or writing by the fire and keeping secrets—like a child, always keeping secrets. I see Carrington not yet grown up, ever. And find her no less of a genius than the others: than Virginia, most revered and beloved of all in the feminist writing domain, than Vanessa, representing art, bohemian love, and beauty, than Lytton, sinuously styled and seductively sensitive, than Duncan, pure, wise, naive, vague, and the artist incarnate, awkward and endearing.

Now that it is all over (Virginia: "A fortnight already gone. It goes too quick—too quick. If only one could sip slowly & relish every grain of every hour!" VWD: IV, 129) and time to reevaluate our view of them all, these Women of Bloomsbury alongside these others, I think we might well come down on the side of gladness that they got so much in, whether through or in spite of their loneliness and unconventional loving. True, we cannot do more than say to the moment in which they seem so very present, as Virginia says to Leonard, quoting Goethe, "Stay, you are so fair," knowing it impossible. Yet the traces, in their art and letters and journals, of their life and its richnesses and multiple sources of joy as of despair, seem strangely nearer than those of other movements which are in fact closer in time to us.

"All our Bloomsbury relationships," says Virginia (VWD:II, 326) "flourish, grow in lustiness. Suppose our set to survive another twenty years, I tremble to think how thickly knit & grown together it will be." Some survived longer than others, but their collective and individual genius lay perhaps in the very vividness and vitality of that lusty relationship, living and working, its roots and branches having so grown together.

3
Virginia

A Work and a Life Deeply Loved

. . . the perfectly buoyant & energised life which is now my aim. Oh yes, I don't waste a moment: I am always on the hog . . .

Virginia, to herself,
May 15, 1931 (VWD: IV, 35)

And so the immitigable day passes. I face up to it without any evasion: this has to be lived I say to myself.

Virginia, to herself,
April 11, 1932 (VWD: IV, 206)

Over Virginia's early life, says her nephew Quentin Bell, there hung the menace of disaster, insanity, and early death. One of her half-sisters was mad, as was her cousin; her beloved and beautiful mother, Julia, almost twenty years younger than her husband, died very young. Julia's staunchest daughter, Stella, who was the model for Holman Hunt's Lady of Shalott, had to take over the keeping of Virginia's famous father, Leslie Stephen, inconsolable as he was upon the loss of her mother. Already his work for the Dictionary of National Biography weighed heavily upon him, as did an unceasing and unnecessary worry over financial security, and Virginia felt—by all these worries—cramped from her earliest existence, even, as she said, in the womb.

The household was unredeemably gloomy. Later, when Virginia's elder sister Vanessa falls in love with Duncan

Grant, she is able to compare the joyous and bizarre Grant household with the heavy-spirited one from which she and Virginia issued: "Oriental gloom," as they described it. Stella, hard-working, conscientious, had a brother George, charming but whose approaches to the girls, particularly Virginia, have been thought to have severely traumatic results on their future lives: thus, her recurrent fits of madness are thought to have been caused by these early incestuous advances as well as the grief over her mother's loss, and the unusual lives of both sisters to have been irremediably influenced by these events.

They had summered at St. Ives, at Talland House, which they now had to give up. Early life seemed to be a series of giving ups: Virginia's madness, sure to recur, made her relinquish—from the death of her mother on—any hopes of a "normal" life, which indeed she never had, as one usually thinks of such a thing. Stella died in her turn, another loved being lost. Vanessa, getting her freedom from the household early, to go off and paint, was another loss—and then later, Thoby her beloved brother and her intellectual "sparring partner," as Quentin Bell puts it, was to succumb to an untimely death from typhoid fever. From all these irrecoverable losses, there was to be no ultimate recovery.

46 Gordon Square in Bloomsbury saw the gathering of the Apostles conversation and reading group that had started at Cambridge, and to which were added various others. The Stephen sisters joined in the riotous and often sexually adventurous discussions with the young men, most of whom were bisexual or homosexual. Eventually, of course, Vanessa was to marry Clive Bell, and Virginia (after a one-day consideration of an offer of marriage by the homosexual Lytton Strachey), was to marry Leonard Woolf—of whose Jewishness she was half-afraid, but whose supportiveness she was never to question, neither in her bouts of illness and madness, nor in her sane and creative periods. And whom she deeply loved.

"You know, The Goat's mad," the others would say, and Virginia herself would speak of her being "off her head." That "marriage of true minds," as runs the title of one of the books about it, was more, indeed, of the minds than of the bodies.

No children, for the doctors would have thought it unwise, because of Virginia's mad spells; no sex, and separate rooms—nevertheless, the life of Virginia and Leonard together must be seen as a happy one. They both thought so, and repeatedly Virginia states that no one can be, can have been, as happy as she was, as they were together.

They alternated between Monk's House in Sussex and London, between political involvement and more literary writing, between their friends and their quiet work, until the worsening of the war; she and Leonard had figured what would be the fate of a Jewish socialist and his wife, and prepared themselves for self-poisoning with gas fumes from the car, and also secured enough morphia for a fatal dose. In 1940, their house at Mecklenburgh Square was blasted by bombs—as was Vanessa's studio, and Duncan's next door at No. 8 Fitzroy Street—and then No. 52 Tavistock Square, for which she was still paying rent.

Virginia, just before her sixtieth birthday, with the rumors of German invasion at any moment and under the stress of the repeated air raids, felt she was going irretrievably mad, hearing bird's voices until she could no longer stand the thought of it or of being unable to write again, for her madness. Considering what it would do, yet again, to Leonard's life, she walked into the nearby river with a large stone in her pocket, making her decision irreversible. On the bank she left her walking stick, and in the house she left notes for Leonard and Vanessa, explaining her action and its reasons, expressing her gratitude to Leonard for that great joy he had given her: "I don't think two people could have been happier than we have been."

Virginia, to Begin With

What's "I?"
Virginia Woolf,
Mrs. Dalloway, p. 108

We must start with a picture of Virginia, because so many of us begin there, and because of her strength—rarely are so-called "invalids" so strong, so vitally valid, and so intensely contagious. Precisely because so much of this tale will not concern Virginia as agent, but as sister and receptor, or as understanding friend and implicit mentor, distant or present, we should begin with her and her views, before asking her to permit us to step aside from her, in order to go on.

I picture her, first of all, as placed just where Vanessa and Carrington are located: she was fondest of "things that stir me to describe them . . . I insist (for the sake of my aesthetic soul) that I don't want to read stories or emotion or anything of the kind into them; only pictures that appeal to my plastic sense of words make me want to have them for still life in my novel" (VWD; I, 168). Like the reference to the words in a play as listened to, as opposed to the word simply seen ("the word heard. Its solidity: its depths," from "Notes for Reading at Random," TCL, 377), the density of the interrelated senses (pictures/words; sounds/words) satisfies the painter in the writer, the declaimer in the listener, in a formal interweaving close to Clive Bell's *Significant Form*. Stories, emotions, overlays of various kinds are to be rejected from the formal use of and reaction to language as such, not subsidiary or subservient to any other thing such as plot or feeling. What Virginia Woolf writes to Ethel Smyth, in 1930, about the composition of *To the Lighthouse* (and, by implication, *The Waves*, more appropriately still) goes along these general lines also, and runs against the grain of traditional fiction-writing: "Though the rhythmical is more natural to me than the narrative, it is completely opposed to the tradition of fiction & I am casting about all the time for some rope to throw the reader" (quoted in NFE, 27).

The study of her "little language" which will follow in no way concerns itself with some hyperbolic miniaturization as perfection, but rather with the old and modest "common voice, singing out of doors," issuing from the great procession of anonymous writers and speakers from time immemorial (TCL, 399). The expression of what is here related to Virginia Woolf is deliberately such as a "little" voice could say, to make room for the voices of Vanessa and Carrington, less sure of themselves by far, and needing a kind of quiet in order to be heard in all *their* depth and experience in their own solidity, as Woolf says of words as heard on stage.

As for the on-stage quality of much of this performance in Bloomsbury, with the set scenes and houses between which our characters rush about (like Vanessa's description of what happens when Bloomsbury arrives in, say, Sussex or the South Seas, written in fact from the South of France), it presents itself as, at once, simple and sophisticated, occasionally sentimental, and immensely funny. Above all, it is enthusiastic, for which, in part, we have wonderful Roger Fry to thank, of whom Virginia was to say, with her own hyperbole, that he was "the only great critic that ever lived," to whom, in fact, she wanted to dedicate *To the Lighthouse* ("You have kept me on the right paths, so far as writing goes, more than anyone") and of whom, traveling in Greece in 1932, she thought that he was the best admirer of life and art she'd ever traveled with, in spite of his "severity" (VWD: IV, 97); the severity has a complement in his constant enthusiasm and expectation of greatness all about him: near the Acropolis, "We wandered; Roger said Awfully swell, awfully swell." And then, in the Byzantine Church at Daphnis, " 'Oh awfully swell—better than I'd any notion of' said Roger depositing his hat stick pochard & two or three guides & dictionaries on a pillar" (VWD: IV, 91). He "oozes" knowledge, she says, but gently, like some sort of aromatic shower. In her letters (VWL: II, 356), we find the identical point of view: "not only the most charming but also the most spiritually gifted of mankind . . . If we could all be like Roger!" And at his death, she lamented: "so rich so infinitely gifted—and oh how we've talked and talked—for 20 years now" (VWL: V, 330). In her diary, Virginia describes several talking scenes with Roger at the center, all typical of Bloomsbury-talk-excitement at its best. The very descriptions act to incite further reading and seeing: "We discuss prose; and as usual some book is had out, and I have to read a passage over his shoulder. Theories are fabricated. Pictures stood on chairs" (VWD: 1, 225). And life lived.

Now that kind of exalted relation to the universe of the mind characterizes Virginia in her relations to others also, at their best. Much in her attitudes to her intimates was based on real admiration, on genuine affection: thus, Virginia of Lytton, who rose in her opinion "the more I read other peoples lives and essays. He had mastered the art of saying what he meant—and in prose how difficult that is! They remain stated finished controlled—even those little biographies of his. Lord, how I wish he'd lived . . . " (To Julian Bell, June 28, 1936) (MFS, 190–91). And Roger, of course, has made more difference to civilization, she thought, than the rest—the more I read of him, she says, "the more sure I am of his lasting" (To Margery Fry, January 14, 1940; MFS, 202).

Her enthusiasm, in abundance, she had to curb occasionally, and this she did, teasing Duncan, for whom, she says, she has to castrate her letters of "descriptions of country and works of art" (To Duncan Grant, March 16, 1913; MFS, 179) since he so hates them; to Julian, she can expand in devastating and at the same time, admiring, remarks about Cambridge ("How I love it and respect it and deride it! The antics, the mannerisms, the sublime remoteness from pop guns and alarms, in this removed place"; MFS, 179), even as she confesses her enormous fondness for Julian himself, without whom all "the bottom of sense and salt is out of our world . . . " (August 30, 1936).

But of course, of all her enthusiasms and passions, her intense love for her sister is always most in evidence. She has given Vanessa, on her 60th birthday, money to hire models to pose for her painting. Ten guineas, whose use, symbolic and real, will ring as true and as important as that of the *Three Guineas* in her book by that name. For it symbolizes art, being a tribute to Vanessa's talent, a gift for her gift. You are, says Virginia, to spend these guineas on "making masterpieces. I'm sure you're the only living painter save Duncan who can." And these injunctions are phrased as parts of a continuity, as if they are not to be separated from life, or the flow of language, being art: "And love me. And have models. And paint me a picture" (June 5, 1939; MFS, 184).

Virginia's attitude to Vanessa is perhaps best summed up by the incident, related in one of Virginia's letters to her sister, where she recounts how she tries, motivated by a painting of a vase and one long flower, to conceive of a room "as a whole" in relation to that picture: this goes far beyond the reaction of a decorator, say, to a central piece, or a writer, say, to a central object in a description—it is, in fact, importantly, about conception itself, about imagining, and—in the long run—about the mind as it responds to art. If she tries, she says, to find the right fabric to cover a yellow checked chair that clashes with a painting of Vanessa's (VWL: II, 259) that means, above all, that she puts the painting first, with its own revelation as that which causes irrelevant things to conceal themselves or be concealed.

If Vanessa issues commands to Virginia to take care of her fragile self, to prepare—after her stories—to write a novel, thus, of greater size than the stories, and (especially) to tell her what size she would like the illustrations of her stories, Virginia herself is fully capable of, and fully used to issuing commands to her sister about her painting: "I should like you to paint a large, large picture; where everything would be brought perfectly finally together, yet all half flying off the canvas in rapture" (VWL: II, 340–41). What an injunction: to command rapture, and demand largeness is to respond to demands and questions about *size* with a truly large answer. Rapture, flying, togetherness, finality, perfection, everything: even reading the terms backwards conveys the urgent desire on Virginia's part which is both projection and empathy. And which remains desire: to this the desirousness discussed in Vanessa's letters is the deepest response; desire as empathy and as art.

Over and over, Virginia tries to find the verbal meaning in what Vanessa paints, even as she knows, respects, and greatly admires the principle of Vanessa's "uncompromising art"—"How I wish I were a painter!" she exclaims (VWL: VI, 236) and, seeing that in fact, in a sense, she is—otherwise, why the extensive descriptions of still lifes, why these vivid scenes?—she continues writing. To Vanessa, for herself, and for us.

So Virginia was seized by sight. A large part of the charm of her diaries, her letters, and her fiction comes from the quite extraordinary vividness of her vision. If Vanessa was, as she called her, a poet in color, she herself was supremely that.

I shall walk along the Thames, she says, all along it, in

the places I used to haunt ... "I shall see" ... "I see," said Ginny, amidst *The Waves*.

And, 24 days before her suicide, she writes to Vita—in full wartime—about fruits and colors and the ripening time for sight: "I suppose your orchard is beginning to dapple as it did the day I came there. One of the sights I shall see on my death bed" (March 4, 1941; VWL: XI, 476). The passage moves us all the more as there was, so to speak, only a river to lend its bed for her death, on the way out to sea, and precious little chance for dapple. So much water, she writes to T.S. Eliot, has flowed under the bridge "that I feel at sea"—time and its continuity have swept away the conscious certainties of self, into lostness. The sun is sinking fast: the last of the suicide notes, as they are printed, ends with Virginia's plea to Leonard:

Will you destroy all my papers. (VWL: VI, 487)

So there will be nothing left of her, as unfinished trace—in this she was the diametrical opposite of Carrington, with all her things unfinished. She is presented here, in her very refusal to remain, to be seen any more.

Wonderfully enough, the edition of the letters does not end on this voice of destruction, but rather with a group of letters found too late to be included in the regular order. They are brilliantly arranged to stop with this undated note to Leonard, thus, the counterpart to the suicide note and plea to have her undone texts destroyed: for the undated letter to her Mongoose ends quite easily and—if we know how to read—hopefully. She is about to begin writing, after sleeping well, and concludes with a resounding phrase: "Shall come back tomorrow for certain."

Engendering the Self: Virginia's Passion

I want to forge ahead, on my own lines.
Virginia Woolf (VWD: V, 56)

What is conceived as writing is born to reading. This work in its long gestating patience is quite as much the business of women as their pleasure, when the two senses of matrix meet, in the womb and on the metal printing plate. "Strong work," as it is phrased in the terminology of medical training, and it is indeed.

Especially as Virginia Woolf conceives it. To her own conviction—and ours too—she writes, on and on, "with fury, with rapture, with absorption still" (VWD: V, 64), bringing books into the world *against the current*, repeatedly comparing her writing to childbearing. The strong work it is, rowing against the current, riding against the wind at top speed ("and having got astride my saddle the whole world falls in shape, it is this writing that gives me my proportions" [VWD: III, 43]) means harnessing a steed and especially herself, for her own extreme dash. It is, truly, dashing writing, taking a strenuous pace.

She notes admiringly the gait of Lord Byron as he writes, and refers it, through her father (thus, as if naturally as well as *familiarly)*, to the male side of the engendering effort: "the springy random haphazard galloping nature of its method . . . He writes cantos without once flogging his flanks. He had, evidently, the able witty mind of what my father Sir Leslie would have called a thoroughly masculine nature" (VWD: I, 181). But in her turn, when she is writing quickly and feels her work in full harness, the joint effort of horse and rider is exemplary and no less male in its appearance than Lord Byron's. "Oh how violently I have been galloping through these mornings!" she exclaims about the writing of *Three Guineas*, the passion of which she implicitly likens to a masculine expenditure of amorous effort: "It has pressed & spurted out of me, if that's any proof of virtue, like a physical volcano. And my brain feels cool & quiet after the expulsion. I've had it sizzling now since . . . " Here the sentence breaks off in its flow, continuing with a "Well, I was thinking of it at Delphi, I remember" (VWD: V, 112). Always the comparison returns us to her excitement at simply thinking of the book. In one of her last letters, she says of the sizzling and fizzing of her ideas that the worst thing is bottling them to order, whereas the best is that initial, uncaptured fizz.

When it is too slow, the gait is compared to hacking, at the most, to a little canter, as opposed to the gallop she longs for, desiring, as she does, to "come out in the open again, when everything has been restarted and runs full tilt" (VWL: III, 209). Her mind, remorselessly severe as she terms it in its ceaseless *labors,* can pluck up the "forces of dominance and power" which are the quality of strong writing in its pride of "ego that erects itself like another part of the body I don't dare to name" (Letter to Ethel Smyth, quoted RN, 25). That ego in its highly eroticized sense remains inseparable from the drastic initiation of a new book like a new birth, made in ecstasy. Of her beginning the portrait of Vita called *Orlando,* writing it on a clean sheet, she says that it floods her body "with rapture and my brain with ideas" (October 9, 1927; VWL: III, 428)—no surprise, then, that such excitement leads to letdown. She is assailed by doubt after all the intensity of the birth-giving, and the relation even of the relation it bespeaks: "The question now is," she writes Vita, "will my feelings for you be changed? I've lived in you all these months—coming out, what are you really like? Do you exist? Have I made you up?" (VWL: III, 474). As the doubt continues, bringing with it the dryness of vocabulary and thought, the mind arid in the dust after the rapturous early tumescence ("In October, my mind was dripping"), now exhausted, she takes to detesting Vita, whom she has so loved. This postpartum depression is her usual "after book gloom," as she admits after the completion of her book on Roger Fry.

That familiar despair is alone able to desiccate the fluid energy which is usually hers in the fullness of the flood of composition, such vital liquidity being the explicit equivalent both of the male act of engendering and the female parturition. Plunging in the swollen and excited current of the composition of *Three Guineas,* she is convinced another novel may "swim up" at any moment. In some miraculous and androgynous sense, the former galloping strength and spurting power of those hard rides when she was fightingly equipped with "my old spurs and my old flanks" (VWD: V, 232) all through those moments flying and flying, meets and joins in the fertile moment the raging current into which she is plunged, to an extent almost unbearable.

The vital Virginia longs, in these fullest moments of being "to invent any way of dimming my own eyes, which are, sometimes, too bright, aren't they? Couldn't we drop some-thing into time to make it thick and dull?" (December 2, 1928; VWL: III, 561). For writing against time and the currents of ongoing life is at once the same plunging into the instant and raging against its "driving whirlwind." It is still, and always, the relation that writing is that brings it near the affairs of the heart and body, explicit love affairs, such as that with Vita—of which Orlando is the excited fruit—and implicit mental ones, like that of Virginia's Roger Fry, partly posthu-mous as an affair, and no less wonderfully odd:

> What a curious relation is mine with Roger at this mo-ment—who have given him a kind of shape after his death—was he like that? I feel very much in his presence at the moment: as if I were intimately connected with him; as if we together had given birth to this vision of him: a child born of us.
>
> (VWD: V, 305–7)

Two-parent engendering, this is: but the omission of Roger's love affairs, including the major one with Vanessa which is so in question here, works against any complete resemblance in this product of their love, in this work about which she was always hesitant, both about undertaking it and the result. Intimate connections are no proof of or guarantee of complete relation or resemblance.

Importantly, essentially, she relates best to herself when she is in labor, in that "working fighting mood, which is natural to me. I don't see myself a success. I like the sense of effort better" (VWD: III, 32). For what she was, after all, engendering, was—both against the current and in top gait— her writing self: "One always harnesses oneself by instinct & can't live without the strain" (VWD: V, 65). The very strain of the metaphors pulling against each other in the double sport of riding counter to, and plunging into the current that is writing, gives it its depth and its invincible, engendering energy of conception.

That Virginia should have chosen, for dying, a current against which she took pains not to be able to fight, plunging into a water that which was strictly unrecoverable from, was no less courageous and no less generous in conception than those engendering acts. I want this brief meditation along her lines to lead toward three other thoughts, equally brief: one about *The Waves* and the idea of a language little, yet sufficient, born in its own waters; one about the presentation of Virginia's self-ending, and perhaps the most important one, hinging into the rest of this book, about the idea of understanding, as Virginia and—then—Carrington, understood it.

A Little Language, for Lasting

. . . the lives of all these books filled the room behind with a soft murmur. Truly, a deep sea, the past, a tide which will overtake and overflow us.

Virginia Woolf, "Reading," p. 164

From the sea of her past reading, there comes breaking into her *Waves* Virginia's question, murmured to herself and implicit for us: as we are passing so rapidly from moment to moment, how can we manage to experience the presence of the most vital forces we know, sharing their vital energies? How can we express those energies, in what sort of language?

In that novel, which she thought of as a poem, intensity of language is openly sought, and wonderfully found, flowing toward the final setting in its massively moving dialogue between the personal and the impersonal, the singular self and our collective death, the natural defeat and the modestly human victory over it. The last and highest note—Virginia's protest against the death of her brother Thoby, here named Percival—"*Against you I will fling myself, unvanquished and unyielding, O Death!*," this italicized conclusion responds antiphonally to the italicized earlier descriptions of the day rising and coming to an end with: "*The waves broke on the shore*" (297). The crash of the ever present waves prepares the coming break of day, in the cyclical renewal, implicit and explicit, of the human and natural worlds.

Virginia's writing is at its height: to this resolution of the writer's mind—in that of Bernard, modest, bumbling, and knowing—and of all our lives, the strong lines of this strong prose is heading. (But modestly: "Heaven be praised," I said, "we need not whip this prose into poetry. The little language is enough" (226). Bernard's final summing-up of his life gives the history of a now elderly man, seen from inside, glimpsed in a mirror, and placed against the pattern of a rise and fall in nature exterior to the self, a *memento mori*. Bernard *knows*, and we know with him: there is no need or room for an object to that knowing: such knowledge, deep as it is, must be quite simply inscribed within the revolution of natural cycles. It is described with equal simplicity, in this "little language," at once all that is possible and also enough.

Even if we do not "whip this prose into poetry," as Bernard says, the book remains a poem in its structure, and poetic in its vision. How can writing render knowledge of this mortal sort, without sentimentality? "I begin to long," Bernard has said before this, "for some little language such as lovers use, broken words, inarticulate words, like the shuffling of feet on the pavement" (238).

The strangeness of this book, exclaimed the reviewers . . . How to render this strangeness or even salute it adequately in our own version of a small and shuffling, even inarticulate language? How better than to weave together fragments of Bernard's long meditation, as he is explicitly trying to synthesize: "Now to sum up" (238), for he is, as we are, tired of stories too satisfactory, of "phrases that come down beautifully with all their feet on the ground" (238). As in Stevie Smith's *Novel on Yellow Paper* (1936), the foot-off-the-ground person is the one ready to go, and not immured already in traditional ways of writing or thinking, finding a certain instability more agreeable.

Fittingly, the soliloquy is, as we cannot help but be, about interruptions—into the just tolerable world of little shopkeepers where "Tuesday follows Monday; then comes Wednesday" (257), where things do go on in small ways ("Lord how pleasant!" "Lord how good!"), there crashes the death of beloved Percival and the gripping regret over past inaction: "the terrible pounce of memory . . . that I did not go with him to Hampton Court." (Hampton Court, where Carrington helped Roger clean Mantegna's canvases: how all is interwoven . . .)

Bernard, in anguish, to avow his not going, arrives at Jinny's, and just "because she had a room; a room with little tables, with little ornaments scattered on little tables. There I confessed, with tears—I had not gone to Hampton Court" (264). So the confessional tradition, long in ritual, is reduced to the little and the ornamental, to the scattered; so ornament is invoked as setting for the unornamented self-lament. For life withers, says Bernard, as Jinny is able somehow to teach him, "when there are things we cannot share" (265).

Now, even should we not hear the echo of other place names in it (for example, *Mansfield Park*, that Austen novel that Lytton read to Carrington, that Duncan read to Vanessa just before her death, that Virginia loved), even should we not remember why it would be appropriate for Bernard to say this to Jinny—or why a person named Jinny should happen to have such noticeably little tables with such noticeable little things upon them—this moment is deeply moving, because of its verbal strength, so thoroughly *sounded.*

But of course this moment passes, like all moments, and the sincerity seems all of a sudden symbolical, and—so as not to let it be dulled to lifelessness and sent to the grave of sentiment, so as not, as Woolf puts it, "to let the lilies grow"— they break it off, to return to Bernard's own "disillusioned clarity." This light reveals the nonentity of it all, outside momentary confessions and stories of the loss of love, outside the unspeakable impossibilities of a single speaker shouting, in himself and for us all, at the meek and mediocre passing by of things. "Was there no sword, nothing with which to batter down these walls, this protection, this begetting of children and living behind curtains, and becoming daily more involved and committed, with books and pictures?" But of his seeking for something unbroken, of his going from one to the other of his friends "holding my sorrow—no, not my sorrow but the incomprehensible nature of this our life," Bernard can only try to tell the story, saying of himself: "I to whom there is not beauty enough in moon or tree; to whom the touch of one person with another is all, yet who cannot grasp even that, who am so imperfect, so weak, so unspeakably lonely. There I sat" (267).

Whatever is inscribed by him against the protective patterns of daily living, in his only little language, and against the cyclical rise and fall of the nature in which waves are continually crashing, will be necessarily already broken, himself necessarily marked by the aging that he glimpses in the mirror. As if his language were to go gray with his graying self, and he to will it vigorous, however uselessly, up until the breaking end: "Must I for ever," I said, "beat my spoon on the table-cloth? Shall I not consent?" (279). Not, plainly, until he has to. This path leads along strong linguistic lines, of that small and yet sufficient courage about expression in the little language of prose. The *project* of prose is the keeping vivid of the moment by language. Paradoxically, the very childishness of this gesture: the beating with the spoon upon the table, the impatience, the outspoken desire and blatant hunger for feeling, all that raw longing expressed in it—is somehow redeeming. Were one to be able to whip this gesture, so childlike, and this prose, so simple and direct upon occasion, into poetry, it would skew the perception by forcing its angle. The strange truth of it all is that this prose, unforced, is so extraordinarily poetic.

This eyeless book, said Woolf. This poem of a novel. This most intense of my writing . . . Whatever we think of truth as being is perhaps best grasped when the passion for language is stilled for one moment, and even that habit, seen through: one day, Bernard leans, quite simply, over a gate leading into a field, and senses all of a sudden that everything stops: "the rhymes and the hummings, the nonsense and the poetry," and a space is cleared—not outside, in the field or by the gate, but in his mind, swept clean of all the dull foliage that habit has nourished:

> I said life had been imperfect, an unfinished phrase. It had been impossible for me, taking snuff as I do from any bagman met in a train, to keep coherency—that sense of the generations, of women carrying red pitchers to the Nile, of the nightingale who sings among conquests and migrations. It had been too vast an undertaking, I said, and how can I go on lifting my foot perpetually to climb the stair? (283)

Our best gestures are so small, for all the too muchness and too vastness of what we are engaged in, making some whole out of fragments, clearing space and coherence from so many details: it is probably impossible, what we feel ourselves called upon to try. Bernard's voice is just that, a trial or an *essay* of the self unfolding, like so many pleats of that ocean folded over like napkins until their breaking or undoing. As for this self in himself to whom he speaks, it is undone, deserted, unseeing, disabled: it cannot even summon its strength to make a fist, and finds all about it withered. "A man without a self," I said. "A heavy body leaning on a gate" (284). Without even the strength to push the gate open except by the force of his own despondency, he sees himself from without as this "elderly man, a heavy man with grey hair, through the colorless field, the empty field" (286). The questions he raises are crucial, and not simply aesthetic: how light can be called upon to return to this world without colors and without self, how the once vivid and colored landscape only remembered can be summoned to come back, how we can—for it is surely not just of Bernard that it is a question—glimpse again some train drawing "across the fields lop-eared with smoke." The very term "lop-eared" has the resonance of a more innocent world, rabbits and children replacing the grey-haired, heavy speaker.

And this time, language being exhausted like the speaker himself, life returns indeed as a form of childhood nourishment, through the pages of a brightly-colored children's book, as they manage to keep and to hold what matters, making it last. Bernard's suggestion that we look at the scenes together, "as children turn over the pages of a picture-book and the nurse says, pointing: 'That's a cow. That's a boat' " (239) is oddly simple, with a whole sense of warmth and possibility, of stability and trust, is in emotional correspondence with the desire manifested by the beating of the spoon on the table—we imagine some child's hand, perhaps plump, certainly impatient. Retrospectively now, these pages of pictures are registered as moments to be seen and turned, turned to and finally from, toward others.

As the interweaving becomes visual instead of oral, the *real* emotion that Pater sensed in the condensation of life finely tuning itself to its most intense moments takes on the guise of truth; the recall is of the past, but somehow saves the present:

> But for a moment I had sat on the turf somewhere high above the flow of the sea and the sounds of the woods, and had seen the house, the garden, and the waves breaking. The old nurse who turns the pages of the picture-book had stopped and had said, 'Look. This is the truth.' (287)

That line of true-seeing, of trust and true-believing returns us to the past as source and nourishment, through the gaze as primordially powerful, efficacious beyond speech. The little language to be found has to combine, then, the visual and the verbal in order to last.

Truth is found and shown by larger-than-life figures: the old nurse here, and, elsewhere in *The Waves*, the figure of the woman writer, at Elvedon: "The lady sits between the two long windows, writing . . . I see the lady writing. I see the gardeners sweeping, said Susan" (17); and the writing scene becomes a stable point of reference, like the picture-book, with the gardeners sweeping all around, and the lady writing "between the windows. And the solitary is no longer solitary" (141). In some deep sense, the nurse showing and the lady writing are both preserving the fragmentary into the possible lasting, over against the exhaustion of language and of life. "All this little affair of 'being' is over" (288), says Bernard, and that very little language would seem, in that case, to have perfectly matched such a little affair as life. After all, the peelings and bread-crumbs left on the table could be seen to undo any expectation of wholeness—any coming of any Percival at all to complete any gathering—no matter how essential a communion scene is being represented, no matter what strength the collective brings with it, past single identity. (Bernard is all of them, and they, him: "Here on my brow is the blow I got when Percival fell. Here on the nape of my neck is the kiss Jinny gave Louis. My eyes fill with Susan's tears. I see far away quivering, like a gold thread, the pillar Rhoda saw, and feel the rush of the wind of her flight when she leapt" (289). The fragmentary and "little" remains would seem to undo any holistic ending, to make impossible the hope of passing anything on as complete: is there any substance or truth in it? (288).

The figures of nurse and writer, and later, mother, act as sole guarantors of the important and the lasting, of what can remain: they can be counted on, as parts of the self, nourishing the self, until "The shock of the falling wave, says Bernard, which has sounded all my life . . . . no longer makes quiver what I hold." So important is the *holding*, that it is stressed at the risk of awkwardness ("makes quiver"); a little language, so moving, can take such a risk, and win.

The point is that the littleness of language in no way contradicts its lasting power; it has to hold out against all the things too big, the songs too loud, the speech too glib, and the phrases too beautiful to ring true among the litter of our lives:

> What is the phrase for the moon? And the phrase for love? By what name are we to call death? I do not know. I need a little language such as lovers use, words of one syllable such as children speak when they come into the room and find their mother sewing and pick up some scrap of bright wool, a feather, or a shred of chintz. I need a howl; a cry . . . . Nothing neat. Nothing that comes down with all its feet on the floor . . . I have done with phrases. (295)

To respond to the large figures of nurse, writer, mother— here, those female figures serving as muse—the fragmentary will do, wonderfully indeed, better than ornamented phrases, and is found sufficient by Bernard, gentle in the hesitations of his speaking self, touching in his aging efforts and modest speech, as his hopes center on catching some last train: "I, I, I, tired as I am, spent as I am, and almost worn out with all this rubbing of my nose along the surfaces of things, even I, an elderly man who is getting rather heavy and dislikes exertion" . . . He dares not even ascribe his whole feelings to himself, not, "I have a sense of daybreak," or "I feel the dawn of hope," or anything of that kind or tone: rather, he ends in smallness, caution, and refusal to blow things up big by language: "There is a sense of the break of day. I will not call it dawn" (295).

Not as resounding a song of glory as might seem appropriate to stand up to the loudly apparent cycles of nature, the crash of Percival's death or of the waves, and yet—just because of its modesty—the adequate preparation for that final fling of the writing self unvanquished and somehow lasting, against the break of day and death.

❦ 4 ❦
Together, with Virginia

Sisters: Virginia and Vanessa

I daresay you'll think I've said nonsense. You can put it down to the imbecile ravings of a painter on paper. By the way surely Lily Briscoe must have been rather a good painter. Before her time perhaps, but with great gifts really? No, we didn't laugh at the bits about painting.
Vanessa to Virginia, about *To the Lighthouse*
(May 11, 1927; VWL:II, 573)

You do know really don't you how much you help me . . . I can't show it & I feel so stupid & such a wet blanket often but I couldn't get on at all if it weren't for you.
Virginia to Vanessa (February 4, 1938; VWL:VI, 211)

My letters, says Vanessa repeatedly, how dull they are; how boring, how ill-expressed; even in her just-quoted, lengthy and moving letter in celebration of that great novel *To the Lighthouse*, she exclaims: "But I am very bad at describing my feelings. I daresay you'll understand" (VWL:II, 573). Virginia of whom Carrington too thought, and said towards the very end of her life, that she was the one person who would understand her, did know, in these cases and many, how to understand.

As with Vanessa's lamentations about the dullness of her art next to Duncan's, about the flatness of her renderings in relation to her conception, the reality is far different from what one would imagine in listening to her. In part, of course, this is the negative magic of saying what you hope not to be true: if the gods chasten those they love, we know they also have had the reputation for cutting down, and more rapidly still, the tallest stalk of wheat for its *hubris*; too sure a self-assurance may be confused with immodesty, over which the threat of nemesis hangs. In part, of course also, the presence of Virginia as receiver might cause anyone to say that she knew her letters to be dull, boring, and so on, as Vanessa repeatedly did ("I know my letters are dull," July 10, 1910; "this is a very boring letter isn't it?," n.d., 1910's summer; "I find it difficult to believe my letters are anything but dull . . .," August 31, 1915).

Yet both sisters' appetite for letters is "insatiable," as Vanessa says of Virginia's, and she feels (happily) called on: "Nevertheless perhaps you'll expect me to write too though as you tell me I'm so inarticulate" (April 6, 1911); of course Virginia has had letters from all the wittiest people around, says Vanessa, but she seems still longing for the letters from her sister, of which she never has enough. Insatiable, Virginia was always to be that: expecting, wanting, needy. She was, to be sure, needed in return, but did not always feel so. In contrast, Vanessa's world seemed to her so full, and so very rounded, children and artists and art all responding to, and encircling her.

Vanessa (of whom Nigel Nicolson, in editing the *Letters of Virginia Woolf*, in volume III, exclaims: "How she takes over this volume," xvii) can indeed almost be seen to take over the entire volume of Virginia's love. Expected, she always was, and also needed. Her protective instincts toward her sister, and her love, flourish exactly as they are necessary. Instances from the summer of 1910, after Virginia's stay in a rest home, are typical in their tone. Vanessa urges Virginia on a path of prudence: "Do restrain your gifts," she urges, "and don't waste them . . ."; she must not exhaust herself in London, must think sensibly. Why must she always be truculent? Even as all fuss around Virginia, continually anxious about her, hovering over her, even displeasing to her in their wrought-up state worse than hers, Vanessa is able to except herself from the others and to know how urgently she above all is wanted, needed, loved, desired. Indeed, the tone that most frequently runs through the letters is not *anxious* so much as it is *desirous*. If only I could feel, she writes on August 8 of this same year 1910, that you would really look after your health. Given Virginia's tendencies to overstrain herself, her sister can only hope she will finally reduce all the stress, understanding what she can and cannot, or should not, do. This may well be, however, what she was least interested in attending to, or comprehending.

Miss Thomas the nurse seems to think—"it's not my idea—that seeing me would be your chief reason for wanting to come back at once." It might just be, at least in part, her idea too: just to see me: her "chief reason" . . . "seeing" . . . "wanting" . . . "at once". The terms of projected (and no doubt also actual) desire are salient and unmistakable. The mental closeness between the sisters is based on similarity: Leonard says you think you are being made to eat unnecessarily, says Vanessa to her sister on August 26, 1913, but when you get in that state of worrying, until your brain is spinning and you are miserable, what the brain needs is actual material nourishment; I know, says Vanessa, because I have been through those states myself and that *is* what is needed.

What is needed . . . the need is, always here, mutual (although most commentators tend to stress Virginia's excess of it), is always double. As delight in conversation is so much a part of the way of living (from Harbour View, Studland: "We talk a great deal," Vanessa writes), we, reading her letters and seeing her paintings, can hear the sound of conversation echoing even in the calm and hieratic figures of the great painting of *Studland Beach* (1911–12), all these years later, even when we may have forgotten the particular subjects of conversation—which she described as being mostly about Sodomites, and the question of that tendency, and of love in general. On the most trivial level of her need for Virginia, Vanessa longs for a simple and prolonged getting-together. If only you could come down for an evening, she says, we could dispose of all the news at once, sitting in my studio and talking over everything; or then, "if you came for longer, we could be less condensed" (from Millmead Cottage, Guilford, August 4, 1911); please tell me all the gossip you can rake together, (February 1, 1917). The program is all planned, as if the stage were set: they will talk, and that is the art of being sisters. "If you could come for two nights we could get through quite a lot of gossip" (June 5, 1917, from Charleston). If that is not possible, please send me all the tidbits you have (just think of your poor country sister both gossipless and sisterless), she pleads, in a wonderful habitual teasing fashion. Send gossip immediately . . . this is the utmost Bloomsbury delicacy—the other pole of the very serious work. "Tell . . . tell . . . tell . . ."—the command performance is also an invitation to constant *exchange*—as Virginia's appetite for letters, news, compliments, affection, is never surfeited, neither is Vanessa's; she and Duncan share Virginia's letters, laughing hard over them, as they share the reading of *To the Lighthouse*, each with a copy, each persuaded of the truth of that telling.

On a level more profound, she longs for communication about that most valued of their undertakings that was their work, for Virginia's judgment on her own, and for their interchange about her sister's writing, from early on ("As I do prefer your descriptions of humans to those of scenery but I might have both I think. Anyhow those of humans give me great hopes of you as a novelist, there's a command for you," August 26, 1919). She longs, particularly, for Virginia's presence at times of deepest joy, coincident often with the times of hardest effort.

Exemplary along these lines is a letter written from Roger's home at Durbins in Guilford, one of the places where she finds herself happy to the point of longing to settle down for the rest of the summer, and where her delight at working is as great as Roger's usual energy, next to which she often feels her own pale: so happy is she painting that she entirely forgets her nerves, her body, and anything else at all. "Why aren't you here too? I wish you were as sensible as I am & as certain about your precious brains—but of course they may not really be worth it." (June 2, 1911). Plainly, such a tease could only be written to a sister whose genius is as unquestioned as Virginia's, and yet is all the more loving and all the more perceptive as, in fact, Virginia is not as sure as she should and could be; the combination of playful affection and teasing is typical and endears Vanessa to the reader as it did, along with a thousand other things, to her sister.

Their closest relation, unsurprisingly, has to do with the high combination of Love and Life that Vanessa read as the very opposite of Sidney Saxon-Turner's "Bloomsbury-Cambridge" style of desiccated living (capitalizing the terms in just that manner and writing them very large on her page): LOVE, LIFE, and also, though it does not appear there, work. Desiccated living is above all opposed to work as passion, and the passionate temperament in work, love, and life lies implicit, and sometimes rises explicit, in this other—and in my view, truer—Bloomsbury's heart.

To Virginia, Vanessa describes her delight in her ongoing art projects, even when the expressions are fragmentary and not full-blown: ("My sketches so far are not very numerous or particularly successful but it's great fun to be doing them," n.d., VB/VW, 1912), quietly at Asheham, together with some paintings, where she always found she could do more "real" work there in a few days than for weeks on end in London. This is her try-out for a life in the country, where she would often have to be alone, but where she could have a larger studio than would be possible in London; she believed her inner resources would easily suffice and in fact they easily did, there at Charleston, and her desirous being, in regard to her sister, could express itself in words, letters, and images, whether detailed, or then faceless, as in the famous painting for so long at Monk's House, of Virginia in an armchair, with no clarification of her individual features at all. This is the picture of Virginia that perhaps best seizes all her aspects, since it defines none.

Vanessa's tease about Virginia finding her inarticulate has no basis in reality, except in her wish to be better able to express her feelings on paper, as she could so well do with her brush. In fact, she writes with great clarity; inarticulate Vanessa certainly was not, nor dull. The frequent letters cajole and discuss and argue, even as the painting sister left her brush for the page (as she said, the highest compliment she could pay to Virginia's genius at the time of the *Lighthouse*), fearing her own inadequacy with words and projecting the fear onto Virginia, who then was free to find her fully adequate.

The same of course is true in reverse, when Virginia

leaves literary criticism for a time to write about art; she writes in *The Nation,* just where Vanessa was to find, in 1917, that article of Roger's which returned her love for him through her respect in reading him. Roger and Duncan and Vanessa have been to look at the young geniuses of the world of art at the Autumn Salon in Paris, and they are discussing Virginia's piece in the cafe enticingly entitled "Le Rat Mort," before a play. "Roger says he likes it very much. It's just what he wanted to get said. He thinks it a great advantage to have art criticism written by those who know nothing about it. For my part I couldn't see any art criticism in it. However it seemed to meet with Duncan's approval too." Of course, the "know-nothingness" of Virginia, in respect to art, just because she is a writer, is as patently false as the "inarticulate" nature of Vanessa just because she is a painter. Roger adds a note to Vanessa's letter, complicating the issue: "this isn't at all what I said but you can read between the lines & allow for Vanessa's artistic distortion" (October 20, 1911).

This balance is effectively set up between the sisters and their stated capacities, incapacities, and talents stated and unstated. Roger's footnote to Vanessa's letter about the play reemphasizes the elements of the balance perfectly: the lines are wonderfully and comically drawn, with Vanessa alone and patently wrong, against the crowd of Virginia-admirers, fake-oppositional, affectionate, and safe.

Since that setup is so effective, the exchanging of roles will continue to work. Virginia's genius will be teased, and Vanessa's great talent encouraged; the dangers of rivalry, except on the unconscious level, will be averted by deliberately minimizing remarks: you will always be richer than I, because you sell better, especially if you get launched in France, Vanessa says. Or: how can a writer write of painting, or a painter write with intelligence? But their own high intelligence and mutual understanding will be set in play and nurtured by their double generosity of spirit, informing all they write and see, in relation to each other, and together, in relation to the world.

To Duncan, on March 6, 1914, Virginia writes of her Nessa, in an ignorance which is a quite certain knowledge, of a myth which is a quite certain truth, deep at the heart of love, informing it with another energy not altogether reprehensible: "People are always asking after her; indeed one of the concealed worms of my life has been a sisters jealousy— *of* a sister I mean; and to feed this I have invented such a myth about her that I scarcely know one from the other" (VWL: II, 146).

Virginia will be called upon to offer criticism and comment on Vanessa's art, and the latter responds immediately ("Well it's a good thing you still think I have some rough eloquence & vigour of style," November 22, 1918). She will also be called upon, by Vanessa in her most serious tone, to share her theories of creation and expression, to tell her "new theories of aesthetics & feelings" upon looking at Vanessa's recent work (July 3, 1918), and sometimes in a lighter fashion, as in the telegraphic request: "Do send all gossip & aesthetics" (July 9, 1918). As for Virginia's judgment and its consequences, Vanessa wonders if her sister could use further illustrations for her work—the prime example of collaboration will of course be this one, with both together on the same project, from their different fields, uniting in the final product. The desirous request is added as an appendix: "Then I write also to say that if you'd really like me to do any more . . . ," November 22, 1918. Thus the open and unembarrassed trace of wanting to be wanted is made unburdensome, not entering the center of the letter, just put after as afterthought. This is tact, and this is also sistering at its best.

This longing is a double one, each anxious continually about the other's reactions—Virginia unable to be at ease until Vanessa writes her about *To the Lighthouse*, Vanessa not really happy until she knows how Virginia feels, seeing her work. Vanessa will, however, be urged, and not just in an appendix, not just to illustrate further, but also (and perhaps more urgently), to yield up her views on Virginia's work, and will usually do so in the flirtatious mode to which both are accustomed: "I have had my copy of your stories. You don't care what I think of your writing, of course, do you Billy? So it won't interest you at all to be told that I was amused, interested & fascinated by the skill & completeness with which it was done. No doubt you are a very good writer . . ." (July 23, 1917).

The essential lightness of her response fooled neither of them, of course, and this was just the way to answer. All the more moving, then, is her reaction to her copy of *To the Lighthouse,* in which she feels "her pride humbled" and her aesthetic judgment incapacitated. Knowing as she does that her opinion matters more than anything to Virginia, she continues to state, nevertheless, that she cannot flatter herself to the extent of thinking her "literary opinion" is really of any interest to her; but she has, all the same, feelings about it as a work of art. Again, she reiterates that her feelings "probably don't matter" at all—how could this possibly be? How could the feelings of one sister in regard to at least a semi-portrait of their parents "not matter at all?" They matter in large part, again, as symptomatic of the desirous Vanessa, wanting to be told her feelings matter, her judgment counts, her admiration helps.

Astonishing, she says about this creation of Virginia's, how she makes the extraordinary beauty of their mother's character rise from the dead, how shattering it is to find herself "face to face with those two again," now that she is grown up. A supreme portrait artist you are, she says to Virginia, able to move the reader personally (as in my case she continues) and impersonally (as again, in my case, and that of Duncan, who feels he knows our mother now), able to understand and imagine relations as a whole. And even here, the odd balance set up between the complementary roles of the sisters comes into play: I'm a bit doubtful about covering paints with wet cloths, says the painter to the writer, but it might be done, she says; "But how do you make Boeuf en Daube? Does it have to be eaten on the moment after cooking three days?" (May 11, 1927; VWL:II, 573).

So that she takes in the remarks on painting (no, we didn't laugh at those bits), makes limited caveats concerning them, and then goes on to the other, domestic and writerly side, as if effective writing were somehow aligned with the actual kitchen, as if, when Virginia describes the dinner scene with the main dish bubbling, she should know how it is made, as if reference were to confirm the real recipe. Virginia's writing convinces.

"Now having made a sufficient fool of myself I hope to

please even you . . ."—why would Virginia be pleased by
Vanessa's making herself "foolish," except that the desirous
and loving being needs confirmation in her very non-foolish-
ness—as with the dullness of letters and paintings in other
cases—and that the tease continues as part of the essential
set-up. I am so enthused that I lose my rationality, over you:
like some continuing and nourishing love affair, this exalted
community of spirit makes itself sensible at the summit of
the most admiring letters of one to the other, where the
shattering and the astonishment are felt, not to the point of
in-articulation, as the jest runs, but in fact to the point of
emotional outpouring.

Virginia's answer to the long letter with its complex of
feelings and intensity of admiration is slow in coming, and
anxiety overtakes the writer. Like some quite wonderful
dance of uncertainty, the give and take of the situation is
itself a dialogue. Don't tell me my letter didn't arrive? Of
course, it was not what it should have been as a statement of
my complicated feelings ("not that I succeeded in expressing
them very well—nor the few but very definite aesthetic judge-
ments I dared to make"). But you probably just didn't notice
my letter amidst all the others; if it didn't arrive, "if you want
to know what I think, I'll try to tell you again. It will be the
greatest possible tribute to your genius I can pay if I do as
you know that I find nothing more difficult than putting my
sentiments into words & then on paper." Yet on the other
hand perhaps you have had my letter, been furious at my
saying all the wrong things, and you think the best thing is
just to make believe you never got it.

The seesawings of tremendous concern, about phrasing,
about feelings, about daring to send their opinions each to
the other about each other's art, the real anxiety about and
anguish in reception, are here visible to the point of pain. The
relation between the parents and the daughters, the daughters with each other, and both of them with language, is
nowhere so clear in its intricate tensions. The very bones and
sinews are exposed; fascinated, we stare at the exposition, or
turn away embarrassed.

A month before, another summit of complication was
reached, this one having to do with the same topic, from

another angle, that is, the maternal relationship. Vanessa longs to have her sister write a book about the maternal instinct, which she has never found sufficiently explored in writing. Now this might seem a highly inappropriate topic for Virginia, who was never allowed to have children, but Vanessa explains how many opportunities for observation Virginia has, and how she can "start with birth, which also has never been described except by men" (April 23, 1927). I could tell you a good deal, she says, as if such communication were as easy, say, as gossip and perhaps indeed it was: she openly describes, and we can but wonder how Virginia reacted to this, how Angelica her little daughter, instead of sucking on her nipples, was given to biting them repeatedly and fiercely, until she was quite sore (January 1, 1919). Let me tell you, begins Vanessa . . . and continues about the passion of maternity, the instinct that should fade, as the children age (give me six more years for Julian), and the rest. As if it were at once to be apologized for and described. The reader, intrigued by the situation and not entirely comfortable with it, may well focus on the idea that Virginia is being called upon to write not only on a topic she knows little about (less, for instance, than art), but about a specific subject, that of birth, on which she might well have some feelings of uncomfortable kinds.

Of course Virginia was close to her niece and nephews, who felt being with her to be an immense treat, and in fact the pictured relation between Mrs. Ramsay and her children will perfectly portray maternal affection, all those years later. But the major question remains unsettled. Why is the sister here urging the pen to give birth to such knowledge—and what sort of knowledge is there to be on the part of someone who has not, precisely, given *that* sort of birth, urged to give pen to *this* sort of birth? What desires is Vanessa expressing, in this bizarre suggestion, as she imparts what inspiration? From the positive side of this exchange, the one I take here, the desire is generous. The very fact that mothering can be shared, birth discussed, and maternal feelings expressed goes to confirm the power of the network *à deux* set up with such an intensity between the two. As if they together were giving birth to knowledge about family relations, sisters, mothers, and lovers, as they do to a certain knowledge about art and letters, love and life:—"why did you bring me into the world?" we have heard Virginia ask her sister (March 17, 1921).

These letters call for strong reading, and for the generosity of spirit that they manifest to be returned. They too serve their cause of bringing into the world a certain passionate way of seeing, of reading, of sistering.

Of all the letters, probably the most celebrated and for many of us the most interesting is the one concerning Vanessa's reading of *The Waves,* in which she finds herself "gasping, out of breath, choking, half-drowned as you might expect" (October 11, 1931). Next time she reads it, she says, she may float more quietly, but this time she is moved and must express herself in these "words which aren't one's medium." She knows Virginia will understand, just as she knows her reaction will have been "expected." In return, too, she wants to "understand what you're about," and thus wishes for her painting project of a "great picture" to be in some sense analogous to Virginia's novel in its own meaning. How can one explain, she asks, and then does so convincingly: "to me painting a floor covered with toys & keeping them all in relation to each other & the figures & the space of the floor & the light on it means something of the same sort that you seem to me to mean."

The interest here is not just in the reaction, but in the metaphors she uses. For the case of childbirth returns, and the actions of relation to a child, as to a grownup: in merging the feelings about giving birth and about Thoby's death, about having a baby and singing a lullaby, she picks up on just what she was suggesting Virginia do in her writing, and— by her understanding of her sister in her double relation to sistering: to Vanessa and to Thoby now dead—avows that what Virginia was doing was, symbolically and significantly, mothering.

> For its quite as real an experience as having a baby or anything else, being moved as you have succeeded in moving me—Of course there's the personal side—the feelings you describe on what I must take to be Thoby [Percival's] death . . . Even then I know its only because of your art

that I am so moved. I think you have made one's human feelings into something less personal—if you wouldn't think me foolish I should say you have found the 'lullaby capable of singing him to rest.' (VWL: IV, 390–91)

She knows, in any case, that Virginia will not find her foolish, will have expected and have been waiting for her reaction; she wants to have understood what Virginia was and is about, and wishes to share that understanding.

That this double emphasis on meaning and on sharing should be exactly what is, here and so well, shared seems the perfect *image for the intention* for these letters—they are themselves about the effort to keep, and the joy of keeping close relations with each other, and about figures and space and, above all, the light cast on them, through understanding, by one sister and the other.

Virginia and Leonard, and Carrington, Alive

What fun life is, how happy I am!
Carrington to Gerald (July 5, 1921; DC/GB)

Nobody shall say of me that I have not known perfect happiness.
Virginia, after a holiday in Cassis, 1925

Sometimes in the last few days I've thought it may be a bad thing to love anyone as I love you.
Leonard to Virginia, 1913 (VW, 149–50)

But I don't really think it can be, continues Leonard's remark; it is only that such a deep feeling cuts you off from the world. The difference between those not in love (he instances Lytton and Norton) and us is that everything is "so thin to them & to me—everything with you in it—so rich" (VW, 146). Never was there a compliment itself of more richness paid to love. The consciousness of the desperate transience of it all, of us all, like that cloud moving across the sky that was then removed from *To the Lighthouse* (when "each lover knows, but cannot confess, his knowledge of the transience of love:

the mutability of love . . . ," VW, 150), somehow cannot touch the depths of that core of common things as Virginia recounts them— a bus ride to Richmond, sitting in the grass smoking . . . sitting down side by side, & saying 'Are you in your stall, brother?'—well, what can trouble this happiness? And every day is necessarily full of it" (VW, 150).

Leonard beautiful on a ladder, Leonard in a house, loving her, that sufficed, until the madness. She would not, she says, wish to live were Leonard to die: so the gasoline was ready in case it was needed for their double suicide, and the morphia secured from Adrian Stephen. So, of all people, Virginia could understand Carrington in her final act, and did. She had sensed it as imminent, as her letter sent after she saw Carrington the last time bears witness. Virginia's notes to herself on Carrington in March and May of 1932 are among the most revealing documents we have:

Virginia, on Carrington

So we went to Ham Spray . . . 'I thought you weren't coming" said C. She came to the door, in her little jacket & socks with a twisted necklace. Her eyes were very pale. 'I sent a telegram, but I do everything wrong. I thought you didn't get it." She was pale, small, suffering silently, very calm. She had hot soup for us. . . . I didn't light the fire, she said . . . She burst into tears, & I took her in my arms. She sobbed, & said she had always been a failure. 'There is nothing left for me to do. I did everything for Lytton. But I've failed in everything else.' . . . I held her hands. Her wrists seemed very small. She seemed helpless, deserted, like some small animal left . . . There was not much time. We had tea & broken biscuits . . .

Virginia, to herself, March 12, 1932 (VWD: IV, 81–2)

So Carrington killed herself . . . And we discuss suicide; & I feel, as always, ghosts [dwindling] changing. Lytton's affected by this act. I sometimes dislike him for it. He absorbed her [,] made her kill herself . . . all this jumble somehow shadowed by Carrington's death . . .

Virginia, to herself, March 17, 1932 (VWD: IV, 83–4)

Talk of Carrington: how long shall we talk of Carrington?

Virginia, to herself: March 18, 1932 (VWD: IV, 85)

A saying of Leonard's comes into my head ... "Things
have gone wrong somehow." It was the night Carrington
killed herself. We were walking along that silent blue
street with the scaffolding. I saw all the violence & unreason crossing in the air: ourselves small; a tumult outside:
something terrifying: unreason. Shall I make a book out
of this? It would be a way of bringing order & speed again
into my world.
      Virginia, to herself: May 25, 1932 (VWD: IV, 103)

For Virginia and Leonard were the last visitors Carrington had before her death, and her reaction to Virginia's invitation then to her to come soon to see them ("I will come
or not," she said) reads as emblematic of her characteristic
ambivalence toward her own action. Now Carrington's
unique way of being in the world was just what Virginia had
repeatedly emphasized to her after Lytton's death, in order
to persuade her to remain. Because Carrington's being herself
was, she said, the best way to represent Lytton, whom she
made so happy, and to whom she gave so much. It would best
bring him back, since he had so loved her special peculiarities:

Oh but Carrington we have to live and be ourselves—and
I feel it is more for you to live than for any one; because
he loved you so, and loved your oddities and the way you
have of being yourself.
      (March 2, 1932; VWL:V, 28)

That note is echoed in Virginia's last letter, which Carrington read directly before her suicide; it was written in the
evening after their afternoon visit, when Virginia, finding
Carrington gentler, quieter, and more affectionate than
usual, had worried, correctly, about her will to live. This final
last letter expresses yet again the original nature she senses
in the younger woman, to whom she "can't help scribbling
one line to thank you—oh just for being yourself" (March 10,
1932).
    Herself Carrington was. She had told Virginia that last
day, that she had failed with everyone except Lytton; about
him, you best understand, Virginia had said to her repeat-

edly. And so she probably did. The same strong verb appears in the other direction when Carrington writes to Virginia, after Lytton's death, that she, of all people, "will understand." That double tribute from one strong singular woman to another, both to each other, is what remains lastingly in my mind here. The point is not just Virginia's being always haunted by "poor Carrington" who was necessarily to be alone in her desolation, as she states it baldly after Lytton's death: "And no one can help you." Indeed no one could, but Virginia's emphasis on the singularity of Carrington and on what she understood reveals her own powers of comprehension, as to what she singles out. Between them, in fact, there was an understanding of singularities, each of the other's, and in that, a corresponding double strength.

Virginia and Carrington each lost their only brother, and mourned always, transforming him into a sort of myth: Virginia, her brother Thoby into the noble rider Percival, the absent center of the group in *The Waves*; Carrington, her soldier brother Teddy into a sailor lost at sea, echoed by Beakus Penrose . . . But, for their losses, their present working passion somehow compensates with its extreme intensity and its innate love, against losing: "Do you know," writes Carrington to Lytton, "I am never quite so happy as when I can paint. Everything else seems to fade miraculously." (August 27, 1923, DC/LS); and Virginia, writing of her work on *The Waves*, expresses the same sort of intensity in the challenge to dexterity, avoidance, and yet aim: "Something new goes into my pot every morning—something thats never been got at before. The high wind can't blow, because I'm chopping & tacking all the time" (January 7, 1931, in her diary: VWD: IV, 4). It is a morning hope and happiness, with a skill in the sailing.

Much else linked them, including a fondness for the pecularities of nature in all its details: Carrington exclaims aloud, as it were for both of them: . . . "Isn't exploring the most exciting thing almost in the world, yes in every direction. This morning I feel everything so actively the smells in the garden, the sounds of the flies and the bees, & the warmth of the early day for its not yet nine o'ck. I feel so full of affections and happy . . ." (DC/GB, July 8, 1921), and again to Gerald:

"the exquisite early morning sky, the beech groves tinged with brown filled me with feelings of happiness that raised me out of myself" (October 6, 1924, DC/GB), and yet again, almost shouting her happiness in the hot sun and the rooks singing. The very focused passion of their relation to the natural—to the species of trees, and of plants and flowers, and of birds: the specificity of these relations, held with such dizzying intensity, was part of their up-and-down psychological make-up.

> What a terrific capacity I possess for feeling with intensity
> . . . Virginia, to herself, May 25, 1932 (VWD: IV, 102)

> Oh dear I see I am all wrong I care far too much for Ham Spray. I am weak in body, and soul because ever since lunch I have been in ecstasies over the beauty of the fields, the sunlight on the top of the stairs, the beech grove, faded and already tinged with brown, and my family of cats.
> Carrington, to Julia Strachey,
> October, 1929 (DG, 427)

In some of her remarks "On Being Ill," Virginia notes the aliveness to each detail around her with which she is graced at times of what her doctors would call manic moods; Carrington could have made the same notes. The passionate attachment of both was always to certain things, never, dully, to undetailed things in general: so Carrington, in one of the last entries in Her Book, from February 1932, two months before her suicide, when she is looking through her old pictures to find some of Lytton to give his brother James, and remembering their life together before they moved to Ham Spray: "Tidmarsh all came back. How much I love places. I remembered suddenly my 'passion' for a certain tree in Burgess's back field. And the beauty of the mill at the back of the house and how once a kingfisher dived from the roof into the stream" (DG, 496). And Virginia, who has shown elsewhere a fondness for this same bird, then wonders whether, reading Sir Thomas Browne's *Vulgar Errors*, "a great number of minds," only capriciously enlightened by knowledge, may not still be ruminating on "whether a kingfisher's body shows which way the wind blows; whether an ostrich digests iron; whether owls and ravens herald ill-fortune ... with more curious speculations as to the joints of elephants and the politics of storks ... "; "Reading," *Captain's Death Bed*, 171). Both women cared, with the gaze and temperament of an artist, about the specialness of things around them.

Both women were Proustian in this specific, certain, focused, and intense sensitivity, and were both, in fact, absorbed in Proust over a long period—Carrington living totally, if temporarily, within his world of perception, on which she comments repeatedly, reading him on trains and ships and in bed: "Proust amazes me," (October 18, 1928; DC/LS), and again the next year, "I read Proust feverishly" (November 2, 1929; DC/LS)—and Virginia saying she is about to read him backwards and forwards (VWD:II, 209). His power of reminiscence and his vivid saturation of prose by the poetry of impression and longing, is often felt again through Virginia's writing, as if she were rewriting him, through her own no less powerful conjuring and imaginative style. A passage about a gate opening in *Mrs. Dalloway*, just to take a case ("For so it had always seemed to her, when with a little squeak of the hinges which she could hear now . . .") brings back to the reader's memory a Proustian reminiscence of a sonority rarely found. Here it is, by chance but significantly a symbol and a signal of something about to penetrate: a sound small, polite, and infinitely resonant.

For the passage does not only recall Talland House at St. Ives, where the Stephen family spent summers—Virginia's "A Sketch of the Past" has her remembering: "You entered Talland House by a large wooden gate, the sound of whose latch clicking comes back . . . ," (MB, 111)—but also, in the memory of Proust's readers, the sound of the little bell at the gate at Combray, when Swann enters and the family, seated under the great chestnut tree hears not the harsh and loud jangle they each made when entering, but "the bell's double tinkle, timid, oval, and gilded." This original figure entering, enters into another language to capture the personal past, revealing the intricate and moving way one figure can be filled in with all the small miracles of a naturally profuse and suggestive setting. The bell, the figure, the gate—these signal the power of the memory, that vigorous instinct which Car-

rington and Virginia could evoke with true Proustian simplicity and richness: "that first Swann filled with leisure, per-
fumed by the smell of the great chestnut tree, of the little
baskets of raspberries and of a snatch of tarragon" (*Du côté
de chez Swann*, 19). Virginia writing of, and at Monk's House,
Carrington writing of, and at Tidmarsh, and then Ham Spray,
will be in some measure empowered by the same longing to
express what is, large and small, most lingering in the heart.

Their intense sensitivity to language, as to nature, makes
them both characteristically prone to rapid and minute shift-
ings of perception, to quicksilver reactions to other people
and especially in relation to themselves. They are joined in a
conscious and perhaps also an unconscious will to spontane-
ity: Virginia's encouragement to herself and others about its
heady freedoms ("Let fly, in life, on all sides") is balanced
by a close attention paid to others: "And care for people"
(November 12, 1934; VWD: IV, 25). It was not a lesson that
had to be learned by Carrington—whose blue eyes were said
to take in at once everything about people, as about things,
near and far off—for she knew it. This sensitivity works nega-
tively as well as positively, in Virginia's profound feelings
about criticism of her work, finding herself through it either
"interesting" or obsolete, and her corresponding belief in
what she calls the thinking stuff "as a web, fertilised by other
people" (December 7; VWD:IV, 193). Carrington's hypersensi-
tive reaction to the opinions of others, about her art and
herself, be it Roger or Gerald, Simon Bussy or Lytton, or
indeed anyone, marks her as of the same mold.

Their interior other life is vividly similar, even in such
small things as are common: Virginia's sensing so vividly, for
example, "the absolute delight of dark & bed" (July 8, 1932;
VWD:IV, 114) and Carrington's equal delight, repeatedly expressed, in settling down in her single bed, even when the
empty house has "a melancholly sound" and the pillows are
very hard. "But it was a pleasure to be alone in this fortress
& watch the fire lighting the room . . . The pleasure of being
alone in my bedroom is very great," or again, the "Pleasure
of lying alone in my room Looking at BOOKS. I suddenly see
what my grandmother must have felt when she refused to
have a doctor at Ivy Lodge & locked the door & died" (HB).

It is the one place where she can be as vague as she likes, can yawn without wondering about the "thoughts" of the coal skuttle, and can exist, as she puts it, "not affecting anyone except myself by what I DO. Not being in the wrong, a great mercy" (HB) (n.d.). A defensive behavior, perhaps indeed, that fear of others' thoughts and reactions, but in any case, motivating her positive gladness in her room alone, or her delight in the silent house, eating "an egg, in a little casserole, cauliflower, & stewed apples" (October 15, 1924, to Gerald).

She was, of course, far more given to an apparently solitary existence than Virginia and than Vanessa, but there is some underground likeness between them all. Their characteristic hesitation, with all its own peculiar ardor, is no less similar: Virginia to Ethel Smyth (January 12, 1941; VWL:XI, 460): "I happen to be very humble just now. I can't believe in being anyone." In being anyone: that is precisely the fate that befalls Carrington in her own mind—and that the death of Lytton aggravates. But it was already present; in a sense, the multiple views of herself by herself—her hands writing, her feet in slippers, her cats all about her—are already part of trying to hold on to a being, to a being she does not always believe in. Virginia calls herself Adeline Virginia Stephen, which she is normally not, chooses a series of nicknames for her different correspondents and for herself with them, and—most significantly—writes her early journal under the name of "Miss Jan"; Carrington calls herself not by the name given to her, Dora, but by a series of nicknames, or this ambivalent non-sexed surname Carrington, and working to distance herself from "anyone" she might be, signs her journal by a name doubly other than her own, misspelling her married name in Her Book. No self-structure, and no self. "I haven't any standards of my own," says Carrington to Brenan (February 28, 1923). Nothing in her paltry life, or in her ill-arranged brain, as she calls them, to make her worth writing to; she bores Lytton, being no one, as Virginia tires herself when feeling, no less than Carrington, no one.

But it is above all the intensity of their love for and their adoration of their companion that joins them: this Virginia understood, with her need for and her talent for recognizing "a marriage that is a tremendous living thing, always alive, always hot, not dead and easy in parts as most marriages are" (VWL: I, 497). Carrington's relation to Lytton was that too, tremendous and living, with all the difficulties that implies, until his death—thus and for that reason, the necessary end to her own life, as she saw it.

Work, work, work. That's my final prescription.

So we read in Virginia's diary (VWD: V, 50), knowing work to be indeed a prescription against emptiness, ("And how much time I have wasted!" she exclaims [December 19, 1921; VWD: II, 152].)

Writing to Gerald Brenan on July 14, 1924, Carrington declares: "I long to start my painting again. It is not in people, & relations one finds happiness . . . Well, not very even happiness, but in one's work" (DC/GB) . . . . But of course, she does not dare go into Lytton's room to get her brushes, for he is working; and, at other times, she has written pages of what she calls nonsense, and not arranged her brushes. The feeling is of unsureness, even in the art, for always, she says, "I feel so uncertain of myself" (May 1, 1927; DC/GB).

That her work meant, finally, nothing to Carrington without Lytton, is and was simply an honest statement. "Cold winds do inhabit here," she wrote in her own journal. (January 6, 1928); that she often felt ashamed of what she had done, that she knew she did not do what she had in mind to, even when she had the time—this is less important for her own short life, than her feeling that "we had collected all our wheat into a Barn to make bread & beer for the rest of our lives & now our barn has been burnt down & we stand on a cold winter morning . . . You can't get away from the fact that Lytton is Dead . . ." (HB).

Work did not get her away from the facts; and so she could not—as Virginia, worried and with good reason on the day before Carrington's death, wanted her to—trust the advice of others "to be sensible." The word is telling, for it is just the word Vanessa used to Virginia, expressing her love and concern. As much as Vanessa, as much as Carrington, Virginia, understood loneliness. Writing was an adventure to be taken up by oneself ("If *The Waves* is anything," she says

[October 8, 1931; VWD: IV, 47], "it is an adventure which I go on alone"). Whether by necessity or by choice, the aloneness can verge into the lonely. Carrington saw no point in creating, with Lytton not there: as I see it, that is not impossible to understand.

Like Virginia herself, she followed the stricture of Henry James that Virginia quotes shortly before her suicide, to "observe perpetually." Virginia has observed her own "despondency," making it serviceable thereby: "I will go down with my colours flying" (VWL: V, 358), and so she did. No less Carrington: "There was a proud look on her face," said David Garnett about her death, in his *Old Friends*.

Colors fly as best they can, in spite of whatever winds they have to face and fly through. "How to keep the flight of the mind?," asks Virginia (June 2, 1940; VWD: V, 298)—such a flight was never guaranteed as easy, anymore than is a "tremendous" living companionship, or the ability to live after the end of it, as with Carrington, or then, and still more terribly, as with Virginia, the end of one's mind itself.

5
Vanessa

A Good Life for Painting

I am painting again quite steadily. Its wonderful.
Vanessa to Virginia, May 13, 1919 (VB/VW)

Virginia saw her sister Vanessa as of an "inviolable reticence" in her work and in her living. This ultimate reserve of Vanessa's, so unlike Virginia's more openly needy and affectionate and cajoling ways, this deep privacy sensible in her greatest paintings—quite especially in those I take as emblematic for this present study, *The Tub* and *Studland Beach*—makes any discussion of her life a more problematic matter than it might otherwise appear. Adamantine outside, and intensely vulnerable within, says Virginia of her sister.

Married to Clive, an inveterate womanizer, she first loved Roger Fry, the art critic, with a passion that he returned and in the long run surpassed—the beauty of both was in their character and in their soul, as each remarked of the other, and in their ways of being. She then fell desperately and forever in love with Duncan Grant, the artist, erstwhile lover of Lytton Strachey, and a man of great kindness, vagueness, and artistic talent. Mainly a homosexual, he was briefly bisexual, and from his union with Vanessa came Angelica, who was later to marry Duncan's lover David Garnett, still thinking herself the daughter of Clive Bell.

Of Vanessa's two sons, Julian, the elder, was killed in the Spanish Civil War: from this great tragedy in her life, she never entirely recovered. Quentin became an art historian and professor, and author of several books on his family and on Bloomsbury. Vanessa was happiest in a quiet life, first at Asheham, and then at the farmhouse called Charleston, not far from Rodmell where Virginia and Leonard occupied Monk's House; surrounded by children, a garden, and friends coming and going, she painted, lived, and loved Duncan with her whole heart. They traveled often to France, where they, with Clive and sometimes Roger, stayed in Cassis, in a little cottage where they could paint outdoors, see the sunlight, and live that elemental life which Roger and Vanessa had both extolled: oh how simple life could be, if we could make it as we chose.

The will to simplicity and a colorful chaos make a good merger. Virginia's description of life at Charleston is priceless, of Clive shouting somewhere in the garden, Vanessa emerging from the patchwork of different-colored flowers, absent-minded and not eager to be interrupted, and Duncan wandering about hazily, with various ties and yellow waistcoats draped about him and paint-stained blue trousers that have to be hitched up . . . and not so terribly different from her descriptions of the life in the Lytton-Carrington-Ralph ménage, with chickens wandering everywhere about and a sort of everywhichway arrangement of living. The pictures make an engaging and instantly convincing backdrop for the informality of life and work and love: whatever order there might be underlying the picture will be interior. I think we should prize both the pictures and the feeling, even at the risk of being accused of romanticism: we are not entirely without textual and lived justification. Carrington explains to Virginia, referring to how Dorothy Wordsworth's room at Dove Cottage has been kept "exactly as she left it," how morbid the Stracheys find her keeping Lytton's study as he left it after his death and asks: "Am I romantic about it d'you think? Oh no," answers Virginia, 'I'm romantic too, I said' " VWD:IV, 82).

With the war, which killed, as Vanessa said, the Bloomsbury spirit, and with the loss of Julian, her own spirit darkened, and her painting too. She is buried in the churchyard at Firle, and a plain black tombstone marks the grave. We could dwell on that, or then remember her in the way she wrote of herself to Angelica in September of the year she died:

"Duncan is painting, I am sitting in my room with the door open between us. The garden is full of Red Admirals and birds and apples" (VB, 361).

Corresponding: Vanessa and Roger

Remember I love you not because you have any virtues or charms for you haven't any—you're old and ugly and rather stupid and no good as an artist and why should I care for you at all? your Vanessa

Vanessa to Roger, 1911

I will try somehow to get things right.

Vanessa to Roger, 1914

The devil is that people like me want so many things and it's only rare Phoenixes like you that have them, and then you're off before one can look around. I do honestly need someone who can talk art and sympathize and criticize.

Roger to Vanessa, 1917

He was always the giver—no one excited me and stirred me as he did.

Virginia, of Roger (RFL:I, 95)

With his black brows and greying hair, his noble countenance, and the dramatic sadness of his union with his mentally unstable wife, Roger Fry was unsurprisingly attractive to Vanessa Bell, with whom he conversed, painted, and had a love affair, from 1911 to 1914; given his eloquence and his passion, it would be hard to describe it better than he does himself, in a letter to Vanessa in 1911: ". . . our so extraordinary intimacy which leaves nothing to be said, scarcely anything to take form in the mind. We arrived so quickly, so almost instantaneously at taking everything in each other for granted and we skipped all those times of mystery and trembling hopes and anxieties and all the subtleties and half-revelations" (RFL: I, 349). Although perhaps the elimination of that initial state of uncertainty could be seen to have contributed, along with other factors, to the final dissolution of their affair into a lifelong friendship, it is as if their double beauty were to have enhanced the scene forever, as it is played out in letters and in paint.

Roger Fry can be seen to have taken for a while the role of Leslie Stephen in Vanessa's life, in part counseling her as an older male, fatherly and demanding. Until her involvement with Duncan Grant, younger by six years, Roger was the most important figure, for her art and herself. Even when she had transferred her love to Duncan, Roger remained admirable to her, as a man and as an art critic, Quentin Bell reminds us, although she quarreled with him about specific art theories and did not admire him as a painter. Roger, aware of the latter, is clear-eyed and forthright on the subject, as was she:

> You're very nice my dear about wishing to like my things more. Of course it is always a bit of a disappointment to me that I like my own work better than you do. But it used to be far worse when I had no confidence in my own judgement and felt that your not liking them was a final damnation; but you know I've got over that and have begun to have quite a good enough conceit of myself. At least I think I get more power every year and that's all one need worry about. I don't suppose you'll ever *like* my things very much but I think you'll respect them more and more because there's a lot of queer stuff hidden away in them as a result of all my long wandering and peerings and gropings in the world of art ... I shall never make anything that will give you or anyone else the gasp of delighted surprise at a revelation. (from St. Tropez, October 7, 1922; RFL: II, 526)

What he could give the onlooker was, he said, a quiet pleasure, with some sort of meaning "tho' mostly one passes it by ..." (RFL: II, 527). This was a constant refrain, the being passed by that he so strongly sensed. Duncan, on the other hand, Vanessa (and others, who bought him in abundance) admired as a painter, and this must have been bitter for Roger, who was so often the recipient of her enthusiastic comments on Duncan's paintings, alone and in relation to hers. When she expressed her opinion about Roger's painting, it was never hypocritical, always straightforward, and—frequently—in accord with his own evaluation, as his critical sense was so very acute. Roger's depression about his own painting comes clearly through in many letters to Vanessa, whom he never ceased to love and of whom he never ceased to be the confidant; in several of them Vanessa's reaction to his work is referred to, sadly.

Imagine the forthrightness of a man who can say this, and how perfect a correspondence he could set up with a woman able to be herself as forthright about her judgment. The like and respect dichotomy, in relation to his work, finds exactly the distinction needed; Fry earned the respect of all who knew him, even as, indeed, his paintings did not "surprise" or "reveal" in the sense that his astoundingly successful public lectures could and always did.

Roger's influence on Vanessa, on her attitude and her art is clear, first through his introduction of the French painters into her consciousness (and that of the English in general), then through and towards a certain way of seeing and coloring, as well as a certain wit and inventiveness. Their almost symbiotic relation for years can be seen as a model of mutual reinforcement and nurturing, in spite of Vanessa's other affections.

Angelica Garnett points out, in a conversation in the fall of 1989, how his energy was striking, continuous, and available at all times, whereas Vanessa and Duncan were energetic only in some domains; how he was gregarious and dealt with the public, while they preferred being left alone to paint. The very force of Roger's enthusiasm gives him his own youthful appearance and attitude (Aldous Huxley, in 1918: ". . . old Roger Fry, who for a man of over fifty is far the youngest person I have ever seen"; RFL: II, 59). Repeatedly, in the letters from Vanessa to Virginia, Roger's extraordinary vigor, energy, and dynamism combined with his rapidity of rhythm occasions remark and admiration (as did, when Vanessa had fallen ill with measles in Italy, his angelic patience and cheerful temper [May 10, 1911]). Roger seems, indeed and miraculously, a man for all seasons, more and more amazing as time went on, right until the end of his life. He could be bumbling and awkward, doing everything too fast and furiously, wearing others out, eating and holding forth at the same time, as Gerald Brenan rather jealously describes him, with his enormous enthusiasm and vitality the key both to his awkwardness and his brilliance. Larger than life he seems now to have been, always initiating things, collectively, like the Omega crafts group, and singularly, as with his life in France with his multiple contacts with French painters and his translations of Mallarmé prefaced by Charles Mauron. Wherever he was, he inspired all the actions of any group of which he was a part, guiding, enthusing, abounding in ideas; always having several projects, he would start several pictures at once instead of one, alarming those about him with his energy.

When Roger stays with Vanessa, they set out with their easels in the morning, wherever they are, and, she writes from Chicester (in August 1915), unless he's there, she generally does not make the effort to go out to paint with other artists, but lazily paints at home. Roger's energy, on the other hand, never ceases to amaze her, and even before she wakens, he has usually been out to take a look at the architecture of some church and gone bathing, at the very least. From Bosham, on the 31st of August (where she is trying to see what it would be like to live in the country, loving the solitude as she has so many jobs on hand and feeling she could easily withstand the winters—a sort of try-out for Charleston and preface to the period at Cassis), she recounts in great detail a hilarious sailing expedition with Roger.

Typically, Vanessa and Clive wanted to start the day slowly, accomplishing what they had to before going on to other entertainments and work, but Roger had to catch a train later and stewed around impatiently until they were ready; just as when they had traveled in Italy, Clive and Vanessa took their time over everything, and procrastinated about most things, while Roger fumed in the foreground or background (where it is harder to imagine him). So on this occasion, they slowly got ready while he did some jobs in the village. Arrived at the boat renting place, they settled down to bask in the sun and watch the children catch crabs while Roger, undaunted, "fussed about" by the boats with the boat men, until he secured a large and handsome boat, took them for a sail at top speed and dangerously fast, stripped off his clothes to swim, changed his mind, obstinately tacked and tacked in the light gusts of wind after they were frighteningly becalmed, and rushed them back safely and triumphantly. Vanessa sees the whole venture as characteristic of his determination to "conquer men & tide & wind & come out in the end with technique triumphant."

Roger was always to be not just the most determined, but the liveliest and the most enthusiastic and energetic of the group, with Virginia (of whom, says Vanessa to Virginia, he was "foolishly" fond, and who always remembered his guiding her with unflagging energy and impassioned insights around the world of ruins and art). To Roger's exceptional being, Virginia's own *Roger Fry* bears firm witness. Repeatedly, in her letters, she celebrates him as the one true civilized individual she knows, as the most remarkable man she has ever met, as "the most heavenly of men . . so rich so infinitely gifted" (to Ethel Smyth, September 11, 1934, after his death; VWL: V, 330). We have, she says, talked and talked for twenty years now. I don't know anybody who gave more. Roger and Lytton and Leonard, all so crucially important to her, seem no less so to us.

In a sense, Roger was, for a time, to Vanessa, as France was to him; not just a model for art and loving, but an entire way of living. Their relation was inter-sustaining, nourishing, and thoroughly admirable: when Vanessa writes him of his beauty, she means, as she says not just his person but his character and, indeed, his "whole view of life." This very beauty has to do, at least in part, with a special mixture of intelligence, intensity, and simplicity, underlying this tale, and making it all the more difficult to tell, intense and unsimple as it was.

Vanessa's tragedy, so goes the saying and perhaps also the story, was that she was not able to love Roger longer. Rare and deep ran their correspondence, in all senses. Their personal correspondence in enthusiasm and warmth, intellect and judgment was unusually close, and no less so, their epistolary correspondence, singular in its profundity of self-exposure, and in its lasting power. Of the abundant notes and letters exchanged, letters which cover a number of years, until the death of Fry, many are moving, and all have that strange and unchallengeable quality of intimacy on every front that counts. Even when they are no longer lovers in the physical sense, because Vanessa has become involved with Duncan—who, in 1918, according to Angelica their daughter, put an end to their own physical intimacy—the relation of Roger and Vanessa has something special about it. Always that air, says Angelica, of those who have been lovers; for us, now, reading the letters exchanged for such a long time and touching so many points of practical, aesthetic, and metaphysical concern, this correspondence is unforgettably vivid and of a high order of intelligent style.

Whether they are discussing a new green dress for her and the dinner parties at which it is worn, or the paintings of Giotto and Matisse, for which she has a particular passion, whether their work or their relation, and the problems of each, or the interweaving of Vanessa and her sister Virginia Woolf, Vanessa's writings to Roger stand, concerning her mind and personality and heart, in the place of the private journals kept by Virginia and Carrington, and so many other artists and writers, those journals with their strange and sometimes uneasy relation to the letters, those journals often best described as situated midway between invention or elaboration, and fact. Her letters to Virginia, discussed in a chapter unto themselves as they have a tone unto themselves, are completely different as befits their relation, but *strangely* different; less strangely, they have more to do, often, with practical detail. The letters of Vanessa to Roger are documents, above all, of the working out of life, love, and work. At first it is a mutual working out, and subsequently, a separate one.

The relation of love to work, and of respect to both bears mentioning as prefatory to the discussion of the whole. One incident can be read, perhaps, as emblematic of that strong interrelation of mutual respect, and as illustrative of Vanessa's largeness of spirit and generosity of mind. When their relation has given Roger so much pain that he in turn has inflicted his own painful feelings on Vanessa, who then forces a lessening of their mutual contact, she suddenly reads an article by him in *The Nation*, and becomes newly acquainted

with Roger Fry the great art critic. At this point, she is sur-
prised to find herself feeling as close to him as ever, and
suggests that should there even be a distance between them
again, she should always start by reading his critical work,
to reestablish the closeness between their minds.

That experience and that remark go far, for they indicate
that her relation to him is based on the kind of respect that
can state itself openly, as here, and will never decrease. In
turn, his respect of her work is repeatedly stated, and he
found it hard to realize, as he had to, that she did not, in
general, admire his own. He was influenced by her ideas
and her painting, to such an extent that he felt he lost his
independent judgment, and finally had to work out his own
method: in a heartbreaking letter which will be quoted at
length later, of June 16, 1916 (RFL: II, 397–98), he speaks of
having to find his own way in painting, to work out the things
he has suppressed "because they didn't meet with anything
in you" and of having to accept what, in him, is not "exactly
like you or what you like or admire . . ." His admiration of
her work is, in fact, as he points out, extricable from his love
of herself. On March 11th, 1919, for example, long after their
own love affair has finished in favor of Duncan, he speaks of
his desire for her pictures as such, more than any others: "I
have such a queer personal liking—a mere *taste* for what you
do and, if you'll believe me, I think it's quite separate from
my love of you as a woman" (RFL: II, 449). Their respect is
mutual, like their affection, over the whole period of their
lives. In a sense, the lesson of their writing is summed up by
a comment Roger makes in a letter to her about the Futurists,
who have had an exhibition in 1912, at the Cologne and
Sackville Gallery: they still have to learn, he says, the "great
design depends upon emotions and that, too, of a positive
kind, which is nearer to love than hate" (RFL: I, 45; in *The
Nation*, March 9, 1912).

Their exchanged letters have, in their own way, a great
design, and were, quite certainly, until the end, based on
undeniably great emotions. At one point, Vanessa exclaims
over the coldness of his letters, and at another, over that of
her own personality, in relation to him and his pain—sensed
as double, in his loss of her and of his own confidence in

painting and being—which inflicts upon her in turn a parallel suffering: but in general the warmth of their unique relation illuminates both of them, and their readers alike. Their relation seems to flourish in fullest light, even in its most anguished parts. Unlike Vanessa's relation to Virginia and to Duncan, both surely more complicated in the extreme, hers to Roger seems open to the reading.

Roger's description of her always is an artist's description, capturing exactly her image as we most long for it to be before us, capturing it with the eyes of love and art alike: "the movement of your head when you look round in delight at being so beautiful and at my feeling all of it so much . . ." (RFL: I, 350; August 1911). What he feels, in thankfulness, is shared by the reader, whose picture of Vanessa is created thereby: "When I think of the other beauties and guess at the shape of your soul, I have to feel immense gratitude that you find a place for me in your heart . . . I don't think I forget you for a single moment of the day" (RFL: I, 351; October 11, 1911). The countryside is lovelier, the colors of it purer, and the sky gayer to think of her there in the background of his consciousness, he repeats, under an October sky.

When their relation is finally threatened, on the intimate plane, by that of Vanessa and Duncan, and she has said that indeed she has had to tell him the truth at last—even though she would have preferred to keep each relation in its own individual slot, without spilling over—and has had to tell him of her love for Duncan, precisely, because it is getting in the way of the intimacy she has with Roger, Roger replies in a letter of hurt that never lessens for the coming years. His pain is all the worse in that he has loved Vanessa as an artist *and* as a woman, both. The fact that both Roger and Duncan are attached to her in both senses, along with the fact that Roger is heterosexual, and Duncan, a homosexual who was only briefly bisexual, complicates enormously the whole *relation* of their relation. Roger, who feels less talented as an artist, is doubly sensitive to the Vanessa-Duncan affair; neither his sensitivity, nor what some will call the tragedy of Vanessa's deep and lasting involvement with Duncan, will abate. This is permanent stuff, then, and Roger speaks courageously in 1914, when he tries to be, on a Sunday in August,

Virginia Woolf. Courtesy, Harcourt Brace and Jovanovich.

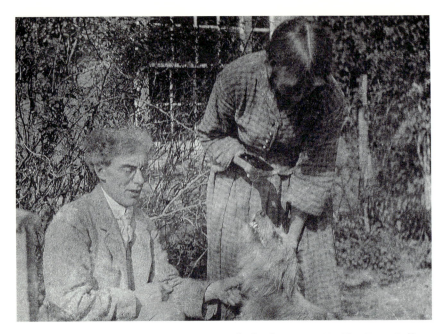

Roger Fry and Vanessa Bell and "Henry," Charleston, 1917. The Tate Gallery Archives.

Leonard Woolf and Virginia Stephen, 1912[?]. The Tate Gallery Archives.

[Left to right] Virginia Woolf (hidden); David Garnett; Vanessa Bell; Quentin Bell; Leonard Woolf; Angelica Bell with "Sally," Mark's House Rodmell, 1940. The Tate Gallery Archives.

Vanessa Bell by Duncan Grant. Private collection.

Vanessa Bell, Charleston, 1930. The Tate Gallery Archives.

Vanessa Bell, Charleston, 1936. The Tate Gallery Archives.

Dora Carrington by Mark Gertler, 1913. Private collection.

Dora Carrington, no date. The Tate Gallery Archives.

Dora Carrington and Ralph Partridge by a river, no date. The Tate Gallery Archives.

Dora Carrington and Gerald Brenan, 1921. The Tate Gallery Archives.

Vanessa Bell and Duncan Grant, La Bergère, Cassis, France, 1928. The Tate Gallery Archives.

Duncan Grant and Roger Fry, Charleston, 1931. The Tate Gallery Archives.

[Left to right] Lytton Strachey, Duncan Grant, and Clive Bell, Asheham, 1913. The Tate Gallery Archives.

So we off'd (shakespear. to depart
to go away.) & had tea at
one of the best & most élitè
shops in Bond Street— Barbellon
& created no small interest
amongst the Brigidier generals
& Ladies of noble birth

and you would have cackled
& stared also my dear
if you had been there

A letter from Dora Carrington to Noel Carrington, 1916. Courtesy, Harry Ransom
Humanities Research Center, The University of Texas at Austin.

Nude—Henrietta Bingham, c. 1925, by Dora Carrington. From a private collection, London. Photograph, courtesy of Sandra Lummis, Fine Art, London.

Nude—Ralph Partridge, c. 1920, by Dora Carrington. The Tate Gallery Archives.

"philosophical" about the whole thing: his self-denigration here, and frequently, reminds us of Vanessa's self-denigration in relation to Duncan, whose work she often finds superior, when she finds her own, often, dull, colorless, and, in fact, failed in comparison. For Roger makes the same sort of comparisons between his work and theirs:

> I've been quite philosophical not thinking too much about Asheham or wondering what thrilling things you and Duncan do and say about art . . . Of course you're doing splendid things, damn you. And mine will always be makeshifts.
>
> (RFL: II, 381; August 23, 1914)

Roger's feeling of being left out, expressed repeatedly and—for the reader passionate about him—movingly, makes its own desperate appeal. Of course, he was to go on to love others, in France and then in England, and of course, he remained the clear-sighted, enthusiastic, and brilliant critic and close friend he knew how to be, but his original relation to Vanessa was, quite properly, unforgettable.

But let us go back, so as to go forward in the telling of their relation in another key, for it was to turn out—thanks, as Roger says, to the admirable abundance of Vanessa's warmth—all right.

The early days, in 1911 and until 1913–14, are full of a matching and mutual adoration even as the artist Vanessa is growing into herself. The peculiar fascination of the correspondence, apart from its own style and substance, is surely this. We are able to watch her in her moods of elation and depression, and to see her style evolving into its various facets, through the representational and the abstract moments, through the mosaic period and the other experiments, through the large canvases as learning devices, to the works of her later years. It is to Roger always that she recounts the experiments and the elation, her work with Duncan and her depression—she recounts Vanessa in a way we see nowhere else. We have to be grateful that she did not, in fact, live with Roger, for we would be deprived of our surest source of knowledge about her being.

The relationship between them is, in the beginning, gloriously physical: February 8, 1911: "Dear I wanted you!" (February 8, 1911); "Roger I do want you so badly. you don't know how often I have wanted you since that night at Genoa. I wish life could be as simple as you & I would make it" (June 5, 1911); "Oh Roger how horribly I want you. I can say it now I'm ill . . . Besides what muse was ever as good as you, & one must recognize good technique if it's not to be lost" (Wednesday, July 6, 1911); "I wanted you horribly . . ." (August 22, 1911). And, just as gloriously and importantly, it is everything else too: "I never can really tell you how wonderful I think you or how much I love you—how charming & adorable & delightful you are to me in every way" (n.d. VB/RF no. 25).

Roger she loves for just the things we see in the pictures of him: his odd intensity, his vitality, like what Virginia says of him, saying no one else excites her as he does, no one else is so completely a *giver*. Vanessa to him: "You have a peculiar springy movement that gives me great pleasure to watch. Also the way your head's set on your shoulders . . . My dear, I do love you" (August n.d., 1911). Her imagination of him is as vivid in its visual detail as his of her, as she openly says in a letter on June 8, 1911, a good example of her loving in thought and writing:

> When I think about you I begin to try to draw you but luckily only in the air. I know the shape of all of you pretty well now—even your hands I think I know almost as well as you know mine. I don't talk about them as much but perhaps I have felt them even more intimately. Do you think so? I was very happy after you'd gone the other day, thinking of you.
>
> (VB/RF, 7)

The Bells find him extraordinary looking, she says, "if not mad," and wonders what they would think if they knew "what she had done" with such an odd-looking creature. With that marvelously odd creature, her inner artistic self seems to find its full verbal development. To Roger, with his odd angularity, singular face, and marked enthusiasms, his life-enhancing quality and his nurturing of the best in others, she can write out the best of herself. Roger is quite unlike anyone else. "I believe you have an extraordinary effect on other people's work. I always feel it when I'm with you . . . What is it you have in you Roger? . . . I don't know how you do it but you make everything bigger and more alive" (VB/RF, August 16, 1911). In 1911, she goes to his exhibit in the Grafton Gallery, but refuses to go to his lecture, saying it would be "too jumpy an affair" for her; his judgments on art she values, and for that reason no doubt shares with him her various ups and downs with her work, all of which is interlarded with her own appreciations of the contemporary painters she finds greatest: Cézanne, Matisse.

She writes to Roger with her hands covered in green paint, writes him when she finds her paintings a failure and herself crotchety about them, writes him of wanting him and longing for that kind of easy companionship they have shared: "I wish life could be as simple as you and I would make it" (June 5, 1911; 7). This very *simplicity*, potential and expressed in their relation, gives a quite extraordinary flavor to the correspondence, its style, taste, and lingering joy.

In that same letter, she describes the painting of her nursery scene, comic in appearance, but entirely new in manner—as if warding off the bad luck that might come if she were to get, as she says, "too conceited," she immediately teases herself and him with an offputting: "probably you'll think it exactly like every thing else I've ever done," just as before she has said of what she was then doing: "in the end I daresay it will be like that awful tea pot you disliked so much" (February 8). To be able to put off on Roger the negative aspects of judgment, whether or not he would agree, serves her purpose and seems, in fact, to have worked out well in that sense. Her nursery scene, she finds comic: over it Clive roared with laughter, saying it was partly Cubist and partly like Simon Bussy (Roger's French friend whose wife was the author Dorothy Strachey, the translator of André Gide). The technique gives her great excitement and experiential delight: "I am trying to paint as if I were mosaicing—

not by painting in spots but by considering the picture as patches each of which has to be filled by one definite space of colour as one has to do with mosaic or wool work, not allowing myself to brush the patches into each other. It's amusing to make these experiments even if they don't succeed. I think this one *ought* to give me something of the life one seems to get with mosaics. I don't know if it will" (June 5, 1911; 7).

Now that very liveliness she craves is precisely Roger's major characteristic, which one senses through his face and eyes and life, and which Vanessa detects and expresses, using the same word "alarming," about his "habit of rushing at everything" (14) as does Lytton about him: "alarmingly intelligent" (July 22, 1917). This is why Roger has such a strong effect on the work of exactly what most effectively opposes the "fatal prettiness" of the English minor arts, all the "very fanciful bright and piquant things," all "gay and pretty," which Roger countered with the strong inspiration of France and its colors totally different, its design more striking than pretty, and its sense of largeness. The Omega enterprise wanted to be just what Roger represented: the opposite of piquant and pretty, rather dynamic, vital, subtle, but above all, collective. (Carrington's account of her visit there on November 8, 1918 gives a rather different picture, however: "Went to Omega & saw Roger looking like an Evangelist preacher all in Black. He took me round the show, & showed me the beauties of his own works. On the whole it was a very DRAB performance. The woodcut book what one could see of it draber (sic) even than the paintings . . ." She prefers Duncan's flower piece to the rest of what is there, and in fact almost always liked his work, preferring it to that of the others [DC/LS].)

Vanessa wanted for her art a certain largeness of aspect which will be the contrary of the little faded-color flowery chintz fabrics we associate with Liberty and (—dare I say it?—) the art of being proper. In her painting, she does as Roger suggests, and puts, for example, a colossal figure in the foreground (finding it a failure and too difficult). But her *Studland Beach* of this epoch is majestically persuasive, with its brooding large figure which is discussed in the section of

Chapter Seven called "A Tale of Two Tubs." Teasing, she states herself jealous of Miss Gill, with whom Roger is painting a still life, envious that he will find her a Picasso, whereas Vanessa . . . But it is exactly here that she finds her own talent and excitement, lively as she longs to be: of a new and exciting idea "itching" in her head that she is about to attempt, she says, endearingly that it is not "a Picasso or any one but (and then she signs) Vanessa" (November 6, 1911; 48). Vanessa is exactly what she learns to be, exactly with all her forebodings of failure and her triumphs of imagination. And of love.

She cannot continue to see Roger so often, and they must limit themselves to two or three times a week, because of Clive's state of mind; and yet all the delight of what she calls his peculiar charm, his "presence and the feel of you in the room" is enough to make the difficulty worth it. He has changed, she says, everything she most cares for: "What an extraordinary person you are. When I see you in your own house I understand that even better. I do like seeing you among the things you have chosen yourself. They all seem like you full of quite peculiar charm and rightness. Wouldn't it have been a pity if I could never have told you any of these things which I have always felt to some extent. I suppose I couldn't have said them unless you knew I loved you" (November 23, 1911; 55).

Her open statements about her feelings extend to reassuring him about his painting, and his work, and his life, when he badly needs all of this. His dependence on her has, at this point, become extreme, and his discouragement, intense. Yet Roger is always, as Vanessa says, a good muse for her, and she wants to be that for him: What nonsense, she exclaims, for him to say he will give up painting without her! He has a great deal that is totally independent of her, and further, he seems to be improving, while she feels she is "getting horribly behindhand doing nothing" (VB/RF, 62). And she continues in another letter, reassuring him, for he feels he has done everything at the wrong time in life. People like us, she says, are always old and sedate when they are young, and then later become young, when they are expected to be the opposite: we are just beginning to find out what is in us. Besides, he has not to forget her affection: "Remember if you're going to creep on to a shelf you must expect to find me climbing up too, and you'll have to make room for me to be beside you there—so don't choose too narrow a one" (n.d., 63).

Repeatedly, she reassures him, separating her emotion from the gratitude she feels as an artist for his criticism and his support: "Roger dear I love you very much and not because of all you do for me but because you are you. Do you know it?" (January 15, 1912), and exclaims how happy she is when they are together, asking him in turn if he is *really* happy with her, and wishing she could tell him "about himself" as well as he is able to tell her about herself. When they make love, in even the most sordid surroundings, it is, she says, like water when one is very thirsty, comparing the feeling to one of Matisse's paintings. To make love "in the midst of quite ordinary things . . . turns them into something else. Not that it wouldn't be divine to do it in Asia Minor too" (October 12, 1912). Cézanne, Matisse, and also Giotto are her favorites: in a November letter, 1912, she has had a Giotto before her all day, thinking how little one can analyze one's feeling in front of great art. "One is simply lifted into a different life and carried off in it" (November 2, 1912; 81). Even if one's love does not work out, she says, "It's enough that one should be in the world and one's lucky to see it." And this was always to be her feeling—that generosity of spirit did not, I think, let her down, even when things went badly.

Roger's letters to her can be private, she insists on telling him, for she gets her mail in her room with her breakfast, so could he please write *real* letters? Somehow his letters seem a little cold: is he bored with her, or tired? "I want affection" (December 27, 1913). She was always to want that, from him, as from Virginia, and to need it.

Then the predictable (was it?) happens, and her painting companion becomes the love of her life, with all the difficulties attendant on that, given Duncan's inclination towards men. The letter is dated by her 1913, but it is likely to be from 1914 (as it is marked in KCL); in any case, the news to which we have already read Roger's reaction is expressed by Vanessa as gently as possible, saying that as long as her feelings for Duncan did not impede those she had for Roger,

there was no need to tell Roger of her preference, even though
that had meant she had actually, at certain moments, had to
lie to him. Can we talk it over, she asks? They have talked
over so much, her feelings of failure beside Duncan, and
everything else.

But Roger seems so morose, and it seems unfair to her
"that I should be able to be so happy with really no more to
go upon than you have. How I wish you could be too" (133).
She "continues to love" Roger, which seems true enough,
assures him he will never be crowded out, and thinks they
are bound to work something out, with two such sensible and
sensitive people, and her need for him; they are bound to find
some way of managing a good relationship, for he provides
something no one else can, and it is, she says, "something I
think I shall always want."

What Roger gave her, although she does not express it
thus, seems to have been precisely that energy and intensity
uniquely his own to which even his expression of his unrecoverable romantic loss of the woman he so loved and admired
bears moving witness. For Roger's account is deeply moving,
that sad story of Vanessa's erstwhile lover, the loser-out to
her lifelong passion for Duncan, so that he was to feel, and to
be excluded from her art, as it came under Duncan's sway,
and from her life, as it revolved around Duncan, with, eventually, his various lovers. In a passionate and distressing letter
from Durbins on February 27, 1915, he laments to Vanessa,
who has suggested he be "sensible" and has pointed out that
her relation to Duncan is as one-sided as Roger's to her,
furious that she can compare her "position" with his unhappy
one. Roger writes a letter that I quote at length, for it reveals
as no other document could, his pain at the betrayal of both
his affection and his working relation to Vanessa:

> it makes me boil over to think you can know so little of
> what I feel and must feel that you should do it. Look—
> you work with him constantly, you're his usual and con-
> stant pal, you play with him, you can spend a week in the
> country alone with him. He gives you everything except
> love and I'm pushed away into my place and only wanted
> when there's nothing better on. All my work I have to do

alone without any help or encouragement or interest, and
worst, infinitely worst of all, there's the past (which you
haven't got), the past and bitter sense of desertion, the
humiliation of losing the whole centre and meaning of my
life. Your life goes on as before: you are still the centre of
all that interests and pleases you. I have to try to piece
together a life of scraps and bits, almost all become
strange and uninteresting and dull to me by comparison
with what I had . . .

I hope, he says, you will never know what I am now suffering,
or rather:

> I hope you'll never know it by experience. If you could
> know it a little more by imaginative sympathy you could
> be more tender to me; you could help me to begin life
> again more—you could not hurt me so terribly. But you
> won't understand ever. I shall try and not show you this:
> I have to write it to relieve the feeling your letter gave me.
>   No, I'm wrong; one day a long time hence you will
> understand; one day we shall be what we once were to
> each other, only it'll be too late to be much good. The joy
> of life will have gone from me certainly. It'll be very
> strange and pale but quite beautiful and, in a way, I shall
> be happy. I suppose you think—you must think—this ut-
> ter sentimental rot, but I can't help knowing it quite
> surely. Only the pity of it. . . .
>
> (RFL: II, 383)

The tone will forever after be different. This is the crucial
letter, as I read them, and the saddest, truest one. Not to be
returned from, in a sense.

In his painting, he is as committed as in his affections,
for he goes "on doing the same thing till something comes
out of it . . ." He had, over the years, great reason for discouragement with his art, far more than Vanessa ever had: as
each will say, from time to time, I have been doing this, but
you wouldn't like it; maybe it is good and maybe not . . . , so
he says to her, in 1921 (September 6; RFL: II, 512): "I wish
to goodness I could show you my big picture, tho' probably

you wouldn't like it. It seems to me it's either rather good or it's quite commonplace a point de vue; I wish I knew which it is." Repeatedly, he exhibits and nothing sells: already in 1894, he is writing his father that he wants very much to exhibit his portrait of Edward Carpenter at the New English Art Club, where Walter Sickert will sponsor him, because the Royal Institute of British Artists has refused him, as have all the other galleries (but it is, he says, the opinion of his fellow artists that counts, March 25, 1894; RFL: I, 157), all the same, in spite of that, he is never cheered up by the public about his work. In 1921, everyone in the London Group sells, he says, at the Autumn Salon of November except him, and his prices were already very low. "It's really getting rather ridiculous," he writes to Margery Fry, "the more so as I now feel pretty sure of where I am compared with other English painters. I no longer have the feeling that I wish I'd done Duncan's pictures which I always used to have. I'd rather have done my own—so that my total failure is becoming quite interesting; the worst of it is it is so expensive" (RFL: II, 517). The impossibility of selling them, he writes to Jean Marchand, his French painter friend, telling him how painful it is, when no one will buy even as presents or "nearly so," and in spite of his not being the very lowest of the least painters—snobbish Londonians look at him that way, he complains, and blames it on Clive, who guides their judgment. His house is full of them, and why continue . . . Turner the dealer wants him to give up, the public "spits me out like the skin and the pips," even as he thinks he is constructing happy pleasant pictures, not difficult ones, so why the uniformity of the "dislike or indifference or contemptuous and grudging approval" he receives in England, as opposed to France—this to Virginia, whose appreciation means all the more to him for the rest of his feelings (June 20, 1923; RFL: II, 540–41). Vanessa and Duncan must themselves think little of his pictures, because they advise Maynard Keynes, and he buys not one of them . . . Not one painting or drawing sells in New York at the Brummer Gallery in 1925, and he has 200 pounds of expenses (April 14, 1925; RFL: II, 563).

Maybe watercolor, he says to Vanessa, but the results disgust him, and it isn't suited to his "positive way of feeling"

and his desire to paint exactly what he wishes at every different moment, for which that medium leaves not enough time
(September 27, 1924; RFL: II, 560). But on other occasions, he
finds the flat colors of his still lifes "rather good." Occasionally
too, he manages to throw off the impressionism Vanessa "in-
fected" him with to find again the construction he used to
have and has always had when fully himself. For just as she
and Duncan took on the coloration of Roger's theories, he
took on the colors of their art, and had then to cast off, finally,
this model given by the other in order to reconstruct himself.
And not just in art; whatever the part of rationalization in
this letter, it speaks truly, if terribly, of love and the abandonment of self it may lead to:

> I am myself again now, you know, after all those years of
> not being. All sorts of things I'd suppressed because they
> didn't meet with anything in you are coming back. It's a
> very queer state. I don't like myself any better, but I'm no
> longer disgusted with it for not being exactly like you or
> what you like or admire . . .
>
> (June 15, 1916; RFL: II, 398)

But only artists appeal to him, and after Vanessa, he
finds it hard to put up with anyone else's intimacy. Of course,
this state of things, as we could have predicted, was not to
last, and after his brief tumultuous involvement with Josette
Coatmellec, his relation to Helen Anrep, with whom he lived
from the mid 1920s on, was a happy one. Still, it was the
Vanessa-as-artist model construction that informed a good
part of his life and art, and this was not to change. On March
19, 1917, he speaks of beginning a painting she is about to
begin also: "I'm afraid I'll make nothing of it and I have a
vision of the wonderful thing you'll make of it which will
make me very jealous" (RFL: II, 407).

Given this jealous state of things—about life and art—it
was all the harder for Roger, who dealt with the Omega
workshops daily, to have Vanessa and Duncan seceding from
them, and seeming ungrateful: he tries to call them back to
order, using even the techniques of blackmail (how much he
has done for her and Duncan), and the rest. The difference

between Roger and Duncan and between their art also is made evident in Carrington's visit to the Omega workshop which she found so drab except for Duncan's flower piece: we cannot help contrasting her description, quoted above, with Virginia's of Duncan's paintings bubbly like white wine. It is all the more touching that Duncan was so eager about having any of Roger's comments on his paintings, even as he knew Roger's to be dull by comparison. Roger was always—as unfortunately he usually seems to have known, in spite of some of his letters quoted here—a finer critic than artist.

And nevertheless, Roger's tribute to Vanessa, in spite of his pain, is entire. On September 16, 1917, he writes of his admiration, in response to one of her letters that questions why he is attached to her, since she finds herself unworthy of such attachment. "Oh, why do I admire you?" His answer is full of the sort of reason for which each of us, I would imagine, would most like to be admired. Because you go directly for things which are worthwhile. You have, he says, "got quit of me and yet kept me your devoted friend, got all the things you need for your own development and yet managed to be a splendid mother." You have been my security in this shifting world, you have made me feel so strangely secure. It is, he says, the genius you have in life and in art. "I who have no trace of genius anyhow, can't help a deep envy of your gifts. But I do admit that it's really the nicest thing to feel that you care to tell me of your worries and difficulties again . . ." (RFL: II, 416; September 16, 1917). Vanessa is able to confide and to make secure, and this, for people of all ages, as the ages wore on.

In any case, she said, speaking of her relation with Roger's daughter Pamela Fry, even age does not matter so much when both people care "about a thing like painting"—nor does basic unsatisfaction. Unsatisfaction was something she was to know: Vanessa's letters to Roger in pain have all the marks of someone who has known, and knows at the present, all too clearly, what pain is about. "But one can force oneself not to expect or even want much more than is freely given— I think any good relationship depends in the end on the one person being able to do that . . ." (1918, VB/RF, 264).

Roger, to Vanessa, on the 14th of August, 1918, from Lady

Strachey's home, 8 Grange Road, Cambridge, writes of his relief, for he has not been able to get her out of his mind, is sorry if his pain has pained her, "but love is so selfish." He had come to believe nothing was there, and that he "was quite bankrupt" with her and that it was only from inertia and habit that she kept up any relationship with him, and that their past work, the greatest thing life could have been for him, was swept out of her mind and memory. "The worst of it was that when I'd written my letter I knew that the thought of life without you was too unbearable and that I must go on loving you at whatever cost. I wanted to tell you all that I was doing and seeing every day and then I had to think that it would mean nothing to you and if that is so I couldn't."

I have put this letter last to make the answering point that to Vanessa as to Roger it always was to mean something, and a great deal, what the other was doing and seeing. For Roger, the real part of life always included Vanessa, ever since he had first known her; and, on August 28, 1919 (RFL: II, 455), he gives her the highest tribute, that of wanting to see her as much as he can, with pleasure and only rare moments of pain: "I think it's really the greatest compliment I could pay you to have thought it worth-while to go on through all those years to get to this, don't you?" The compliment is great, and Roger continues to love her, yet to feel "a little out of it with V. and D.," who quite naturally, as he writes to Margery, share all their feelings and "don't know how much they tend to leave me out and it's rather difficult to be alone in company" (May 21, 1923; RFL: II, 536). He knows they do not know, and always, speaking out of suffering, he knew what he was telling of. Vanessa also was well-aware, knew of what such solitariness felt like, given her attachment to the unpinnable-down Duncan, in all his "voluptuous creamy grace" as Virginia was to put it (VWL: III, 216). Of Duncan, Angelica writes: "He possessed the instinctive wisdom of an animal, never undertaking responsibilities that belonged to others, never promising more than he could perform. He bobbed on the surface, gently irrepressible, impervious as a duck to water, elusive as a leaf on a pond" (Introduction to *Duncan Grant: Works on Paper*, catalogue to exhibition at Anthony d'Offay Gallery, 15 November–18 December, 1981).

Never did he cause complications willingly, preferring to avoid all controversial issues, says Angelica. He seemed seamlessly open, and only afterwards, she now muses, now looking back in 1989, does that very deliberate absence of complication seem to her to have been a lack in him.

Perhaps it was indeed a tragedy that Vanessa could not love Roger as he would have wished; but it was, at least, never a tragedy of unknowing, but rather, of the highest intelligence. The letters speak fully, and with that intelligence, of the pity of it all: of art, of pain, of love, and far more.

Vanessa and Duncan, to Roger

But all my pictures are failures now I'm very much depressed about them.
                    Vanessa to Roger (February 7, 1911)

Like Carrington painting in the same house with Lytton, whom she so vastly admired, Vanessa painting alongside Duncan leaves us, in her letters to Roger, a remarkable record of her feelings about her work, and about her fellow artist whom she so loved. They are vividly concerned with evaluation as with development—according to Quentin Bell, their enormously self-deprecating point of view is often a part of what we might call magic thinking or magic writing: saying the worst about yourself means that at least that cannot be true. If you say your paintings are not good, you have, as it were, done your best to ward off the sins of pride. A second possibility is, as he suggests, the important fact, already mentioned, that both Vanessa and Virginia preferred their sketches to the finished product—thus, her frequent disappointment with her completed work. It is interesting to note, along these lines, that Carrington had exactly the same reaction, starting equally early. In a letter to her painter friend Mark Gertler, of December, 1913, she laments: "What a damned mess I make of my life and the thing I want most to do, I never seem to bring off. My work disappoints me terribly. I feel so good, so powerful before I start and then when it's finished, I realise each time, it is nothing but a failure" (DG, 23).

Duncan himself had no such preference for his work over Vanessa's; when they worked together, he considered her painting the equal of his, as indeed very often it was, and sometimes, more than that.

Another possible reason, one that might be particularly convincing to a female reader of the scene, is simply that in insisting on the value of his work, she was warding off the thought that it was not always as great as his facility would lead one to believe. This innate self-persuasion can function without necessarily taking on the dramatic tinge that Angelica lends it in her *Deceived With Kindness*, where she states it as an overvaluing, precisely because in loving someone who could not completely return her love, Vanessa was obligated at least to show him as larger-than-life in his artistry.

One of the more interesting slants on this whole correspondence of Vanessa with Roger is this self-evaluation contained therein in relation to Duncan: I am insisting on the corresponding value of these letters because it is partly in that relating of the relation to another (as in letters), or to the self (as in a diary)—that the self-challenge lies. It is not just that the female creative artist chooses to make her life and her work alongside the man she loves and admires, whatever his (sometimes changing) relationship with her, but that her recounting of this ongoing development of self and work to the other has its own challenge for the self and for the reader, both the initial one, of the letters as they were sent and the message as it was gotten, on one side, and the subsequent ones, of the correspondence as it stands, two-sided, relative, and complex.

For that reason, I have been dwelling on Roger's own reading and work, as well as on his own relation to Vanessa, before looking at Duncan's, to her and to their companionship, enduring, amazingly, for fifty years. Her great good fortune, in spite of the solitariness which all her critics will stress, was that she had, and knew how to appreciate, as well as such a sister, such fellow artists, such lovers, and such friends.

Vanessa's unrelentingly frequent statements, to Roger, of artistic despair are interwoven with more hopeful statements about experimentation, but the very noticeability of ups and down in any letter, revealing or not of her inner life, is startling in the light of what we are accustomed to think of as her anchoring of the chaotic but working life at Charleston. These letters are the clearest statements of her growing up through Roger's love and admiration, even while loving Duncan and suffering thereby.

Among the things Roger is able to intensify and enliven, partly through his intense love and admiration for her, is her own relation to her art, and to Duncan, whom she loved to the point of passion. Her letters to Roger are of interest in their smallest details: she is much less given to the grand style and the wider scope of things than he is. In their intimate style and authentic generosity of spirit, they instantly affect us. Her honesty about feelings—for we can only assume that to be the case—permits her to display depression and elation, experimentation and discouragement, her fear of failure even as she hopes for success: "I'm very much excited about my nursery scene—though I think it will most likely turn out a failure. But it may be useful to me as an experiment" (June 8, 1911; VB/RF 8). We have the feeling of an artist trying herself out, and unwilling ever to give up.

These are not just confessions of her own variable states of mind, and of the sensitivity of her feelings, but also reflections on painting in general; this intricate relation of art and life, of creation and emotion, depression and the desperate urge to continue, fascinates the reader familiar with *Studland Beach,* for instance: "I succeeded this morning in making yesterday's failure still more of a failure and have given it up in despair. It's really very difficult to paint on the beach. One can't get any composition and one's colour changes completely when one brings it in out of the sun." And the letter continues: "I've been trying this morning on the beach to paint your subject—the one with the colossal figure in the foreground but its a failure. It was too difficult" (August 22, 1911; VB/RF 43).

An overwhelming intimacy is thus created between painting and feeling, between reading and seeing, in these letters, themselves relations of the highest order. A letter of November 16, in the same year, shows the intertwining between enthusiasm and doubt and love, describing some chrysanthemums and snapdragons she is painting against a blue handkerchief: "I rather like the design," she says to Roger, "but perhaps you'll think it ordinary. I'm not sure it isn't really." And then she dwells on the delight of his presence and "the feel of you in the room."

But in the next week, we are privileged to see the entrance of Duncan in her life, sent somehow like a snapshot to Roger, who was probably not exactly overdelighted by the scene so sent: in the bizarre interaction of its parts, it was bound to be painful. "Roger—aren't you jealous. Duncan came to tea yesterday & number of things happened to stir your jealousy. First we invented a new art." They covered the canvas with lacquer in different colors, and then painted it with figures, a procedure they intended to keep secret, that led to an "exquisite" result. This alone is indeed enough to incite jealousy in someone with Roger's particular sensitivity about being left out of their work; it gets worse. "Then Duncan asked me to sit to him. But very likely that won't come off. Perhaps you could paint me at the same time which might console you." Here there enters a whole strange eroticism of gazing and being gazed at, especially when both the parties are painters, and it cannot have been very consoling for a third painter to have to entertain that thought. "And then—what do you think happened? I had my bath in his presence! You see he wanted to shave & I wanted to have my bath (he stayed to dinner) & he didn't see why he should move & I didn't see why I should remain dirty & Clive was there & didn't object—& so! But I'm afraid he remained quite unmoved & I was really very decent. I felt no embarrassment & I think perhaps it was a useful precedent!" (November 23, 1911). The fact that she is writing to him, says Vanessa, should remove all trace of jealousy in Roger. Absolutely; but such was probably not the outcome, given that the admixture of art on art to tease on tease was exactly such as to inflame.

In this double revelation, of Vanessa to Duncan (unmoved, given his lifelong predilection for other sorts of bodies) and then of that exposure to Roger, who was indeed probably jealous, given his sure predilection for Vanessa, she marks the importance of this scene—suggestive of a future situation and her future close relation to Duncan—by placing an exclamation point after the adolescently excited rhetorical question and almost giggly response: "And then—what do you think happened? I had my bath in his presence!" To which incipient jealousy, having brought it about, she gives an instant consolation, again, the arch suggestion they both paint her together; that the setup should be so very odd, with its revelations and its flower-laden decor—for the room is full of chrysanthemums,—does not detract in the slightest from her outpouring of affection for Roger, and how extraordinary a person he is, particularly when seen at home, among his chosen objects all resembling him, replete as they are with "quite peculiar charm and rightness."

In fact, the elements continue for a time to be interwoven, her painting with Duncan and her relation to Roger: she and Duncan paint indoors and she finds herself less impeded by working at Duncan's side than she would have thought, but continually assumes his superior vision: "I always think why didn't I see it like that? But as I have come to the conclusion that I didn't see it like that I no longer try to think I did" (September 11, 1912; VB/RF 74). She gets used to working with Duncan, but never conquers the feeling of his superiority: he has, she feels, more genius, more originality. Thus she calls upon Roger, on whom she is used to relying, for his judgment, and also for that listening presence that permits artist and writer to grow.

When we learn that the physical relations between Vanessa and Duncan ceased after the conception of Angelica, part of the story Angelica tells, as she tells of the ensuing sadness and deprivation of her mother, we have to make our own sense of that situation, as we do of the not so dissimilar situation between Carrington and Lytton Strachey. Does the self-deprecation of these two women artists depend, and if so, to what extent, upon their relation to that *other* who cannot—as the common expression goes—satisfy them sexually or romantically? For that is the sense Angelica makes of Vanessa's story; we must make our own.

Now the issue of the intelligent and creative woman making the terrible effort of working alongside a man she finds more creative and more intelligent has to be addressed:

these letters raise that question, as do those of Carrington to Brenan, about working in the same general space with the brilliance of Lytton ... Vanessa refers not to Duncan the beloved for judgment, but to Roger the art critic and ex-lover, aware, as both of them are, of the problem of listening and address: as she tells him of the problems of these comparisons, that she believes Duncan's paintings are "of course" more original, hers duller, she also wonders at her own telling: "My dear—why am I writing all this?" (October 12, 1912; VB/RF 72).

Her way of writing about Duncan's art holds two emotions in an instructive balance. Her envy ("of course") assumes already that Duncan's work was necessarily going to be superior, and her feeling of pre-failure. But then she makes a courageous statement, in the fact of non-mastery, that trying whatever experiment, even should it fail, is often related more to the use principle than to the mastery one.

Two days later, she feels an improvement, and instantly relates it to Roger, whose conviction she needs, whose approval she desires, along with the view his perspective, being other, can offer to the self; but she already reserves the right to judge herself more leniently, should his authority show reservations as to the quality of her product: "I've done a much better watercolour today. I think it's really quite good but you know one can't tell when one's just done a thing & perhaps you'll hem & haw over it & I shall see you don't like it & perhaps I shall think you kind to its merits & perhaps by that time I shall quite agree with you" (January 24, 1913; VB/RF 85). It reminds us of Virginia so desperately seeking Leonard's approval for her work, and her seesawing over her own merits, and of Carrington's own uncertainty. In this resides a large part of the appeal of these women for us, that they were so very much less certain of their gifts than we are of them now.

Two weeks later, discouragement ensues on the heels of Vanessa's moderately, if modestly, upbeat sensation: "I am now quite convinced that I have gone back & in fact I believe I have retrograded dreadfully. I have been going on with my still life & at the end of two more days work at it, I think it has become dull & realistic. Oh dear. I am depressed" (February 5, 1913; VB/RF 92). The worst is her gradual belief that the world will judge Roger Fry to have forsaken his trust in her talent, through exaggerating what she has told Duncan about Roger's reservations over certain watercolors—he will be, since their love is ending, in the arms of someone else and she, alone, since "I, alas, am not in Duncan's."

But their painting side by side continues, and will always continue, and this is the crucial point: Vanessa as artist was able to work, and often happily, alongside someone she loved and respected. I am not altogether sure there is a lot more to ask for than that. They work together on their projects, and this she recounts to Roger. For example, the atmosphere of London needs cheering up: bright colors are perhaps the solution, and she and Duncan take to painting as they have not done before: "The young lady is dressed in yellow, the young gentleman in dark blue with a pale green shirt front and the background is in Venetian red ridges but I don't think they're very realistic. We're leaving a good deal of white in ridges so as to give brilliance and there are black lines too between the colours" (September 15, 1913). And in September of 1914, she describes how she and Duncan paint two modern dress dancing figures in red and black and white and cadmun yellow and a little green, "trying to keep them rather light and full of accent" as it must be to offset London greyness. Together they are working on color, they are opposing the drab.

For the real point is working together, as Vanessa explains to Roger: she and Duncan are just on "friendly but quite cool terms" (August 20, 1914; VB/RF 136); they do nothing together but paint, and talk nothing but painting (August 25, 1914; VB/RF, 138). But it is precisely this working together that hurts as much as the living together, as Roger has made clear in his letter of August 23, 1914, terrible in its lucidity not just about his personal relations, but about his art: it bears requoting, for it is at the heart of the issue: "I've been quite philosophical, not thinking too much . . . or wondering what thrilling things you and Duncan do and say about art . . . Of course you're doing splendid things, damn you. And mine will always be makeshifts" (RFL: II, 380).

Vanessa continues to describe their experiments in art,

nonetheless, and it seems clear that this is part of her openness and giving nature; she speaks and writes both to Roger
as friend and Roger as art critic, about what really matters
to her. For what has always and essentially mattered is her
art. That she and Duncan were able to join, somehow, *within*
their art, painting the same subjects so often and simultaneously, has something very wonderful about it. And that she
can share it with Roger, who has loved her, has itself more
to do with mental generosity than with cruelty. The same
impulse seems to be working when she cautions Virginia, as
late as March 1919, not to let Roger know that she and Duncan
are in the bath: this casts, says Virginia [VWD: I, 259] some
light on Roger's point of view, even at this date, even given
the complications of the situation. He was intensely and understandably jealous when Vanessa was bearing Duncan's
child, believing, as he said, that she would never again have
any interest in him or his work; not only Duncan, but their
child, would be bound to come first in her heart. In a deep
sense, that jealousy never abated, in spite of the cessation of
physical relations (by Duncan's decision) between Angelica's
parents shortly after her birth; it went much further than
an only sexual jealousy, given Roger's all-encompassing and
drastic adoration of Vanessa.

It did indeed take him a long time to get over loving
Vanessa, if he ever did, and Vanessa was fully aware of this.
Never was she either, in some sense, to stop wanting him,
loving him, needing him, and above all, counting on him,
even for her expression to herself of herself—it is as if Roger
were to be her surest means of self-representation—thus my
emphasis upon these letters.

If I could always have you as a model, he had said in
1912 (RFL: I, 357), "I should be a real artist, really truly and
without doubt . . . . because you have this miracle of rhythm
in you . . . in everything you do." So losing her is in a sense
losing, more than would ordinarily be the case, losing a sort
of easy comfort which had the delight of reasonableness.
Their relation, with all its strains, with the impossibility of
"perfect ease and abandonment which we mustn't even think
of ever having—even that becomes easy" (RFL: I, 357; 1912).
When it became uneasy in the extreme, over Vanessa's devo-

tion to ambivalent Duncan, Roger says bitterly of his disappointment: "You won't understand ever," he said. "I shall try and not show you this . . . No, I'm wrong; one day a long time hence you will understand. . . . Only the pity of it" (RFL: II, 383; February 27, 1915).

As for understanding, it echoes as a theme throughout all the letters exchanged, all the conversations, all the recountings. So little and so much understanding seems to have been done by those involved here, and those coming after (Gerald Brenan's "It was not possible . . . to understand it" of Carrington's death, Carrington's assurance that Virginia would best understand . . .); so many references to Roger's and Vanessa's concern about which of them understands what, about what is fitting. In the best times, Roger has enjoyed the luxury of intimacy of seeing Vanessa in any mood whatsoever, never bothering "a moment about whether I'll understand" (RFL: I, 357; 1912). When she no longer loves him, he understands indeed, but tries not to show her his most utter despair.

Roger continues unhappy, even though Vanessa claims she does not feel she has changed, or that her basic affections have altered in relation to him. She is less contented with her life than he seems to think, and certainly does not find that God has arranged it to make her happy, as Roger enviously suggests. "Happiness" as such she would not have chosen over her deep and intense relation with Duncan. I will always want you dreadfully, she says to Roger, and I will try to make it work out right. And so she did.

It is to Roger—significantly—that Vanessa describes, briefly, the pain she has with Duncan and his lovers, in particular, of course, Bunny Garnett, and describes her feelings of inadequacy about art: now the question is implicit here as to what extent the close intimacy between a self-doubting female and the gentle, generous, and talented homosexual she loves may be as dangerous to her own consciousness of worth as it seems to be enabling. It is so problematic an issue that it raises hackles on both sides of the argument: my view is that in the case of Vanessa (and in fact, in the case of Carrington, although Lytton and Duncan were scarcely the same type), the relation may well have been, in spite of her vast loneliness and the question of her self-esteem, profoundly helpful more than harmful. Duncan enabled, respected, and loved Vanessa, even though—of course—she found herself wanting (in both senses of the term) with him. Her love for him was in great part enabling, anchoring, empowering, for her art and for her life. We have only to read his letters to her to love him ourselves . . . He was genuinely sorrowful about the pain he caused in those who loved him: he writes to David Garnett: "I am so fond of Nessa I am ashamed she should be so fond of me and you are fonder of me than I deserve and I must just abjectly love both of you and hope not to be too much noticed for it" (VB, 141).

But, in spite of her attachment to Duncan, Vanessa continues—as I have pointed out—to need Roger's affection as well as his judgment: she could rely on both, and that she could confess her need of them saved their relation. We have, I think, the sense more of honesty in her writing than of some ploy to ward off arrogance or bad luck from self-congratulation: she feels morose about her painting, doesn't want to show him, and finds her decoration boring (n.d., 1914; VB/RF 126). And again, worse: "I am in the depths about my painting. Duncan has been doing most lovely still lifes besides his long scroll. I am plodding away at two different still lifes one of which seems to me really bad & the other at present nothing much. So I am rather depressed." (Monday, September, 1914; VB/RF 138); and still later, she finds herself again "painting very badly lately & getting rather depressed over it," and falling into "fearful muddles" (May 21, 1915; VB/RF 164).

Like Carrington's repeated feelings of depression over her own painting, this refrain of the woman artist alongside the other who seems to her to be doing lovelier, more important, more challenging work, can scarcely go unnoticed. "Duncan & I have been going on with our sketches of the church. His is an odd rather old fashioned picture—a strong effect of sunlight with a great deal of very sharp detail. Mine is now a complete failure & I have given it up . . . (a summer Tuesday, 1915; VB/RF 178). She has started, she says, another church sketch, about which she can only hope that "it won't become dull too." Why do all her sketches and paintings so easily take on some dull and muddled effect in her view? Is it in the view, or in the work? ("I have worked at my still life of bottles & apples since you were here but it has got into a stodgy muddle & I think I shall have to give it up. I get so depressed about it" (Friday, 1915; VB/RF 180). Is this a psychological or artistic judgment? Is she hoping Roger will contradict her, supporting her as she does Duncan?

We have no way of knowing what she was hoping; but the quite remarkable frequency in her letters of this complaint and the prevalence of female self-devaluation much along these lines seem quite visibly correlated. The intensity and enduring nature of this self-judgment is heartrendingly familiar. Vanessa is notable both for her honesty and her ability to connect with the man who had so loved her and who was the perfect receiver of her outpourings, both humorous and self-deprecating: she and Duncan have both undertaken what would seem an impossible task, doing Fra Angelico reproductions in watercolor blown up 10 times (!) on the walls of her bedroom. Duncan's she finds "very lovely," while hers seem to be neither herself "nor Fra Angelico & I'm rather desperate about it" (May 10, 1916; VB/RF 196). That "desperation" seems always allied to the fear of "dullness," early to late: "I have been trying to paint much more solidly & have done a still life which at least isn't a watery colour as most of my oils are—but it may be rather dull I think" (June 22, 1916; VB/RF 200). Although we may find her oils not watery, and her paintings not in the least dull, her modesty about her own creation appeals, as they do.

But she always cared about painting, and about seeing some design—thus, doing large pictures is increasingly important for her, since she feels she can see the design therein more clearly. Perhaps more clearly than in her life. It may be sensed that some of the passion for her art comes from a lack of mutual passion in her love—or do we read it into the letters? In any case, loving Duncan as she does, she is immensely grateful for Roger's praise of him, and actually thinks he might better be able to appreciate "this curious literary thing" in Duncan's painting. It is a sort of double generosity she shows: when Roger praises Duncan's genius,

Vanessa is able to respond in kind, about Duncan, and then about Roger himself, speaking of her two supports and main loves, her generosity stretching perhaps a point with her prudence, for she says, about Duncan what a delight it is to be with some one "so alive & creative . . ." (1918; 271).

Roger, feeling not always creative, and decidedly less alive without Vanessa's love, must have found it—as perhaps we do—difficult at times to take Vanessa's outspokenness. In the long run, her views on herself, whether mediated by her views of others or by theirs of her, are deeply instructive for whatever it is in female creation that longs to be sure, and remains still unsure of itself. She is positive of the value of her love and feelings, of their own open expression, and, most importantly, of that incredible privilege of being able to recount the intelligent creating self to the intelligent creating other. Her reliance on Roger might well teach us to recognize and appreciate a like privilege in relation to some other— whatever other it may be our most great fortune to find— who will read us, and through whom we can finally learn to read, and perhaps to better value, ourselves.

Duncan to Vanessa: Painting and Living

You must take this dull letter as pure affection, which it is.
Duncan to Vanessa, July 10, 1922

What was it like to be Duncan, so adored by Vanessa? Good-tempered, easy to work with, affectionate, Duncan— whom we remember from all the accounts and the pictures, with trousers always too big and held up (or not) with what- ever was around, Duncan trying on various hats and turbans, Duncan attracted constantly to new fresh young faces and bodies, but always longing to get to his paints, Duncan biking in to Victoria from the country in 1917—Duncan has left us an extensive record of himself in letters, especially to Vanessa, and in an autobiographical account in the Tate Archives. Only the letters to Vanessa concern us here, and because he spent so much time in mid-week in London painting, (and carrying on various relations) there are many of them, perfectly preserved, from "your loving Bear," as

he termed himself. When she is away, or he is, he misses
her urgently, and her "brats," Angelica, his child by Vanessa
in 1918, but also her children Julian and Quentin, with
Clive; when she is away: you are badly needed, he says . . .
come back soon . . . please, he urges repeatedly, do not feel
lonely, please, he urges, and not only when she is pregnant
with his child, take care of yourself. Duncan comes over to
us with a warmth which many seemed to find lacking in
Vanessa (her "iciness," her diamond-hard "reserve," her
"solitariness . . ."), and conveys a sense of responsibility and
accountability which we might not have expected: You may
rest assured, he says, that I will not show your letters to
anyone, and he underlines anyone. Vanessa did, all her life,
count on Duncan, and when she felt him turn away from
her inside with his other love affairs, it seems to have been
harder than anything else for her. Duncan was, of course,
adored, from his youth to his extreme age, for his sweetness
as for his seductive Bohemian character; and he had the
enviable gift of adoring others. From the boyish and over-
whelmingly emotional letters from Lytton Strachey to him
at Cambridge ("Beloved, do you know how happy it makes
me to think that you love me?", October 6, 1905, when they
believed they had discovered the inmost secrets of things,
each thinking the other's love more noble than his own) to
his love of David Garnett, of George Bergen, and of Paul
Roche, the range of his involvement was as great as his life
was long.

When he is with his male friends, from Bunny Garnett to
all the others, Vanessa could only suffer in silence—she knew,
and loved him all the same. Her letters to him at the time in
which he was with George (quoted in VB, 236–38) are deeply
moving and instructive about her depth of love for Duncan:
"I think—I know—we are too much for each other for things
not to come right in the end. It is ignorance and uncertainty
that sometimes makes it so difficult for me now . . . My dear,
I don't tell you I love you, but that I know you love me and
the knowledge makes me very happy. . . . ," and, in a later
letter, urges him not to come back until or unless he can come
back emotionally altogether . . .

Duncan cared immensely about her, and he was loyal in

his way. Why, he asks Bunny Garnett, can she not believe he loves her as much as ever? His love for George gives him

> more power to love her instead of less. And when she is not here I feel too that something is wanting in my life, however happy I am alone with George.
>
> The truth is I want them both. I want too much I suppose. Sometimes I find the tears rolling down my cheeks simply because I love both so much. That is a detestable form of self pity. But at the same time I cannot help thinking that if Nessa could see into my soul at such moments she would see that everything is all right.
>
> (March 2, 1930; VB, 239)

He cared also about Charleston, its plants, fruits, interior decorations. When he was at the farm and she in London, she was to bring inks and dyes from the Omega workshops to wash the doors down, with the same urgency that she was to renew their whiskey and claret supply. Duncan's eye for color finds an outlet in his descriptions: a brown crock with a red top, an emerald green lampshade, a shining tin—all these the lamplight in the letters catches, as the evening light holds a crowd of rooks accompanying David Garnett and Duncan on their way home. It is all a picture, and much else besides.

Of Vanessa's art, Duncan is solicitous and admiring: her pictures give him pleasure of a "most real" kind, and, he repeats, this is no idle compliment (DG/VB no. 48; 1175). He has the power of reassuring her, and does so with solicitude, frequently begging her not to be depressed, and insisting she has no idea how important she is to the world in general and to individuals in particular. It matters, and not just to him, that she should paint, and he longs to see large things and small done by her—he wants a large abstract by Vanessa in his room, and wants to see everything she is doing . . . and her still life again.

Duncan's constant refrain to counter her depression, her melancholy weeks, her exhaustions and endless worry for other people without one moment's rest reinforces our suppositions about the more than ambivalent tone in her letters to Roger, having to do with Duncan and her art. (As for Roger himself, still in love with Vanessa, Duncan hopes he isn't too gloomy for her, and is furious when Roger mistreats her, from jealousy.) Duncan, again with his sweet temperament, was always eager to have any criticisms anyone could make of his work, wanting to put them to profit. Please remember, he asks her, any specific criticisms or suggestions Roger may make about his pictures, of flowers or any others, for those suggestions might help him: his essential modesty appears in this letter (July 7, no 65), as it does elsewhere and often. This, even as he was less than admiring of Roger's paintings (two cases of them arrive, and he exclaims "what a great bore they are" [May 16, 1920]). Modest, but also honest he was.

At moments, he seems as discouraged by his painting as we have seen Vanessa disturbed by hers and Roger by both of theirs: the big picture he is painting is depressing him, for he seems to lose the effect of the whole for the parts. As Vanessa needs support, he gives it: "I long," he says, "to see your cushion cover and your mantelpiece. I know they are lovely and that you only need a little of any encouragement to think so yourself." (DG/VB, nd) As with Lytton and Carrington, Duncan's opinion was exactly the one Vanessa needed, and Duncan knew it, and gave it when it was wanted. Moreover, he wants to see one of her still lifes again, now that a bit of time has passed: again, he always has a sense of the exactly opportune moment: "it will be interesting to see it with a jump. As for my big picture I am very much depressed by it & have had to put your farm picture to the wall because it depressed me still more it is so very complete & I go on & on & always repaint silly little details that seem not to matter in the least to the general effect." What a long letter, he adds, "from your loving Bear" (October 9, 1920).

And, how boring are my letters he says—clearly, the self-denigration is not all on one side. Indeed one might even see it as part of a double generosity, each wanting to give the other the best of himself and herself; indeed, it seems, on re-reading, quite like the modesty of genuine love. I do not believe we should undervalue it.

Crucially, urgently, of course, Vanessa was jealous of his lovers; for good reason. And Duncan was good at provoking jealousy: writing in his diary, where he hoped Bunny Garnett would read it, was his account of one of his very rare episodes of love-making with Vanessa in 1918, after Angelica was conceived: he wrote that he had "copulated on Saturday with her with great satisfaction to myself physically. It is a convenient way the females (sic) of letting off one's spunk and comfortable . . . That's one for you Bunny!" (VB, 172). One letter on the subject of David Garnett can speak for the others:

> As for Bunny, I do wish you had talked to me about him. I never realized that things were so strained until he came to Charleston & then I thought & so did he apparently that he had much better not see you. I do hope you won't make yourself miserable about it. Because you know it isn't necessary either to see him except casually in the future or even I should think to have an emotional scene. Perhaps if you could write & simply explain the situation it would be easier on him to know how best to behave.
> (n.d., DG/VB, no. 560; 1196)

But Duncan hides little from her: she reads of his attachment to Marc Allégret the future film director, the good-looking (but clearly heterosexual, says Duncan) nephew of André Gide, himself a self-designated pederast. He says he is only slightly intoxicated with Marc, but can never find a moment to see him, unable either to figure out whether Gide is jealous or not. These letters exemplify Duncan's honesty; his straightforwardness—as so many witnesses point out—redeemed in some measure the great suffering his openness and his inclinations repeatedly caused.

Overall, the very warmth of the letters from Duncan to Vanessa, recounting, caring, reassuring, casts at least some light on the reasons why she was able to bear the situation. As for the reasons behind the situation itself, they are perhaps not entirely unrelated to those for which Carrington sustained her own no less painful situation; in neither case are they simple, nor are they simply masochistic. Not understandable, as people are fond of remarking? Perhaps just not ordinary—but no less valuable for that.

Vanessa's Art

. . . what a poet you are in colour—one of these days I must
write about you.
    Virginia to Vanessa, February 4, 1940 (VWL: VI, 381).

This tale I am telling, this mosaic with its three interconnected parts, its stories of the other and the self in all its complications, crucially involves the issue of mentors and models. All
the stories are different, as we would expect. Roger's stories of
international movements and the liveliness of interconnected
arts, Vanessa's stories of France and England, of love and sister-
hood, art and abstraction, color and austerity, dark and light,
feature and featurelessness, Virginia's stories of sensitive vision
and imagination bound up with seeing, as with telling and not
telling, Carrington's fictions and arts of love and living form
the complexly illustrated tapestry from which we read and see
and choose our own stories of these figures and their lives and
work.

Roger told, in any case, a strong story, and since Vanessa
was always to be in the sway, to some large extent, of this man
she had first seen as an "enthralling companion" for them all, she
took to it. When he led them into the French waters both she and
Duncan had already taken to, they swam in enthusiastically. In
some readings, as he failed Carrington in not supporting her
art, he failed English art in not supporting its practitioners in
the true sense of their own individual and autonomous leanings,
and in choosing to have the French model prevail.

Cézanne was, in a sense, the reigning spirit in these years:
he had, says Clive Bell, founded "a new movement," and in the
wake of that movement there was Bloomsbury. Roger's account
of his meeting with Cézanne's paintings only after the artist's
death, having heard of him "vaguely from time to time as a
kind of hidden oracle of ultra-impressionism," thus, having
expected to be fairly unreceptive to him, is succinct and elo-
quent: "To my intense surprise I found myself deeply moved."

Moved, and for always; the relation of Fry to Cézanne is characteristic of him at his most gloriously intense. A vividly described scene has Vanessa bringing into the room a tiny canvas
by Cézanne given to Maynard Keynes, of some apples, with
Roger holding forth about the roundness and greenness Cézanne

was able to capture until other apples were never to seem so apple again. "The apples," says Virginia, "positively got redder & rounder & greener" (VWD: I, 140) as Roger spoke, with his enthusiasm leading to exaltation, just as in his lectures with their vivid excitement Carrington and the others comment on repeatedly. He made others want to see, to paint, to live. Roger and the apples on the canvas: buzzing around it, says Vanessa—whose own Cézanne connection was immensely strong, and visible in her painting—like a bee around a blossom. In this incident we can glimpse, and understand, Roger's enthusiasm with its almost frighteningly specific focus, bestowing a kind of freshness on everything around.

A great deal of discussion has taken place about the preference of both Roger and Vanessa for French over English art; like the accusation against Roger that he supported Carrington's decorative mode over her painterly mode, these preferences are in large measure undeniable and unattackable as they are unavoidable, rather like the sexual preferences of the figures involved in this book. It is quite true that France was of an overwhelming importance in the life and taste and art of the Bloomsbury group, against some of the currents in contemporary English art. More crucial in a sense for the subject of this book is the reaction of Vanessa, uncowed by major figures like Matisse and Cézanne, and constantly preoccupied about her painting in relation to that of Duncan: but that is the difference between the vertical influence of the admittedly great creators, from whom the contemporary artists are delighted to, and moved to learn, and the natural horizontal rivalry of those contemporary artists with each other. The case is all the more complicated with Vanessa, of course, insofar as she consciously or unconsciously wishes to aggrandize Duncan's work in relation to her own, from a series of reasons, some of which we have seen, others of which we can suppose.

Now the connection between Vanessa's art and that of France leaps to mind and to sight. The flat surfaces of Cézanne and Gauguin, their particular palette of colors, their portraits and their still lifes, the ways Matisse had of treating sunlight and windows and especially studio interiors, all of this is clearly traced in her work, and does not lack for documentation. A very few examples will serve to illustrate the overall importance of this influence: I will take them from the Tate's collections.

Vanessa speaks over and over again of her painterly relation to Cézanne: February 7, 1911, to Roger: "I am trying . . . to see the Cézannes after my struggle with water colour which grows more and more difficult and fascinating." At a later point, she will try, precisely, to wean her painting away from the feeling of watercolor, but at this point she is plunged into it. January 22, 1913: "We have been trying to paint in water colours; today again . . . I can't master the technique but I believe one might find a way of using it. I mean to go on trying." And two days later: "I've done a much better water colour today." The technique she did master, and carried it over into her oils, with their great flat washes of color, like those of Cézanne. Many of her still lifes could be profitably compared with his, such as the *Mantelpiece* painting I shall be discussing shortly—particularly in its way of massing the elements and the distinctness of their form—but I want to concentrate at the moment on figure painting.

Cézanne's *Gardener* of 1906, with its carefully almost-centered figure, crossed legs and great dignity, is seated in a Provençal setting, with a great flat blue swash of color at the left, then a great ocher swash: the figure in his ocher hat, his ocher and blue shirt, his blue trousers and green shoes, weds the ocher and blue at the left to the grey and green that are the colors of the right-hand side of the picture. Overhead, a grey and blue surrounding color again merges right and left, so that the whole coloring, both forceful and understated, lets the figure with his shaded eyes occupy the center easily. This rendering in its strength and gentleness can be fruitfully compared with Vanessa's pictures of Virginia seated in her chair, particularly the earlier ones of 1912, one in a canvas chair with her legs crossed (SA, 182), the other at Asheham, now in the National Portrait Gallery (SA, 183), the first with an entirely featureless face, the second with the vaguest outline of eyes and nose and mouth. These make a startling contrast with Vanessa's picture of her (SA, 186) of 1934, graceful in her well-defined chair in the library, but with features clearly drawn. The strength of the first two is unsurpassed,

particularly, I would argue, the first with no features at all.
(The same effect is found, and equally successful in Vanessa's
portrait of *Frederick and Jesse Etchells Painting*, where the un-
defined faces stand out strongly against the dull green wall,
which modulates into a bright green rectangle of grass outside,
with a lighter rectangle just above.) The frontality of the pose,
the slightly off-centered position, and the intimate contact—
in spite of, or perhaps, if it does not sound too perverse, because
of—the absence of definition, all of this is highly reminiscent
of Cézanne's *Gardener*, and his well-known portrait of his
mother, done in the same blue as that of the Gardener. The
feeling of force, through form, color, and understatement,
seems close indeed between these portraits, of a same mood
and approach. This French influence has dissipated by the
time of the later portrait of Virginia, as is obvious.

As for the influence of Gauguin, it is visible in the effect
on Vanessa of such landscapes as the 1890 *Harvest at Le
Pouldu* with its simple forms and flat sweeps of color, with
its swirls and pilings together of rocks and sea, its mysterious
atmosphere and uninterpretable blobs, all fitting together in
a whole that is more symbolist than realist, where a dog is
painted red to contrast with the blue shirt of a woman rather
than for mimetic reasons. I would compare this with her
magnificent *Studland Beach* of 1911–12 with its turned-away
figures and strangely symbolist feeling, as if the true meaning
were to be situated out somewhere far beyond the picture
frame. The strange distance in mid-ground, between the two
observers at the left bottom corner, with their hats clearly
marking them as non-participators in the scene, and the
group at the top right corner, with its huddled figures in
contrast to the tall woman in a long white costume, before
the tent-like cabin, staring out, as if in a celebratory rite—
that strange distance is accentuated by the long sweep of
ground against sea, and of color against color as in the Gauguin. Both, I would contend, are celebrations of a certain
mystery, of uninterpretable and inexpressible *acts* and *pre-
sentations*, set at a distance from the observer which stresses
all the more the gap between understanding and seeing. As
the discussion of Vanessa's *The Tub* will emphasize, this very
mystery of certain of Vanessa's early canvases is disquieting

to the observer: thus the multiple interpretations of that canvas—why are we forced to stare into the interior of an omega-shaped tub, as if it were stood on its edge to plunge the spectator into an abyss of contemplation like that of the oddly long-legged naked figure beside it? The strength of the mystery, like that of *Studland Beach* depends on the unpinnable-down feeling of some rite from which, forever, the spectator is to be excluded, from which, forever, we are to be kept at a distance.

In Vanessa's own reflections on *Studland Beach*, she acknowledges the unyielding matter both of the subject and the composition, and of the special background: for, as she says, "It's really very difficult to paint on the beach. One can't get any composition and one's colour changes completely when one brings it in out of the sun . . ." (1912, VB/RF 34), and later, still to Roger: "I've been trying this morning on the beach to paint your subject—the one with my colossal figure in the foreground but it's a failure. It was too difficult" (1912, VB/RF 43). Difficult the painting is, and oddly angled, but the colossal figure of *Studland Beach*, centered and hieratic, has an effect not easily forgotten, as if both near and distant, simple and deeply problematic, in the facing-away of the figures, their groupings, and their size. The importance of this canvas is likely to be, I think, a lasting one.

Finally, for the French influence, Matisse's *Interior of a Studio* of 1903–4 has not only precisely the colors of Vanessa's *Gordon Square* painting of 1911 (dark brown and green) but the same play of light and dark, of window and table or easel, of vertical lines against round ones, the same foreshortening and angles which give the effect of plunging us into that interior. The triangular stool in the center takes us into the painting, as if leading the lines of sight by an irresistible thrust. The way in which the canvas to be worked on is set against the brown of the armoire, the way in which the light to the left is set against the dark directly to its right side, the way in which the textures of wood and fruit and flower and pottery each sharpen the feelings of the others, and the ways in which the yellow of the half-lemon, the grey-green of the place and the red flowers in the blue jug with its darker-blue spots work in such muted harmony are the ways of Vanessa's early Gordon Square interior with its triangular structure, its window, and its muted dark colors taking in the observer, quietly and inescapably, and, also, her still lifes at their finest.

Among the latter, the ones from 1912 to 1920 seem to demonstrate the most receptivity to the French lesson, and yet to have an indefinable other quality. As for the vexed question of the comparison between Vanessa's and Duncan's art, similar though they may be at some points—to the extent that the public was capable of confusing them, and to the more harmful extent to which Vanessa was apt to compare hers unfavorably with those of Duncan, as is illustrated earlier in this chapter—I want to lead up to a comparison of the two canvasses of Vanessa and Duncan at the same time on the same subject and their ultimate *difference* via a brief note on a few other of her still lifes from this period.

Such pictures as *The Pumpkin* with its enormous round central eponymous objects in a dish from which it lopsidedly emerges halfway, and its sparse other fruits and vegetables scattered around on the folds of a tablecloth, has the force of a Cézanne apple-piece, yet its drastic cropping (just before the top of the stem) gives it all the more thrust (SA, 233). The same drastic cropping, even more severe and even more strengthening is found in her *Pineapple and Candlesticks* of 1915 (SA, 234). Here the deep and glowing coloring—all purples and yellows—gives a royal note to this fruit, framed as it is by other lesser fruits surrounding it in a bowl upon a plate, and again by the candlesticks to either side, the tops of which, like the top of the pineapple itself, are severed by the top of the canvas. The effect is quite extraordinary, conveying the same density and presence on the image as might an intense crescendo upon a musical note: the image sings out vibrant, like a positive equivalent of the French poet Apollinaire's final lines in the great poem "Zone," ending

> soleil
> cou coupé
> (sun
> severed neck)

into which goes all the surge of blood and all the radiant light at once, as the modernity of Paris is summed up, at sunset,

by this intense recreation of legend (decapitation) and landscape.

Vanessa's strength in this wonderfully inventive period
is often that of her vivid imagination, and of all the illustrations one could choose, the *Still Life on Corner of a Mantelpiece*
is perhaps the most vivid of all. It is of particular interest
since, in 1914 also, Duncan painted this same group of objects
on the same corner of the same mantelpiece, and as differently as one could wish, to establish a possible contrast.

Duncan's picture, simply called *The Mantelpiece*, of 1914,
is far more crammed than Vanessa's, and less revolutionary.
It shows at the same time less difference between the colors;
the white and ocher on the left side, balanced against the
beige on the other, and the grey and red forms at the bottom
converge in the dull yellow at the top. Most importantly, the
canvas is square and muted, except for the yellow-green hat
box, which Vanessa will reduce to a simple white form, and
the gathered mass of objects is seen straight on, atop a violet
and beige supporting ledge.

Vanessa's picture, on the other hand (SA, 239), is most
remarkable for its high rise, from the triangular ledge
straight up towards the top, seen from below. This odd angle
taken has the peculiar effect of making all the objects stand
up and out: there are fewer than in Duncan's, for Vanessa has
eliminated or reduced to abstraction that which did not fit
in with this triangulated vision. The composition, wonderfully full of echoes and wonderfully odd, with inexplicable
forms verging on the abstract, has a white diagonal stem
echoing a white box (no off-white of the muted Duncan variety here) and a large pink fruit echoed by a deep rose box; it
plays ocher against yellow, with a strange mediation of pink
or rose, plays a triangle against a rectangular shape and a
round one, and uses vivid green and bright white as a shock
after the yellow and ocher and beige-green and brown tones;
its balances its objects on abstract shapes, but with a dull
yellow ridge of support, the color picked up by other lemon-
colored shapes within the picture; the objects are non-refer-
ential, abstract, indeterminable, of purplish brown and ocher
and dull brown, with a streak of grey and a light grey background.

The picture is, beyond a doubt, exciting; without doubt

as important in Vanessa's *oeuvre* as the nursery scenes and the other interior scenes, the equal, I think, of the great *The Tub*. The strange singularity of its piling up and its soaring perspective is all the more singular seen by the side of Duncan's tame rendering; this one illustration suffices to give the lie to her feelings of inferiority with the paintbrush.

Some of Vanessa's other scenes have almost the power of this one; a far quieter example in the Tate, but one well worth mentioning, is the *Chrysanthemums* of 1920, where a quite bizarre color combination of white and pink and black flowers, with darker ones, sit, three in an off-white jug which is reflected in the shiny black table, and again, in an abstract series of stripes of color in swashes to the right of the jug, the white and black and rose stripes sinuously echoing the colors in the painting, and representing their outer curve as the echo of the curve of the jug, twice: in reality and in reflection. Vanessa's art, largely about echoes and flat surfaces and new coloring, is as much about its reflection as about its real subject, or better, that *is* its real subject.

Above all, her early explorations in the fresh freedom of color, brought over from France, with her own "austere sense of geometric design" are responsible for the great screens with their angular figures crouched beneath tall triangles like tents, like trees, like the essence of line itself. These haunting works make, with those extraordinary featureless portraits, a giant step in the art of this semi-figurative period. Among all these pictures, the celebrated featureless pictures of Virginia: *Virginia Woolf,* 1912, in a folding chair, frontally placed, and *Virginia Woolf at Asheham,* 1912, in semi-profile, in an armchair (referred to earlier), hold the observer in an odd and hypnotic sway.

Surrounded as they are in our minds—and as was the case at Monk's House—by the austere geometry of the Omega furniture, these figures seem to represent—in their own strong forms, in their refusal to express anything in particular—the world of art which Virginia describes as a place "where no stories are told." But then, of course, it can be a place for starting to tell our own story afresh.

❦ 6 ❦
Carrington

Such a Short Life

I really prefer inventing.
Carrington to Gerald Brenan (DC/GB, June 8, 1921)

Dora Carrington was born at Hereford, England, on March 29, 1893, in a middle-class family, to Samuel Carrington, a railway builder for the East India Company, who had retired in England with his wife, the far younger Charlotte Houghton, the rheumatic governess to the children of one of his nieces. Carrington (who, from her Slade student days to the end of her life, never used her own first name), idealized her father and detested her mother's fussiness and general what-will-people sayness. "I loved my father for his rough big character, his rather rustic simplicity and the great way he lived inside himself . . . ," she says in one of her letters to her fellow student Mark Gertler, with whom she was to carry on an intermittent love affair for years, as she did subsequently with Gerald Brenan—her restless nature encouraged breaks, reunions, re-breaks, and reconciliation, all with an intensity rarely found in what we think of as "ordinary lives."

Her other close men friends at the Slade, C.R.W. Nevinson, Paul Nash, and Stanley Spencer, encouraged her in her art, as Roger Fry—whose criticism she greatly admired, and who was to give high praise to Gertler, for example—never did. She rarely exhibited and felt a failure, constantly comparing herself not just with Piero della Francesca (one of Vanessa Bell's favorites also), or with Tintoretto and the other great artists she so valued (to Rosamond Lehmann, March 15, 1928: "It's rather maddening to have the ambition of Tintoretto and to paint like a mouse" [DC/RL, KCL]), but—more closely and more tragically—with the brilliant talkers and creators of her acquaintance, closely or loosely attached to Bloomsbury.

Her ambitions for herself never included a standard marriage and children model—she retained perhaps in herself too much of the child for that. Having met Lytton Strachey through Virginia and Leonard Woolf, she fell in love with him in rather extraordinary circumstances: on a walk, he was attracted by her boyish figure, and tried to kiss her, whereupon she determined to have her revenge. The next morning she crept into his room with a pair of scissors to cut off his beard (a somewhat unorthodox castration scene), but when he opened his eyes, she promptly, irrevocably, and—in my view—quite marvelously fell in love with him. She then devoted her life to amusing him, nourishing and nursing him, becoming his steady companion in their two houses, Tidmarsh, then Ham Spray, until the end of his days.

Lytton, being homosexual, feared her devotion in its dependent form, and encouraged her relationship and then her marriage to Ralph Partridge, to whom he was also attracted. In order to avoid his leaving her, and because Ralph wanted it so desperately, Carrington married him, and they set up a ménage à trois, in 1921, at Tidmarsh Mill, near Pangbourne, a home Carrington located on her bicycle, when looking for a suitable place. The house was rented through a fund set up by the Strachey brothers and some Bloomsbury friends, in view of a calm retreat for Lytton, who asked Carrington to be his housekeeper.

They remained there until the dampness became insupportable to Lytton's frail constitution, and then moved in July 1924 to Ham Spray, near the Hampshire downs, which Carrington had always loved, and near which she had been born; Lytton had bought the lease in January of this year. Riding in this country on her white horse Belle, she was happier, perhaps, than anywhere else, as happy as on her frequent walking tours of England and Europe. Lytton's royalties from his *Queen Victoria* were sufficient to purchase the house. Carrington decorated it as she had (and continued to) other rooms and homes, even as she painted inn signs, did tinsel paintings, and glass paintings, all of which made money as she feared her serious painting would not. With the consequence that she had less and less time to pay attention to that painting, from which in any case the constant visitors to Ham Spray were a grave diversion—they were never to see the paintings, which she kept hidden, like a part of her life which was secret and seemed unvalued. And yet she loved painting and was often elated by it, turning away as if it were from a success which would be incompatible with her management of Lytton's home and her control—to some odd extent—of his life.

"I am not strong enough to live in this world of people and paint," she was to write in her diary, that has come down to us as an oddly distanced document, misspelling her own married name, perhaps significantly, "D.C. Partride: Her Book." The time taken up by the constant entertaining and performance of amateur plays, films, and trips to London when she could afford them, to say nothing of the almost constant emotional involvement with men and also women, as if in some compensatory mode for her deep and abiding love for Lytton, was forever inimical to her dedication to her art. Of this particular outcome, she was all too well aware and about it, increasingly sad, and yet, consenting. Victimized as much by herself and her self-doubts, perhaps, as by circumstances, she continued her various love affairs: lengthily, with Gerald Brenan, who always adored her ("once she got under your skin, you couldn't get her out," he was to say in his memoirs) briefly, with Henrietta Bingham, daughter of the American Ambassador to London, as well as a number of what we might call crushes on various women, including Julia Strachey. Carrington often lamented being a woman, and was always to feel ambivalent in the psychological and physical senses. Her last involvement occurred after Ralph became more and more enamored of Frances Marshall (whom he was to marry after Carrington's death), with Bernard or "Beakus" Penrose, a sailor, ten years younger, and who reminded her of her brother Teddy, killed in the War, but whom she lived to think of as a sailor lost at sea. She had an abortion, Beakus tired of her, and she felt old, sad, and unfulfilled, attached always and utterly to her love for Lytton. When Lytton was dying of undiagnosed cancer of the stomach, Carrington tried to take her own life with carbon monoxide fumes, but was called back from the garage when it was thought he was going ("when I gave my life for you, you should give it back," she wrote him in her diary when he later lay on his death bed). Just before his death, she said, he whispered he should have married her, and to that she clung. But six weeks after his death, having tried to live without him and "liking it not," she borrowed from a neighbor a gun to kill the rabbits eating her lettuce in the yard, she said, and aimed it at herself, after arranging the rug to make it look like an accident. But the catch was on, and it did not go off; she fired again, but the aim had slipped, and she shot off her side, and had to be given morphine when the doctor came. In her last moments, she asked him to go down to the liquor cabinet, for he looked weak at the sight of her and she tried to reassure Ralph she would not die: "I have bungled," she said, "my life and my death."

It was a death that could be blamed on no one; she had been preparing for a trip to Europe with close friends, and had presumably not made up her mind the day before. One of the events of that preceding day has been evoked: Virginia Woolf—who, in spite of her sharp tongue and occasional mischief-making, was always fond of her, as Carrington was of Virginia, for her wit and charm and gaiety—had inquired if Carrington would come to see them the next day. "I will come," said Carrington, "or then not." That the latter course was not inevitable seems sure. What is sure is the intensity, a rare one that we should value, with which Carrington loved Lytton. That so many have misunderstood her and her love is in large measure the reason for this present book.

Tormented for much of her life by nightmares and feelings of drastic insufficiency, Carrington nevertheless succeeded in quite an extraordinary fashion in showing and sharing a unique style of living, thinking, and writing which is—at its best—delightful, and—at its most depressing—profoundly troubling. It clearly indicates a woman's often problematic stance towards her own work, the time she has to make for it, and the intertwinings of her relations with those about her, and their own work, values often opposed to values. Carrington's vastly low esteem of herself and her work, coupled with the vividness of her observations, written and painted, of nature and other people, makes a case study for psychology enthusiasts, to say nothing of her obvious father fixation in her adoration of Lytton, and of her habitual secrecy and guilt feelings. Thus, it will be said, with some justification, her inability to sustain any prolonged heterosexual relation.

Her epistolary styles, diverse and convincing, are her real relations: Carrington's unpublished ventures into short fiction, drama, and poetry, pale remarkably beside the variety of tone and temper in her letters profusely and drolly illustrated, and always quite exactly vectored toward the recipient. They are alternately cajoling, flirtatious, tender, gossipy, encouraging, affectionate, digressive, and focused. Her acknowledged bisexuality finds a parallel ambivalence in all her attitudes, so that she advances and retreats, discloses and hides, offers and withdraws with engaging rapidity. Rarely has there been a more seductive subject of self-writing and other-writing.

Carrington alternated between a secretive delight at solitude ("The pleasure of being alone in my bedroom is very great") and a playful passion for gossip: "All the very intimate and indiscreet things I meant to tell you in France," she says to Sebastian Sprott, one of her favorite correspondents, have to her regret been forgotten in English discretion, back at Tidmarsh. "I confess I rather enjoyed for once the company of anyone as stupid as myself," she teases him, before enjoining the homosexual Sebastian about Lytton's comfort, "as one mistress to another" (DC/SS, KCL). The funny informal brightness of her letter-writing art is matched, at other moments, by her extremes of "melancholly," as she always spelled it, and by her nightmares and dreads, coupled with sharp feelings of guilt towards anyone she was ever involved with. Even her all-encompassing love for Lytton was to her "the most self-abasing" sort anyone could have, predicting, as she did, and in part correctly, years of misery for herself;

and yet it alone seemed to her worth creating for, giving up other lives for, making herself interesting for, and dwelling upon. Her touching request in her celebratedly tragic letter to Lytton about her decision to marry Ralph bears quoting in this context: "Once you said to me, that Wednesday afternoon in the Sitting-Room, you love me as a Friend. Could you Tell it to me again?"

Above all, Carrington's peculiar genius for friendship and its written testimony outshone her other writing, if not her painting. To Gerald: "But I have, since we always write, do we not, the truth to each other—the capacity for being a remarkable friend" (DC/GB, June 8, 1921). Indeed she did.

And in the domain of diary-writing, that most ambiguous exercise of the secret and the manifest, she ranks no less high. It is here that we are able to glimpse her life with all its intensity, its loneliness, and its most appealing personal peculiarities, finding as it does its truest fulfillment in its self-writing through the letters to others and to herself. "I feel there is nothing to prevent my now fervent image of the nymph who turned into a stag so perfectly that it could be no disgrace . . . ," she observed in a letter to Gerald Brenan. This, in 1924; but then, in 1931, in a letter to Rosamond Lehamnn, after quoting from what she calls Lytton's creed ("it's *no* good being anything but what you are and the great thing is never to do anything one doesn't feel genuinely inside oneself"), she continues in a self-accusatory mode, familiar to all too many women, endowed with high talent and cursed with a still higher creative ambition: "For really I used every excuse not to do any proper painting. It's partly I have such high standards that I can't bear going on with pictures when I can see they are amateurish and dull" (June 1931; DG, 464). Carrington's likeness in this aspect to Vanessa, whose repeated self-accusations of dullness (in her letters to Virginia, in her paintings next to Duncan's, in relation to what she knew she could do) is remarkable. As Virginia quaked under negative reviews and feared them beyond the bounds of reason, so her sister practices her self-denigration partly as negative or magic thinking; but in Carrington's case, the undervaluing far outdistances that of the others. And that is why I want to make such a case for Carrington.

Her paintings and even her decorations are perhaps indeed underrated; but all of the things she was not, she was most not dull, within her art or in her violently differing styles of expression and of being. Carrington often seems to speak for the best of, and in us, even as she accuses her own self-irresolution; in one of the last years of her life, she wrote that, without any relations to complicate her, she would like to do more painting. "But then," she continues, "this is a resolution I have made for the last ten years. However I seem lately to have become more certain of some things . . ." (January 1, 1928; HB). Whatever the uncertainities and the extensive self-doubts that plague woman creators like Augustus John's more talented sister Gwen, like Paula Modersohn-Becker of the Worpswede group, like Camille Claudel, Rodin's mistress, or even like Vanessa Bell, each of them living to the side of a stellar male or recognized male artist, the vivid style and unique character of each of these women stand out in their expression, quite frequently, of those very doubts themselves.

When she dropped that letter from her married name, in writing on the cover of "Her Book" her name as D.C. Patride, she fulfilled, as if for us too, that promise she made to Mark Gertler, her first love, that she would never be anything but what she was, no adoption and no adaptation, no settlement. "To you," she wrote him about her forthcoming wedding and her refusal to take another name for her own,"I shall ever be Carrington, and to myself." To us also.

Those High Days: Gerald and Carrington

What everyone can see is that you are attracted to those who are less attracted to you, and Repelled by Reciprocity.
Gerald to Carrington, no date, and not sent

Of all characteristics in human beings I dread jealousy and possessiveness the most.
Carrington to Gerald (GB, 178)

He fell in love with her, just sitting in an armchair, when, on some late summer afternoon one August, she "passed across in front of the window, outlined against the setting sun. She just passed across and all at once something overturned inside me and I felt that I was deeply, irretrievably in love." Apart, they got along, and were lovers, warm upon the page; together, they were problematic, with ups and downs constant in their relation.

Gerald has been overpoweringly attracted, he says, by her white legs, green dress, and brown hands, as she dangles them in the stream near Watendlath. Far later, Carrington laments: You are the only person who notices what I wear—this green dress, who will see how lovely it is? He writes her passionate letters, forgetting(?) that Ralph will ask to see them; please remember to put all your passionate stuff in the p.s., says Carrington, so that Ralph can read the main letter—you forgot again. And she hides his letters under the little bookstand outside her room, drawing it for him with its little hollow under the bottom shelf: there, your letters go there. (And Vanessa said to Roger: you need not worry—I get my letters all by myself, at breakfast, so you don't have to be so cautious.) How the secrecy and surreptitious correspondences heighten the pleasure of the words, hidden and so magnified in sense.

You have decided, says Gerald to Carrington, to live without a heart. Only material things matter to you. You would be happy to drop me after six or seven years as a lover, without any qualms at all. Agreed, writes Carrington: "I get on your nerves. No one else does. You can talk and be happy with other people far easier than with me . . . there is something that produces unhappiness between us. I think what you say is true—I mean, that I do not care enough" (GB, 85). In fact, though, this was the case with all her lovers; when Gerald reads Mark Gertler's letters to her, he feels "that everything he had written to or about Carrington might have been written by myself. She had brought out in each of us the same agony of mind, the same baffled exasperation"(GB, 102). Or boredom and impatience, and the feeling that they were not "conversationally attuned to one another." Never was there ·to be any "attuning," just a modest reshuffling . . . and realignment. She would make small gestures of propitiation, out of guilt ("Thus she rarely came to see me without bringing me a present, although she must have known that the only present I wanted from her was herself," GB, 104). He, self-willed, egotistic, and impatient, even in his own terms; she stubborn and guilt-ridden, quirky and secretive. They are always fighting and almost loving, and loving and almost fighting, wherever they were.

But why, Gerald asks Carrington, in another undated letter, do I so attack you? "There is something quite unbearable in my behavior and very much that is good and kind and sensible in yours . . ." I am uncontrolled, I frighten myself, he says, I am just exercising my imagination, and on the other hand, there is so much to respect in you: "your feeling for the country, your life in it, etc.,—being the most essential part of your character" and indeed, "protect myself, detach myself as I do, I am always in some way in love with you." All this in one letter, so that the outpourings from Gerald to Carrington are a fitting response for her own, as they were, in correspondence, a perfect match.

You are medicine to my every bad mood, he compliments her, in all seriousness—with you, a cup of coffee is superb pleasure ("Is it not a most curious & complicated drink? Has it not got a strange and fugitive aroma?") (And is he not a superb writer? Carrington had, it seems to me, great luck in her lovers and her livers-in. Vanessa too.) Among other things, they share this intense delight in the everyday detail that Vanessa shares with Duncan, as she had with Roger, as Carrington does with Lytton, and with Virginia. Gerald makes fun of Lytton's extravagant taste as Mark had, when Carrington abandoned him for the elder and less manly man (which abandonment and its irony he illustrates with a ferociously vivid drawing of the comparative physiognomy of himself and Lytton): of course it is essential that you have to find him his caviar, help him live in the lap of luxury, live with him there . . . .

Quite naturally, the great difference in age and maturity of all kinds meant that the setup of Carrington and Lytton was to be marveled at, from the outside as from in. Carrington's description of herself and Lytton, seen in the great discrepancy of their ages, as they take tea—illustrated in a letter to her brother Noel of 1916—shows not just her whimsy but her true ability to see herself from without. They looked, she said, to the others at nearby tables, like one of three couples: a distinguished Belgian philosopher and his niece, or then perhaps the Duke of Norfolk and his daughter, or then (and most delightful) Lord Alfred Tennyson's ghost and Wordsworth's little Lucy revived. Carrington was never to lose this naive Eloise-at-the-Ritz quality of teasing about and reveling in her own improbable situation.

Different indeed from the relation between Carrington and the far older Lytton is the double childlikeness of Gerald and Carrington, splendidly alive as they both are to each other and to it. Ralph could see, says Gerald, how unlike him we were, neither being "dominating nor aggressive . . . we were unworldly and ingenuous . . . and he also found us irresponsible, vague, muddle-headed and general unreliable (sic)" (GB, 31). That is a description close to the bone of the two of them, and describes at once their exchange of letters and their waxings and wanings in the exchange of love. It is our good fortune that this odd symmetry is particularly visible in their innumerable letters, virtual and real—for Gerald did not send, although he prints them—his most aggrieved letters, full of violence.

Carrington holds on, he thinks, to Ralph more and more, in order to hold on to Lytton, who was always somewhat in love with the heterosexual Ralph, and who remains attached to him. As for Carrington, and Ralph, and Lytton, and Gerald for that matter—for she never gave up on anyone she had once loved, unless, explains Gerald, the demands became too oppressive, as in the case of Mark Gertler—she writes to Gerald, about her feelings for Ralph: "I will certainly never love him, but I am extremely fond of him. I believe that if one wasn't reserved and hadn't a sense of what is possible one could be *very* fond of certainly two or three people at a time" (GB, 24). She explains herself openly, convincingly on this subject: "My chief fault, if it is one, is that when I am with a person I forget everyone else all my other relations, & feel only *this* person I am with, and *these* present moments exist" (DC/GB, July 26, 1921). And, echoing this felt confession, she responds a few weeks later to Gerald about their relation, and her others: "I have loved everything that has happened to us together . . . . But I will not pretend I am faithful. It is true what you say I love to (sic) many people" (DC/GB, September 7, 1921). That system you have set up, Gerald implies, must find its correspondent in our own. We must, he says, build up a secret and private vocabulary in our letters, for I have a real passion for communications that are allusive, that must be unlocked, until the ideas spill out.

Gerald often writes like, and often thinks like, a child: so too, Carrington. This double childishness, touching at its best, seemed sometimes to fill in for the sexual relations which were so frequently skewed, not infrequently by that childishness itself—Carrington wanting them just when she could propose them, and otherwise, openly refusing or just putting up with them. In a startling scene, recounted in all its vivid detail by both Gerald in his memoirs and Carrington in "Her Book," fictionalized but clear, she comes to his room at 12:30 at night, to his bed, where he is weeping, lies beside him as if consummating a sacrifice, insists he make love to her, as it is her duty to be there, and then "The moment after—'Have you finished?' And she got up and left the room" (GB, 105), refusing to kiss him goodbye even the next morning. Her mysteries and her fantasies were singular, like her entire being.

And this kind of mystery appealed to, kept alive, the passion of Gerald, as is consistently clear in his relations with her, and with others: his intense complexity and almost feminine subtlety of understanding perfectly suited him to be close friends with Virginia, for example. And his attitude toward Roger, so distinctly his opposite, was precisely that of someone who wished for allusiveness and secrecy: his description in the spring of 1925 to Carrington of Roger and Helen Anrep having a picnic lunch on his stairs (for Helen shared the same address) is indicative and hilarious. They are discussing the problem of Boris, Helen's husband, and Roger is speaking loudly (the opposite of allusive he was, to be sure), and Gerald is revolted, in a sort of puritanical way, as if by the antics of the elderly, too noisy, too everything. They are simply indulging what he calls their "November love," as they exchange jokes, throwing pellets of bread at each other, "grinning and blithering," and make a perpetual "silly flirtation" out of their intellectual conversations. Roger is particularly shocking to Gerald—and the tone is one of a sort of puritanical younger man: this is often true in his letters to Carrington, where he rails against Lytton's love of luxury, and Carrington's indulgence of him in it and in all else. Noticeably, Gerald will describe the aroma of his own coffee freshly made, as opposed to this view of Lytton imagined to be consuming caviar every day as if it is his due, and Roger taking in great mouthfuls of cold wine and chicken, and "effervescing" in every way possible, holding forth as he eats. Gerald, quite humorlessly, compares him to an old kettle "spitting," and is offended by Roger's using his immense intellectual equipment to such idle end (GB to DC, May 3, 1925).

Now there is more to Gerald's feeling about Roger than just the shock at such inappropriate behavior on the stairs (*his* stairs, as he does not fail to imply.) Carrington has compared the friendly and supportive relation between the ex-lovers Vanessa and Roger, now that Vanessa is with Duncan, to what she thinks she and Gerald could have as a relation now she is with Lytton, and with Ralph . . . How could such a situation as theirs, says Gerald, given the sexlessness between Vanessa and Duncan, possibly throw any light on our future? Only when he is forty, if he is living in Rome, married to someone else, and Carrington is still "imprisoned"—the very word takes aim at her situation—at Ham Spray, could they possibly have any kind of calm relation. Tranquility, such as she demands, is impossible in their present situation (to DC, June 23, 1925). Calling hers a "useless daydream," he begs her to discard it.

In any case, that intimate friendship Carrington describes, so enviously, between Roger and Vanessa will never work, he says to her, because your notion of friendship is faulty. Better we not see each other; when you are happy you do not need me, and when you are unhappy you do. Your own concerns matter to you alone, and you do not know how to share. The difficulties of your character do not detract from its essential beauty, he says, but we cannot be friends like this. Please avoid seeing me.

On the other hand, he writes later (January 29, 1925), Carrington and Vanessa are not so unlike. His dislike for Roger, intense and concerned with issues of fittingness added to an instinctive antipathy, does not carry over to Roger's former love Vanessa, whom Carrington would have enjoyed seeing at a recent party, where she was constantly accompanying Helen Anrep, with her arm thrown around her neck, and her hand holding Helen's: with a "more ironical look" than he had ever seen in any woman's eyes. But, he goes on, Vanessa—whom he confesses he greatly admires—is too much like Carrington herself in character for him to talk of her more: though in Carrington, Vanessa's "sparkle and irony and malice" are lacking. (This seems a rather odd statement to make to the woman you say you love, that another woman's sparkle is something she does not share.)

How *could* Carrington sparkle constantly? Always the sense of guilt: that she is wanting both in what she can offer, and in what she is. To Gerald, she writes: "You want perpetually from me something which it is not in my power to give and I feel always a sense of guilt and depression because I cannot give it to you . . ." (GB, 111). It is, she says, that I hate being a woman, and making love fills me with rage afterwards; because Ralph no longer treats me as a woman, there is less strain between us. "You pressed me out of myself into a hidden suppressed character, but when I returned I turned against this character and was filled with dread at meeting you again. It is really something unconnected with you, a struggle in myself between two characters . . . . Probably it would have been easier if I had been completely Lesbian" (GB, 111). As it is, she says, she feels a tin of mixed biscuits, and a muddle . . .

All these elements persist in her relations with her lovers: with Mark, Ralph, Gerald, Beakus, and of course Lytton, who, in not loving her entirely, as he could not, could furnish a sort of judgment with which she only too readily concurred: but the diagnosis is, of course, like all such efforts, a bit too easy. All her relations seem a writing-out of character, attempts at discovering some other self that would convince her, as her own so sadly and so often did not. And yet, her magnificent letters bring into being and into their own sort of coherence a self which is unmistakable, lovable, definite. The patchwork they make is perhaps the truest picture we will ever have had of Carrington.

After Gerald sets up house with Gamel Woolsey in 1930, Carrington makes a patchwork quilt of her old dresses for their bed—surely a singular gesture. Is this attempt to cover them over just a bizarre longing to get on top of, lie on top of, control the situation, pitiful in its inefficacy? (It even got there late, as the weather grew colder and colder, and she worried increasingly over it . . .) A peculiar sort of revenge, a quilt of her dresses in patches for the bride Medea-like, with mental poison worked in? (I am sorry, she will say, it is not ready yet . . . as if it were a welcome gift, eagerly awaited.) Or then a benevolent, willed participation in the life of others, taking relish, as she did in arranging, assorting, plotting?

For she delighted in planning and setting up schemes, playing pranks, mischievously working things out so a visitor to Ham Spray mistakenly thought his lover was in the house, sending to Clive Bell a fake letter from Bernard Shaw protesting Clive's criticism in *The New Republic*: when Clive writes him, for a good argument, the real Shaw replies, in a bewildered postcard that he knows nothing of this. It is all like a continual practical joke. To facts too straightforward she adds a gloss, a fib, a twist; to relations too smoothly running, hers or another's, she may add a fillip by a smallish, if potent, lie, so that it will boomerang. Carrington is genuinely an original, and in that lies much of her appeal, together with her enthusiasm, her vulnerability, her intensity, and her changeability: bouts of depression, followed by periods of high glee. Just as much as the Stephen family, and Virginia, she manifested what the psychologists would call cyclo-systemia, and this up-and-downness rubbed against Gerald's own violent swerves in mood with too much friction for a possible living-together relationship to have worked out between them. So it could only, in the long run, be quilted over, with pieces of Carrington's own and too apparent used apparel offered atop the other relation, spread out awkwardly, a collage of fragments used up.

Loving Lytton: How Difficult Things Are

But you must tell me if I become a pest, a mosquitoe (sic)—
I am going to work very hard until you come back for it
would give me pleasure if one day you liked my pictures.
Carrington to Lytton, April 3, 1918 (DC/LS)

Oh Lytton how difficult things are. I wish I hadn't such
plural affections.
Carrington to Lytton, August 5, 1920 (DC/LS)

Carrington's relations were, in general, difficult: to people as to things. Her relation to clothes and their relation to others was always a bit odd, but absolutely consistent. At the death of her brother Teddy, she persuades her mother that David Garnett is an impoverished and shabby farm boy, and has her send him some of Teddy's garments, which, says David Garnett, did not fit at all (DG, 126). We have seen her cutting her own old clothes up into a bedspread for Gerald and Gamel; she has, some years before that, sent Gerald Lytton's cast-off ties, which he loathes, and, after Lytton's death, will distribute parcels of his clothing among his friends. During his life, furthermore, she adopts one of his pairs of undershorts as her own, and amusingly illustrates the difference with a drawing: they droop loosely around his waist, whereas they cling to her tummy, giving her the feeling of great strength, she says: "I shall never part with your (drawing of undershorts). It is now mine. I feel like strong man with electric sparks flying out" (November 8, 1917; DG, 86). And she loved, as we have seen, wearing his old jackets and coats cut-down for her: from this amply illustrated standpoint, her wrapping herself in his clothes after his death is far less grim, more fitting with her personality than might be some masochistic dwelling upon things as such. Yet they are ineradicable from our minds, these scenes of her longing to huddle in his jacket after his death, and above all, her putting on his yellow silk dressing-gown when she is about to shoot herself—these huddlings in his things seem to fit together in some strange pattern of making herself over in his image, and of the refusal of her own image, unnatural to herself.

The images she is given of herself by others: by Ralph, when he informs her of the low opinion Lytton has of her, that he has related to Virginia and Leonard, and that they have repeated to him; by two of Beakus's girlfriends, who report to her his feeling of her aging, when she is almost forty, thus, the year she died; by the disinterest of Henrietta Bingham, whom she loved; and by the constant recriminations of Gerald, after Mark and Ralph—these, together with Lytton's inevitable rejection of her as the wrong sex (oh, and how often she agreed) cannot fail to have taken their toll on her self-assurance, already feeble.

If only . . . if one day you liked my pictures . . . the "if" in this relatively early letter in Carrington's long correspondence with Lytton Strachey carries no force of assurance, nor indeed was there ever to be a great build-up of certainty in Carrington's self or in her work, whether they be judged from within or without. Tiresome, she says of herself, boring to Lytton, wearisome in letters and person. Unable to do the large things in art she has envisaged and planned, taken up with the small—tinsel pictures, flower pictures, decorative boards and papers and bookplates—she delays what she could have done.

Sadly, her moods about painting and living seem drastically connected: feeling dull in the one, she has no heart for the other:

> I've felt so stupid lately, and then I get dreadful misgivings that I am boring L.—sometimes I literally dread lunch as I used to in old days. I dread being alone with him, I dread my vapidity, & the almost imperceptible wince he gives, when I offend his good taste, or irritate him with my stupidity. Its rather too Russian at times, my terror, & the way I plunge deeper & deeper into the bog. . . . My painting is going badly somehow I have no heart for it. It starts so well, & then I lose grasp & heart & the pictures remain unfinished
>
> (November 27, 1921, DC/GB).

The effect she made on others, early to late, somehow corresponded to that persona of smallness and childishness she struggled against, lived through, and wrote with. During a visit to Scotland, in 1918, she describes an impression never completely shaken off: "Everyone calls me 'dear' and strokes my hair like a dog" (July 5, 1918; DC/LS).

It all fits together—the childlike delight she took in everything, from puddings ("Qu'est-ce qui est plus doux que le miel and spotted cake. I write in the middle of a French lesson you will perceive. De quoi riez-vous toujours?," July 2, DC/LS; 1916) to newly purchased red boots, from her endless reading (Thomas Browne and John Donne, Jane Austen and Chekhov and Charlotte Brontë and Proust) to hiking and biking and sketching—pleasures so intense as to be unforgettable, so described as to be endlessly seeable, as we picture her with her mop of fair hair and deep-set brilliant blue eyes, riding along on her white horse, hearing the "bunches of little birds in all the bushes along the road, on haystacks and barns, making a deafening noise of chirping," peeling off her jerkin in the dazzling sun, riding by the yellow crocuses and snow-drops in the garden, or, walking over the hill at Hurstbourne Tarrant her home, in the pelting snow with the dark rabbits "running in the dusk over the white common, and huge owls leaping through the air," longing to "rush in sledges down these hills," her passions alternating with exhaustion and headaches and loneliness and her intensity never letting up until one of her last notations before her suicide, unforgettable, about the first place she had lived with Lytton and full of her longing backwards: "Tidmarsh all came back. How much I love places. I remembered suddenly my 'passion' for a certain tree in Burgess's back field. And the beauty of the mill at the back of the house and how once a kingfisher dived from the roof into the stream" (DC, 496).

Her ceaseless and headlong engagement in and for the things around her is just as ceaselessly transcribed in her letters, especially to Lytton, in tones ranging from the tragic to the playful; a cat leaves its traces walking across the paper, so she outlines it; or she "wiles" away a few minutes before a journey to the W.C., writing "for no other reason I assure you mister Strackie, yrs slightly affectionate Carrington" (April 2, 1917). Lytton made a perfect correspondent, answering always in the tone she had set, responding sometimes with sketches for her sketches, of a sponge and a hairbrush to match her red-boot drawing, with French for her French: " 'Quelle vie!' *(my* French lesson, too) . . . and thus I shall laugh no longer" (July 3, 1916; LS/DC).

But Carrington's joy in everything is juxtaposed frequently with all the discouragement she feels at the way in which just such a multiplicity of diverse enthusiasms and endeavors (the other side of those delights) never added up to something larger, something she felt she might have created and always missed. The very love of everything wears her out: "I love this country too much," she says of the valley of the Tarn. "I get so tired with enthusuisms (sic) & mental painting, inside & then I proved rather drab company in consequence, because I get so tired . . . I almost cry when the evening is over & I have to leave . . . to come inside." The streams and the hills and the sheep fill her with "such longings" that she becomes miserable instead of happy, saying "perhaps its too exhausting to live in country so beautiful— I expect only poets can bear it" (August 4, 1921; DC/LS). Often she feels just "on the brink of a great discovery (as in April 15, 1921; DC/LS), on the verge of painting "the best picture I have ever painted," and then nothing is completed. "I must toil," go the letters to Gerald and Lytton, or, "the spirit of work is upon me," and then, quite often, nothing is finished. She was better at beginnings. "So many unfinished things," says Frances Partridge of her studio as it was left . . .

To Lytton, March 19, 1919, just before a visit to Spain to see Gerald Brenan: "I despise myself as much as you do—or ought to—for the way I've allowed all these trivialities to disturb my work. But it was partly also I came to a standstill inside. I hope to be able to push on faster when I come back." The trivialities were, of course, and were always to be, to a large extent, work too: painting a trunk, painting inn signs, decorating rooms—Dadie Rylands's in King's College, Cambridge, or Lytton's own, at Ham Spray—and, just as in the case of Vanessa and the Charleston group, the decorations were seen as part of life. That very exuberance of the aesthetic mixed with the quotidian is, we may think, enviable. Who would not choose to so mix up work and life, art and the daily?

Carrington's personality infuses all her letters with zest and misspelling, with a sort of full-livingness unquestionably her own, inimitable, and eccentrically appealing: like a little girl, but with genius. "Pull quigly and leggo slowly," reads the sign she hung above the toilet at Ham Spray, says Frances Partridge, and Dadie Rylands remembers with delight how, from one room, she would suddenly materialize by your side in another if you wanted to speak to her, with a childlike charm. How unlike anyone else she was, how greatly to be uniquely cherished, he reiterates in a conversation of 1988. Do not put her, he said to me, with anyone else. She was unto herself. (Indeed, I see her so, even though she appears here with . . .)

From "Atalantis" ("Atlantis, not Atalantis, please," answers Lytton), she writes to him on April 11, 1916: "I sliped (sic) down the stairs a brief while ago & smashed the banisters to pieces also my spine & cerveaux. So coma has set in. You made me lonely yesterday, wretch," she continues. But, she laments, on August 12, 1917, I am not up to entertaining you: my letters are wearying, poorly expressed, stupid. The reader longs to interject how, on the contrary, her letters are enchanting—would that we all had such correspondents. But the self-puttingdownness is apparently ineradicable: the time you have spent with me this year, she says, has been a waste for you, "for you might have spent it working" . . . (August 13, 1918). I am, she says, ambitious for you, and so she was. Would we perhaps have done her no good in being, in our turn, ambitious for her? She lived and wrote and painted in a way unlike anyone else: our ambitions would have to have taken, then, that fact into account, and so must they now.

Nevertheless, the difference between Carrington decorating alone, painting by herself, working in a medium other than that of the adored Lytton, and Vanessa decorating and painting with Duncan and Quentin, from furniture and woodwork to churches, working in the same medium as Roger at least partially worked in, may be more serious than one would think at first. The very reaching out that Carrington manifests in her letters to all her correspondents reveals both a protean ability to strike different tones depending on the receiver, while keeping her uniquely childlike, flirtatious, witty, and sympathetic personality intact, and a quite desperate dissatisfaction with any one relation as anchoring, except—of course—that with Lytton, and that has, precisely, its limits. And the consequence of those limits is loneliness.

The letters might be said to be strongly vectored and directed, yet the author is unmistakably and unshakably her somewhat strange and definitely appealing self. They reveal also, as does her journal, a singular and massive sadness. Vanessa, unto herself and—from the time of the death of Julian—enormously depressed, seems at once more able to concentrate on her work and to act out her own role as homemaker and as artist. Vanessa's grief and distress allowed her still to be part of the Charleston family as it was constituted, whereas Carrington was far more ambivalent about her role as Lytton's companion and entertainer. "I've been so happy with you," she writes in 1918, on January 5, "But I'm afraid it was rather uncomfortable and the mopsa tiresome. But that will improve," followed by such notes as that of November 22 of the same year, "My very dear Lytton, I am dreadfully sorry now that I was so tiresome, & worried you."

Even her role as letter-writer seems to her an uneasy one: is she up to Lytton's style, and, above all, capable of concealing her feelings since they weigh on him?—this incapacity for living up, for writing up to snuff is irretrievably tragic. She should care less, she should write better, she is not, she thinks, what she should be. It is this undervaluing of the self in relation to the other that we recognize as habitual in some women and that we want, most desperately, to refuse as permanent, even as we see it playing itself out, in Carrington, in Vanessa, and—presumably, some of us—in ourselves.

Carrington writes:

> It is more difficult to write than anything else—partly because I care so much, & you said it embarrassed you. But rather is it not because it (is) wearying—& so badly written?—do not laugh old cynic—But I should like only to offer to you the most worthy telling. Since you deserve the very best. Sometimes I feel because it is so poorly expressed, & the stupidity so great, that you do not believe

in it. Norton told Alix it was of course just the infatuation of a schoolgirl for a mistress—But since last summer I have never thought of anyone else. Every moment when something definite is not being done. I am thinking of you . . . But my ambition for you is great, & lately I have felt that perhaps Time, which you might have spent working, was wasted with me this year. You must always refuse to see me if this is so—Dear Lytton if you knew how much I thank you for what you have taught me. Even if the results are not very apparent!!! (August 12, 1917)

A schoolgirl for a mistress: her words speak exactly what she means, again, without embarrassment. Now, of course, Lytton answers he considers her letters perfect, asks she not improve them, explains she cannot expect him to share her "flattering view" and exclaims how much *he* has gotten from *her.* And of course, wonderful as it is to receive that letter, Carrington's repetitions of the self-demeaning attitude will mark their future correspondence, and life. Or rather, what she expects of herself, making his life contented and herself indispensable, will be plagued by worries and eternal lack of time for all there was of—wherever is there not?—too much to do.

Carrington has always, she says, "so much gardening and stupid things to do that I get dull and tired in the evenings" . . . (May 13, 1920, to Lytton). Always there will be an almost: of Tidmarsh, where they first lived, with Lytton's friends chipping in for the price, and Carrington in the official role of housekeeper and companion for him: "I am so happy because I truly believe it will be good living here, & you will be contented, almost."

But whatever is it that is not, at least sometimes, marked by an almost? Carrington, I think, expected too much of herself, and therein lies the urgent inescapable pain, in the over self-expectation; not necessarily according to what others think, but according, alas, to the self and the concept of self one retains. We wish, over and over, there could be some satisfaction of a permanent sort along the lines of her occasional outbursts of happiness: "But it's truly rather wonderful to be living with you" (January 16, 1918; DC/LS).

About her intense love for Lytton—let those who accuse it of being so unsatisfactory take a moment to read the letters exchanged: letters of love as real as any others, even if the part that had to be missing was just that assurance of a complete love—she is lucid indeed. At times, reading a Greek anthology (July 7, 1918; DC/LS), she longs to be a boy to give him "that peculiar ecstasy"—to make him happy for all he gives her. But at others, her tone is other, and her longing, different, one not for ecstasy given or received, but for calm:

> Dear, May I tell you how much I love you tonight, so much that if you were here, I should hug your Thinness into Nothings—Did you want to strangle the thing you loved ever? so it would be over once & for all. No more crescendos. No more horrid earthly dullness. Calm & well regulated which nobody knows better than you how to bring into Force! But I know, for when Mark wanted each day to be wildly chaotic, I hated it because it had no connection with one's life & was so devastating.
>
> (January 21, 1918; DC/LS)

Her imagination, her style, her expression are not just convincing, they seem imbued with a lyricism that I would call deeply literary in the best sense of the term: "How I long to steal away from here, & climb the height of Firle Beacon, & one day perchance you would come walking up & I hidden in a hillock would see you pass. And after whisper to the April Hare in his hole—*That* man I love. For he is Lytton Strachey" (April 3, 1918; DC/LS).

Among the lessons Lytton taught Carrington, there was one she found it hard to learn. That one was being what he called one's own God, not caring for other people's opinions. It seems to me that was the one she continued to struggle with right up until the end of her own days, but that among those opinions, there was that of Lytton himself. Repeatedly, we read such notes as: "I felt I had been a BLOT on the landscape . . . & very selfish and altogether unbearable. But Lytton must forgive me. I do not often feel ill & I won't ever again" (November 1, 1920; DC/LS), or this: "You are so kind to care enough to bother over anyone so tiresome as . . ."

(August 27, 1923; DC/LS). Thus, when she thought herself "bad" in his terms as well as in those of society and its expectations, wanting just to dwell among his clothes, opinions, and memories, she interiorized the judgment of others to the point of self-condemnation. This, we sense as the private tragedy of Carrington—not that she loved so much, or so unwisely; but that she felt herself always not up to the style of, the substance of a love she thought Lytton deserved. The judgment leveled against the self is, in the long run, the one that most harms and most limits.

A Very Personal Art

As usual I feel I am on the Brink of a discovery, on the verge of painting the best picture I've ever painted.
Carrington to Lytton, April 15, 1921; DC/LS)

Carrington was an enthusiast. Carrington's art takes much of its charm and instantly recognized spontaneous quality from just those traits of character which all her friends recognized, allied with her delightfully (and sometimes tragically) apparent childlike sense of life.

With enthusiasms, she was indeed wonderfully and abundantly endowed. They extended toward her art, in its outer and inner forms, those mental paintings she felt inhabiting her, toward the landscape she rode about in, toward various people whose appearance she took to. The ways of keeping those enthusiasms alive included not just the shifting around of the elements, like the pictures in her dining room, but also the reinvestment of herself in her undertakings, so that to some extent exhaustion and enthusiasm alternated.

How much of the enthusiasm is able to be conveyed to the observer is oddly beside the point. It was a Goya exhibit in 1920 that provoked her into dreaming and thinking only of art; it is Constable's portraits that urge her to work away at her own; and it is a Giorgione, the Cézannes (it is hard for her to admire even Van Gogh after Cézanne!), and above all the El Grecos in Munich that affect her heartbeat and make her determine also to "alter my ways and start painting everyday again" upon her return to England.

All her life, everything she read, all the paintings she saw, provoked reactions in her stronger than one would "expect" but that is exactly the point. The violence of her reaction to the landscape, whether about her in England, or on her walking trips to Spain or France, cannot be overstated, and it has parallels in the other parts of her life, private and public. At an exhibition of the newest French art brought over to London, she will exclaim that it all looks tired and warmed over, including the Matisse canvases; reading Proust, she will see the world differently, for "Proust amazes me," she repeated to Lytton. On November 19, 1929: "I read Proust feverishly. It is horrifying the vision he gives one of human beings. It's very stiff reading." Never does she take in her reading passively: she reacts with fever, with amazement, participating in the judgments with all the passion of a child and an enthusiast.

Her impressions are intimate always, for the things she cares about. Reading *Pride and Prejudice,* at every chance she gets, she will take it for her own as if it had been written, by Jane, for her innermost feelings, and indeed as she speaks of it to Lytton, it might have been: "I don't think I can face another book by Jane until my excitement is slightly abated. I can't believe you can possibly enjoy P and P (sic) quite as much as I do. You CAN'T. You CAN'T. Because I was always in love with the proud Darcy from the beginning" (September 8, 1920; DC/LS). Her instant affection for the least attainable male, like an obstacle to conquer, a haughtiness to be brought or won over by some possible effort or human miracle is telling: in conception and construction, Jane Austen's novel and Carrington's life bear certain similarities. Elizabeth Bennet was to win Darcy, and Carrington—in some sense at least—to win over Lytton. Even the traces of Jane Austen, like her house, cause unspeakable excitement in Carrington, who has the art and the genius of personalizing everything: thus this personal art she believed in, and made, which is at once disquieting and convincing.

Her nervousness was increased by her uncertainty about the judgments of others, in regard to her painting. Precisely because she so rarely showed it, she was of a rare sensitivity about it. Writing to Gerald, she complains, partly in teasing and partly not: "and when you do see my paintings you never notice them. I often observe Mr. C. your indifference to my masterpieces. There were two in Lytton's room. You peered at them but because I didn't tell you who they were by, you thought them, mere (ver meer's?) & shrugged your shoulders. And had you asked to see any pictures at Ham Spray, or letters, or—you might have been shown them . . ." (June 21, 1927; DC/GB). And then, three days later, when Gerald has protested that indeed he did want to see them, and had said so, she is made aware, as often, of her hypersensitivity on the subject: "Did you ask to see my pictures?—I can't remember—I only remember thinking you didn't want to very much, or you would have persuaded me. But I know its my fault, I am so tiresome, & it is boring, having to intreat (sic), & beg, & pray, to be shown pictures—& unless you do that I hardly believe anyone wants to see them" (June 24, 1927; DC/GB).

Yet in spite of her disbelief about others and her talent, her touchstone for her work is, from the beginning of her friendship with him, Lytton. Referring, in a letter to Lytton, to the picture of himself lying down with a book, which is perhaps her most famous painting, she says, "I have a bout of work descending on me which is a relief" (June 7, 1917). She will finish it soon and, on August 5, "You know those paintings are going well. I am so glad. It's really a good thing you are away—as we both work so industriously" (DC/LS). Painting—whether canvases or tiles and decorative objects— was at once her passion and a sort of heavy duty: so much painting to do, she cries, in 1930, I oughtn't to go "caravansing across Europe." Carrington's manner of plunging so entirely into what she does, whatever it is, bridges her true painting and its passion with her reading, excitement meeting excitement. To Lytton, she relates her putting off and her gritty going on: "I must go back and finish my painting" (September 22, 1923). Lytton is the litmus paper against which to test the value of her work: early on, on 1917 (July 23), she writes of her determination in a typical letter: "Now I am going to work solidly everyday & all day . . . When you come back I will show you all my work. Only up till now so few things have been decent enough." In a strange manner, the desire for working well and that for being loved, or showing her love sufficiently, are interlinked: "I hope you'll like my works when I show them to you" (August 13, 1920; DC/LS). If she is good at what she does, Lytton will approve, seeing her fondness, as it were, carried out. "Lytton, you give me such a happy life one day I really hope I shall be an artist & then you'll see my affection" (December 10, 1920; DC/LS). Surely, Lytton could scarcely fail to see her affection, so that this kind of work wish is identical with a desire for what cannot be, put here in ellipsis. If I could show my love enough . . . But I cannot: "I wish the paintings were a little better . . . " (September, 1930; DC/LS).

In so much of Carrington's life, as in her work, there seems to appear a divergence, which she often notices, between her intention to do the paintings of which she has so strong and clear an image in her but which, so often, remain only mental, and her realization of them actually on canvas. Thus the frequent lamentations about procrastination, about not getting to work on what she knows she can, and should do, about letting the small stand in the way of the large. The initial excitement, that originary enthusiasm, has to be sustained, and often when it is, the determination is nonetheless diverted in its actualization.

Unlike the others whom this book concerns, Carrington did not believe sufficiently in herself to work as hard as she knew she might have. Over and over, she repeats that she will get back to it, after all this wasted time: "Duncan and Vanessa are patterns of what I call good artists. The amount of work they do, and the way they proportion their lives with pleasure, and work," she exclaims to Gerald (July 14, 1926). But her determination is clear, and applies to every kind of painting Carrington does: "I shall stay on as I want to work"; "I shall start painting every day"; "there is no excuse—except a distaste for work—to prevent me painting them!"—"I long to do some proper oil painting . . . for once my head is crammed with ideas"; "I'll linger here if you aren't going back As I am painting so hard & rather reluctant to stop . . . No I must go on with my painting."

I only linger here because of painting, she will say. . . . This passion for painting is surely what matters most: this intention, and this excitement, more than any exterior proof of her painting, any exhibition—it may seem unusual to us that Carrington did not more often exhibit her paintings, did not show them to others. But it is surely the creation, not the showing that matters, the latter interesting neither psychologically nor personally. The painting should suffice unto itself: exhibition, and self-exhibition are only the ordinary move most artists usually make out beyond the painting self, making the painting itself neither more interesting nor more significant to the self producing it.

Reflections on Tiles and Tinsel, A Quilt and a Window

Of Carrington's decorative work, much could be said. All the inn signs and book covers and groups of tiles and room panels show at once an original taste and a sense of humor characteristic of her more than fertile imagination. Rooms leap to life under her hand, and it is very much the same vivifying spirit that we trace in all the memories of her domestic touch—from the decoration of Lytton's rooms at Ham Spray (fireplace, woodwork, walls, and smaller details) to the garden she so carefully tended, and to the meals served (over the details of which she kept watch, no matter who was in the kitchen, working along with them: lemonade, blancmange, and raspberry jam, we are of a total purity, she writes Lytton), caring about the colors for presentation as well as what was presented therein: thus, dark blue plates and a green jug figure in the recounting of the day, along with homemade preserves, each thing counting for eye and palate. Her eyes is as keen as Duncan's for such details. I almost think, she says at one point, I shall invent a new kind of still life, made up of washstands and towel horses: everything was observed, and it all mattered. Her affection for the William and Dorothy Wordsworth model of the alliance of domestic and intellectual sharing accords well with her manner of being, doing, and caring.

Yet always the pressures of conceiving and carrying out anything, no matter how small, seem enormous, as does the relief when anything is done. Her projected imagination holds more interest than the realization: for Lytton's chief cat, King Tiber, she plans a patchwork quilt with 300 tiny squares (I feel exhausted already), "and in the middle will be—a portrait of a cat. Just to make you say 'how typical'— and having said that I shall change, & put a large basket of Fish in the centre" (October 18, 1928). Elsewhere, in their house and others', lampshades, bookplates, painted china and trunks, painted glass and glass paintings, decorated gramophones and wood panels, and the like proliferate.

Three of her decorative genres could be considered particularly problematic or interesting from the point of view of their connotations. First, the painted tile, upon which any conceivable subject seemed to fit, whether houses or sunflowers, cats or fish, but the principal thing being repetition, a certain boredom would inevitably set in. Something about the very numbers of items paralyzes the mind like a localizable burden: the quantities are usually stated, for this is serial and not serious work, and is often done for compensation. "I have done six Fish tiles for our bathroom,"; "only three more Flower pictures to do. I started working at 7 o'clock this morning" (October 14, 1929); sixty more tiles to do, two hundred more tiles to do, I painted 18 tiles, will have to go back next week and do another 20; I will, she says, get those tiles done by tomorrow . . . can I finish the tiles by this weekend? they have not delivered the tiles, and so on . . .

And yet, as concerns the tiles, such a blank and totally undetermined surface presents an openness of action and interpretation that should delight the hearts of contemporary readers. A note to Lytton with no date reads: "The terrible thing about Tile painting is to come to any decision as to what to paint on them . . ." My head is full of IDEAS, she says, but my room looks rather like a Tearoom in South Kensington, with tiles everywhere . . .

As for the choice of tinsel painting, the singular and effective isolation of the image against a background as far from the "realistic" as possible makes a statement in itself about the relation of the painter to the subject painted. The latter is seen directly, with no intermediary of the daily and the normal, set off rather by all that is most unnatural in the ordinary sense.

We might liken this to the paintings of the Byzantine epoch, where the gold background establishes the hieratic

"Still life on the corner of a mantelpiece," 1914, by Vanessa Bell. The Tate Gallery.

"The mantelpiece," 1914, by Duncan Grant. The Tate Gallery.

"The Tub," 1919, by Duncan Grant. The Victoria and Albert Museum.

"The Tub," 1913, by Duncan Grant. The Tate Gallery.

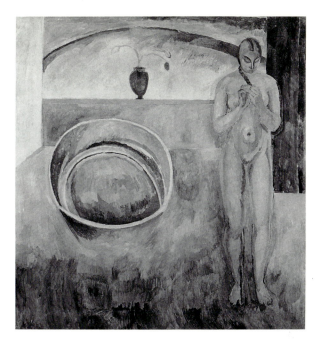

"The Tub," 1918, by Vanessa Bell. The Tate Gallery.

"The Nude," 1919, by Vanessa Bell. For
Omega Workshops Woodcuts.

"Firle Park," c. 1915, by Vanessa Bell. Private Collection, London. Photograph, courtesy of Sandra Lummis, Fine Art, London.

"Studland Beach," 1911–1912, by Vanessa Bell. The Tate Gallery.

"Mountain range at Yegen, Andalusia," 1924, by Dora Carrington. Courtesy, Frances Partridge.

"Farms at Watendlath," 1921, by Dora Carrington. The Tate Gallery.

"Mrs. Box, Farmer's Wife, at Welcombe, Cornwall," 1919, by Dora Carrington. Courtesy, Joanna Mason.

"Jane Marra Grant, Lady Strachey," 1920, by Dora Carrington. National Galleries of Scotland.

"Biddesden Window, Hampshire," 1931, by Dora Carrington. The Tate Gallery Archives.

"The Mill at Tidmarsh," 1918, by Dora Carrington. Courtesy, Frances Partridge.

"Lytton Strachey," 1916, by Dora Carrington. Courtesy, Frances Partridge.

Woodcut—Lytton Strachey reading, by Dora Carrington. Harry Ransom Humanities Research Center, The University of Texas at Austin.

value of the figures—that they were religious then, and profane in our epoch as they were in Carrington's, makes no real difference to the genre and how it is set up. Some of Duncan's paintings have the same hieratic atmosphere and unmodeled figuration, although he declares, in his autobiography (Tate Gallery Archives) that he encountered Byzantine art too late for it to have any effect on him. In any case, it lends a definite feeling of otherworldiness, of another time and place, to their art. Carrington's choice of this un-realistic medium for many of her own creations speaks loudly, if we know how to listen, of her relation to the world. Even in her most amused and amusing moods, a peculiar and appealing reticence has a way of sneaking in, that dissimilarity with the others, that *distance* she sensed in herself from the ordinary world. In her paintings and watercolors, the unfamiliar angles, colors, and perspectives all stress such self-distancing.

But for the moment, a word about the singular genre of the window painting of which Carrington did a notable example at Biddesden, the house of Diana and Bryan Guiness. (It was from the latter that she was to borrow the gun with which she shot herself . . .) Here, having spent some time doing china painting, she then painted the outline of a cook against the window to the left, and a cat sitting on a ledge to the right, so that anyone looking at it from the outside would be convinced by its naturalness. (When she was in the middle of it, and wrote Lytton about it, he, finding the project agreeable, responded that he hoped, as well as finishing the painting of the cook, that she had "been happy in the sunlight." Such was far from being the case, as she describes the adventure at length. At any rate, they were all "pleased," as Carrington says, with her triumphant joke, which she painted with rain streaming down:

> I got up at half past 7 this morning in order to start my picture at Biddesden early. . . . The moment I started to paint—it came on to rain. So all my paints got mixed with water. My hair dripped into my eyes & my feet became icy cold. However I finished it and Diana was delighted.
> (October 29, 1931, to Lytton)

So she took a hot bath and painted china all evening.

The little-girl nature of her imagination which so appealed to those fond of her comes out here in all its charm. Carrington was, of course, to create works of a more "serious" nature—but the very fact that they alternate with these others is of importance for her ebulliently original character.

Woodcuts and Signs

It is Carrington's woodcuts, some of them used to illustrate Virginia's stories (such as "The Mark on the Wall"), that are frequently the best known of her productions. Their quite singular charm was recognized and admired by Virginia, Vanessa, and many others outside the Bloomsbury group.

About Carrington's art of woodcutting, we have some documentation. We know that on October 27, 1920, for example (because she recounts it in a letter to Lytton), she sees that she is holding the instruments quite wrong (Little John Nash teaches her, and seems to think it "quite unnecessary to cut one's fingers"), and learns also to transfer the designs. She is not yet producing the sort of masterpiece she would like ("But oh where is a Bewick?"), yet the woodcuts have a quite remarkable flavor to them: endowed with an interior life, I would say about the human figures, which seem animated by something undefinable. Her animal woodcuts live quite independently, with a charm as much their own as those wonderful creations of Bewick's (of which Ruskin was so fond, particularly, of his little pig.) Carrington's odd child-like quality, at once quaint and effervescent, penetrates in the quality of these woodcuts as it does in her letters, indescribable but definitely there to be experienced, in a quite other way from that sensible in her paintings.

Painting Portraits

Carrington reflected a good deal on faces. For example, she was particularly taken by that of Anatole France, finding it remarkable: "I would have given much to have painted him" (January 23, 1919; DC/LS). This relation she had, like all good portrait painters, to the faces of others, gives something peculiarly *warm* to her portraits.

The range of Carrington's art of portraiture is perhaps best exemplified, on the one hand, by the so-decided contrast she was able to depict between the extremes of elegance and grandeur, as in the portrait of Lady Strachey, and of simplicity, as in the farmer's wife, Mrs. Box; and, on the other, by the renderings of those she particularly loved: her father, Julia Strachey, and Lytton. Given the psychological as well as artistic importance of the latter, I shall only consider those, of which they are a number.

Lady Strachey, painted in 1920, was one of Carrington's few commissioned portraits, and the sitter by whom she was the most impressed. She sits distinguished in her chair, but not of it, more upright than its structure, and facing our left; she is thus to be seen against the current of our normal left to right reading, a fact which renders her appearance still more majestic and isolated than were she to be turned in the direction of our eyes. Her distinction is all the more greatly stressed by having the chair and the sitter framed between two upright columns on either side of the painting, just as her body is framed by the two reverse panels of her robe, thin stripes of orange against black. Carrington discusses, in a letter to Lytton, the aspect of her sitter: "This morning I went to paint her ladyship. She is superb. I was completely overcome by her grandeur and wit. I am painting her against a bookcase sitting full length in a chair in a wonderful robe which goes into great El Greco folds. She looks like the Queen of China or one of El Greco's Inquisitors" (NC, 55). And, writing to Gerald, when she has completed the painting: "I've finished a portrait of his [Lytton's] most eminent mother, Lady Strachey, who is 80, quite kind, but the most witty virial (sic) woman alive today. You would I am sure include her in your Book of Female Odes" (February 5, 121).

The quite extraordinary way in which Lady Strachey's left hand is held, with the forefinger dominant and the others closed, is the point of focus here. It gives a firm indication, beyond any shadow of a doubt, of a strong character, used to pointing things out. We have only to compare that hand, and that seated pose, those witnesses to a life upright and unbending, to detect in Lady Strachey's mountainous presence an integrity as grand as her statement about herself in her robe. It is interesting to note that in her *Friends in Focus*, a selection of her photographs over the years, Frances Partridge gives a picture of Lady Strachey seated in an informal chair, facing the same way, and with her hand held in exactly the same fashion, saying of the latter: "The force of her personality and intelligence is plainly seen in the position of her left hand" (27). It is, then, not at all that Carrington invented the favored position of the body or the hand, but that her ability to pick out those details and focus upon them is linked as much to the eye of the painter as to the personality of the sitter. She has brought to the foreground that intelligence and that force of self-presentation which also struck Frances Partridge, who represented them with equal force in her photograph with its own angle.

The portrait I wish to compare and contrast with the one just looked at is that of Mrs. Box the farmer's wife (1919), who was, says Carrington, delighted with her picture. She sits as if wedded to her large stuffed, and plainly comfortable chair with its back rising high, her elaborate white coif with its multiple folds fitting into its lines, peak for peak, and her arms enclosed within its arms, whereas Lady Strachey has the folds in her hair itself and wears no coif for covering. No pose could more tellingly contrast with Lady Strachey's sitting forward against the back of her chair, with her head higher than the chair's top: Mrs. Box's chair includes Mrs. Box, whereas Lady Strachey projects herself, by sheer strength of personality from hers, her physical and psychological being scarcely of the sort to be *included*.

Most of all, the different hands tell different stories. Mrs. Box has clumsy, almost childish hands, with the fingers nearly the same length; the hands are cupped in each other and in her lap, and fall comfortably below her slightly protruding stomach, visible under the vertical folds of her pinafore. The homely pattern of the ample blouse and pinafore, the dots and stripes and scallops on the suspenders, as well as the folds in the coif, whose lines are repeated in the stripes on the sleeve and the folds of the skirt: all these details are complex and yet homespun in feeling, simple even as they are ornamental. Her facial expression is that of a person somewhat on guard, of a peasant reserve radically other from that of Lady Strachey. The scrutiny of Lady Strachey's eyes and the determined crease of her mouth make an absolute contrast with the suspicious gaze of Mrs. Box, and her weathered cheek, as do her majestic hands with the cradled hands of Mrs. Box. The personal as well as artistic ability of Carrington as painter was that she could enter into the being of each sitter with empathy and capture the essential difference of each. These two portraits in their diametrical opposition show Carrington's intense sensitivity to the reading of persons. Herself so unique, she captured the unique essence of her sitters.

A case in point is the painting of Annie's portrait (Annie the lovely young cook, whose escapades with young men are often chronicled by Carrington). The letter to Lytton is undated, but is presumably from late October or early November 1921, and shows the clarity of her initial perception, the mental so clearly at war with the manual: "I am so excited about my picture of Annie. If only I can carry out my intentions it ought to be a very lovely picture. But I find my hand is such a rebel at obeying the head's orders." (We might associate this, by extension, with her rebellion against OR-DER in general, from that of the paintings in the dining room to the sociological bourgeois order, and even the bohemian kind of order at Charleston: Carrington makes a glorious maverick.) On November 12, Annie's picture is going well, she writes. But it is so terribly cold working, in spite of all the fires and lamps; repeatedly, in her painting of decorative objects as in her larger assignments or self-assignments, she complains, understandably, of the cold. The warmth has, and does, come from and in the painting itself: warmth in work.

Of course no person was nearer to her warmth or to her passion (the one for art as well as the one for reading) than Lytton, who is pictured always with a book; this was his usual pose for portraits, and it says a great deal about his own reserve, and self-protection. Only in photographs, such as the informal ones Frances Partridge was able to take, does he face the camera and the person behind it. For his portraits, those by Roger Fry or Carrington notably, he is seen always with a book, his long legs crossed almost always, whichever way he is facing, and almost always in a chair whose form he seems to fit, whatever it be. Lytton-and-book is a familiar figure, and the quite remarkable portrait by Carrington in 1916, of Lytton lying down which I will discuss at length in Chapter Seven rivets the gaze, in a combination of intimacy and forbidding hieratic iconization with all the more force as we are unused to seeing him anyway but seated, those long legs in some symbiotic relation to some book.

Whether he is reading by a fireplace, or in the garden at Tidmarsh or Ham Spray, the pose is the same: legs crossed or stretched out, book clearly in sight, distance from observer kept intact. The relation is always to the book and not to us. Typically, in a garden portrait at Tidmarsh (NC, 54), his hat is on the table, ready to hand, and his legs are crossed elegantly, the left over the right, his hands holding the book in an exact parallel line with his left knee folded over, as if both were to be intentionally indicating the lack of closeness and intimacy. In a later picture at Tidmarsh, of 1922 (NC, 68), he is almost facing us, turning a bit to his left, his book resting on his right leg, easily crossed over the left. He is included, even his head, in the armchair, and the feeling is somewhat informal, particularly as his right hand droops straight down below the right armrest. This is the extreme of comfortableness, as far as Lytton is concerned, and the constant and typical library background, those eternal books, importantly stresses his intellectual absorption. That absorption is all the clearer in the picture of the lying-down Lytton with his beard, book, and blanket all of the same color which will illustrate my contention, in the last chapter of this book, that Carrington's most expressive self-portrait of her emotions was, in fact, that portrait of her love. In so painting the man she adored, she was, in a sense, painting what mattered most to herself about herself, through him. Whatever exclusion of her own consciousness is represented by that most singular of images, by the barrier of beard, book, and blanket, it is one she clearly painted and gave us, as well as herself, to understand.

Landscapes

Even in the very early *Hills in Snow at Hurstbourne Tarrant*, of 1916, one of Carrington's rare finished watercolors, painted from her parents' home, a singular feeling, again about distance, is captured that is to be repeated in many of her subsequent landscapes. It is a troubling distantiation between the place we look from, and the place we look to, stressed as if deliberately by the empty space in the center, with one side almost straight, and the other curved towards us. A row of pickets separates us from that space, like a barer version of the bare trees of winter. The curved top of the snow-covered hill facing us is dotted with trees seen smallish, both the curve and the trees set in echo, the former with the curve of that empty space of snow in the center, the latter as if in an arranged series: large trees bordering our gaze, near us, medium trees after the central space, a group of still smaller trees on the right-hand side, and the smallest ones atop the hill.

But the distance stands out clearly as the central mode and focus of the painting, exactly what Carrington described in a letter to Mark Gertler (quoted NC, 51) at that time: "Today it is snowing white and a piercing wind. But I love the hugeness of it and the great space between one and the hills opposite."

This sense of distance, on one hand, and an odd, almost eerie closeness felt to other objects depicted or imagined, haunts the paintings of this artist so wonderfully odd. It is, I think, responsible for the strange quality emanating from her work, as if everything seen were to be transformed by the relation to it, in terms of near and far, familiar and foreign, there and absent. And indeed in her unchallenged masterpiece, that *Mill at Tidmarsh*, 1918, of which Simon Bussy speaks so highly, these elements combine in a way that at once invites the observer into the scene, and leaves the observation bewildered. Her vision, of which she thought only a part was successful, gives the same effect of crowding and closeness, and of almost hieratic distance as the great portrait of Lytton, and the other noted land- and object-scapes I shall be referring to. Indeed, the stranger and more original of

Carrington's flower pieces have this singular paradoxical structure of closeness and odd-angledness, seen as if from another place, whether in plunging perspective or in a sideways set, an anti-natural choice. I have chosen to restrict myself here to a few portraits and landscapes, but the points made here could easily carry over to the rest.

If the *Hills in Snow* just discussed is set side by side with *The Mill at Tidmarsh*, remarkable similarities are to be seen. The white empty space in the center of the former is carried over and translated as the black ellipsis at the center of the Tidmarsh mill, the hollow through which the water is to stream, and its *reflection*—for indeed it is the curve and the reflection of that emptiness, turned black, that make up the cental gap in the Tidmarsh picture. It is in correspondence with the black swans, who are brought in for the occasion by the imagination, black hole and reflection calling for black symbolic swans. The reeds in the water serve the same purpose as the pickets in the Hurstbourne picture, sticking up from the base of the painting as if to measure its ground, whether the matter be snow or water.

The crowding of the house and the trees bunched up together, red and orange and brown against the green of the water and the black of swans and hole, reminds us of other disturbing work done in exactly the same period, for example, by the German art colony at Worpswede near Bremen (where Paula Modersohn-Becker painted), where there is that same atmosphere of gloom and myth, of homeliness and menace, of domestic peace and legendary darkness all about, particularly with the way in which the eye is made to follow the clear and engulfing lines in a central-point perspective, toward that black hole, as if by an ineluctable current, inescapable.

The vertical lines of the picket fence and the reeds play against the horizontal lines of the wood house, the dark moments of the picture against the central opposition of white wall and black hole, the outlooking windows against the inturning of the picture until the mind is dizzied by its own reflection. Most onlookers would, I think, agree with Simon Bussy about the worth of this picture.

Nor are its lessons lost. The three pictures I want now to

discuss take their unmistakable strength from a quite noticeable play of presence and distance, of curves and strong up-
and outstanding lines, together with that strangeness of perspective. *The Farm at Watendlath* of 1921 (now in the Tate
Gallery), strikes the eye at first as principally a primitive
painting, above all in the shapes of the two white-clad figures,
tiny in the road outside the grey-white houses, under the blue
hill, in all of which there is something immensely naive and
touching, down to the stones in the little stream at the base
of the picture. The outlook seems as innocent as that of the
little girl standing there gazing at the house, as the white of
the sheets hung beside the house stretching back to the trees
at the left, whose line is continued by a stone wall winding
in a serpentine fashion up the hill, its stones echoed in the
stone wall at the right, continuing the picket fence by the
house on that side, and then the dispersed stones by the
stream. The same shape, that elliptical one already seen in
the empty central space of Hurstbourne and the reflection of
the Mill House in the river, is here caught between the path
and the house door, and, as if in a mirror image, like that
reflection, behind the house, of the lowest hill, with its stone
wall ridge dividing it and accentuating the repeated elliptical
shape from in front of the house. Above that hill, and behind
it, the immense curves of the other taller hills, comforting
in their roundness, but not unlike great overlying buttocks,
stress the femininity of the scene. The same rounded forms
are to be found in the orange and green full shapes of the
Mountain Ranges from Yegen, Andalusia (1924): hills and
mountains had a particular appeal for Carrington—even as
the idea of mothering did not. Her attitude in this can be seen
as more masculine than feminine, or at least ambivalent from
the gendered point of view.

Withal, a great sophistication is responsible for this effect. Like these latter mountain ranges, with their high
curved hills taking up the space until the sky has only a small
piece of the picture, this massively hill-oriented painting at
Watendlath is constructed as a witness to the memory of the
act of painting itself. "I sat," says Carrington describing this
picture's making, "and drew a white cottage and a barn . . .
sitting on a little hill until it grew too cold . . . . The trees are

so marvellously solid, like trees in some old Titian pictures, and the houses such wonderful greys and whites, and then the formation of the hills so varied" (NC, 57).

That immense overarching curve of the background hill, visible in the Hurstbourne watercolor and in the Watendlath painting, is translated in a 1920 painting of *Tidmarsh Mill and Meadows* by the lowest branch of a tree at the left, extraordinarily curving all the way across to the right side of the picture, which is framed on right and left by immense and dark tree trunks. This organizing curve stretches from above the cart and its wheels in the foreground, over to embrace the top of the median tree, harmonizing the wheels along with it, and the same central dark space at the bottom of the house, now seen as small and without menace, making of the picture a quiet and calm statement on happiness, notably in the absence of human figures.

Another strong picture of this same cart before the house, *Cedar Tree at Tidmarsh*, also of 1920, has it standing spare and central against the dark green and navy blue and brown of the branches, that green echoed by a paler green in the foreground, and against which the orange and pink highlighting stands out most strikingly, whereas in *Tidmarsh Mill and Meadows*, the effect is gentled by the light and the distant beauty of the mill; the cart seems an adjunct to life, a simple trace of the work laid by for the instant.

The final instance of this overarching curve I want to consider appears in an oil of 1923 (there is also a watercolor sketch of the identical scene), entitled *Fishing Boats in the Mediterranean*. The hills in the background here are low-lying ones, and the trees upon them, as well as the houses nestling into them, by the backs of the sea, have that primitive look commented on in the Watendlath picture. But the hills are taken under the wing, as it were, of two crossing gigantic poles, which reach up against the sky, in the same way as that overarching branch in *Tidmarsh Mill and Meadows*. I would place this alongside the Watendlath picture for the same mood, that of a naive confidence in some organizing principle for the scene, not a logical one but no less comforting for its human projection upon the natural: here the fishing poles and boats, there the walls stretching up against the hill, as if to mend what nature could not. We might think of the American New England nature poet Robert Frost in contemplating Carrington's sense of landscape and the place of human constructions within it; they seem often in the same mood as that of Frost, whose walls and lines and vision are so deeply about some form of mending. Carrington's greatest pictures always seem aimed at binding together more than at display. That is, I think, the secret of her peculiar warmth even in the midst of that haunting binary sense of the present and the distant and that oddness of perspective which is felt in all her landscapes.

Flower Paintings, Excitement, and the Vanitas *Tradition*

One flower painting by Carrington—*Begonias,* of 1927—that she gave to Olive the housekeeper until 1929 at Ham Spray, has haunted me since the time I first saw it. Everything in it: its angles, its colors, its presentation, all are odd. In it there predominate, almost clashing, the colors orange and pink and green. Not only are those not my favorite colors, by a long shot, but I could not have conceived of their fitting together: perhaps indeed they do not fit, any more than Carrington herself. In it, the vase of flowers sits at an odd angle, as if one were to be looking at it from the top, and simultaneously, from the side. The table on which the vase sits is tipped up, and the whole appearance is unusual. Against the form of the begonias in their strange pink and orange, the flowers outlined in black on an off-white cloth under the vase look stranger still, painted unnatural flowers read against flowers painted real, black and white read against color, pattern against pattern. You might say these doubly different flowers had been painted by someone who saw the world in a different way, but who was perhaps unaware of that: the effect on the viewer is startling, as I see it.

For Carrington, painting flowers was in no sense painting lesser things; it is in fact in relation to these creations that much of her excitement is visible. On the 15th of April, 1921, Carrington writes to Lytton that she has not done even four hours that day "for the great godess (sic) ART," but finds it unimportant, because she has painted four tulips, each lovelier than the last. "As usual I feel I am on the Brink of a discovery, on the verge of painting the best picture I've ever painted." As usual . . . on the verge: the phrasing is characteristic of an enthusiast about work and living, an excited perceiver whose intensity kept her on the edge.

Now it is, I think, no accident that Carrington's relation to the painting of flowers is so highly charged: Ah, she says, I must paint this today or, at the very latest, tomorrow, for these flowers will die . . . Even for those of us who react unexcitedly in general to the painting of flowers as a genre, preferring landscapes or portraits, for example, to still life, some of these pictures seem couched in direct speech. Carrington's reaction to the particular and the perishing has something remarkably moving about it and its specific hereness and nowness: here, these flowers, now. This face on this person will endure, for a while, this landscape for longer; but these flowers just brought me, (or given me by Dorelia, and found in her garden: WHY, oh why, is Ham Spray, alone among "all the gardens of flowery England," such a shambles as a flower source?), or that I have just gathered in my own garden, or that mean something especial to me in this moment—here, in the dining room in Cap Ferrat, these flowers on the table: "Tomorrow I must, in spite of everything, paint them—oh dear, there seem such hundreds of things to do: tiles, pictures, tidying-up, unpacking . . . ," (March 19, 1929), but these flowers, now. They preserve friendship, loveliness, nature, and art together. Like Virginia Woolf's justly celebrated *Moments of Being* held firm and lasting with all they comport, nevertheless, of the particular and the monumental, or exactly because of the precise perishing they undergo. As in her beloved Proust's great preservative and salvatory project of permission—the artist has the right and duty to save the moment for us all—each true artist makes something specific into something, precisely, of moment.

"I've just finished a picture of a Begonia, but I don't know if its any good. = Tomorrow I shall start another picture" (September 11, 1930; DC/LS). Begonias, fuschias, and Dorelia John's garden: these in combination give a curious sort of "internal peace," and an ability to start always over: tomorrow I shall start . . . It seems rather a waste, says Carrington, to have so very much material and be able to make nothing of it. Yet she made of it, I believe, quite a good deal.

Paintings and Personal Endurance

So it is with Carrington: a few of her flower pictures convey the positive side of the whole *memento mori* tradition: not "look upon this, for you will die," but rather: "see this now, and keep it, against dying." Her greatest pictures are able to join presence and distance in this fashion. So her haunting and celebrated portrait of Lytton lying down reading, in the form of a *gisant* upon a tomb, in its closeness and yet its intimate connection with death imagery, both draws us in and holds us at a distance; the same applies to *The Mill*, with its deeply foregrounded dark hole, similarly joined with death imagery, as is its passage under the house like a tunnel reflected in the stream—which also draws, against our very will, the observer into the painting until we wake up with the feeling we are behind it.

I would place the *Farm at Watendlath* among the greatest of Carrington's productions, in part because of its combination of presence and distance. On the side of presence, I would list the primitive lines and observing figures in front of the farm as they appeal to and speak convincingly of the child in all of us, looking on the scene in its greys and blues and white: mother and child holding hands upon a path, looking back at the house held forever against the extraordinary feminine lines of the hills, like breasts and like, also, the *Mountain Ranges at Yegen*, with their similar shapes against the horizon. The laundry is reassuring on the line, the horizon is high and the feeling is primitive, primary, as if at the beginning of something, or of many things. It may well be that such a personal reaction parallels that of Carrington's reaction to Jane Austen: I cannot read anything else by Jane until I recover from this excitement. These pictures, I believe, will preserve Carrington's likeness as an artist well past her, and our, time.

❦ 7 ❦
How We See,
How We Are

Seeing the Self

This tale of art and life would seem, using Lytton Strachey's expression in one of his letters, to have in itself a
strange "writeaboutability." It is, however, complicated by
the difficulty of picturing, in language, the art it specifically
concerns: art is a world, says Virginia Woolf, "where no stories are told," and the points of view taken upon it by the
participants, involved with each other in a sort of group
politics, and then by the latter-day disciples, enthusiasts, and
commentators, are each set at a different angle.

If, elsewhere in this book, I am sketching a feminist picture of a particular danger for women, and their absorption
in their other—to the seeming or real detriment, of their own
self-valuation, as specifically in the cases of Vanessa and
Carrington, it is all the same notable, and no less part of the
feminist picture I choose to paint, that through this other, as
Virginia through Leonard, the self can often be found, and its
experience intensified. As Roger was, for a time, nourishing
for Vanessa, and Gerald and Ralph for Carrington, so in the
relations of Vanessa to Duncan, and of Carrington to Lytton,
there can be found another tale of mutual sustenance—if we
care so to read it.

So the tales of self-portraiture I care to end on are, in
some sense, all of them, ambivalent ones, for differing reasons. They are tales of multiple exposures, of ups and downs,
of concealment and openness, of secrets and revelation: these

women, so very good at seeing, self and others, had—as who does not? but so lucidly—their difficulties with being.

All the relations of these creators to their own art were fraught with complication: Roger's estimate of his art was not always of the most transcendently cheerful, no more than Virginia's or Vanessa's of theirs, or Carrington of her own. (Or for that matter, as we have seen, Duncan's of his . . .) To Vanessa's repeated laments over the dullness of her pictures compared to those of Duncan Grant, those obsessive and haunting declarations of lessness and drabness in regard to the beloved other that Duncan was, Roger's own laments over his paintings (often in relation to the paintings of Duncan and Vanessa herself) make a strange rejoinder. As if we were each of us, always in relation to the other as to the self, to have our own stinging self-doubts. But that is only part of the story as we tell it eventually to ourselves, and sometimes to each other. No matter how long and how arduous a story it proves to be, and whether it be celebrated or modest, the telling is bound, in the long run, to matter.

Virginia: Becoming What We Are

What one envies more than anything is simply life.
Virginia Woolf (VWD: II, 158)

What I most am: very rapid, excited, amused: intense.
Virginia Woolf (VWD: IV, 260)

Where shall we go? How happy I am.
Virginia Woolf, (VWD: IV, 288)

Perhaps even more than in the case of most writers, Virginia Woolf's selves—expressed in her actions as recounted by others, her letters, and in her journal, for herself—are often quite distinct, even different. She of course maintains she dislikes herself in her letters, finding them artificial, redolent, "sprayed about" with the perfume of intention, from a mind of bubble and foam—whatever atmosphere she means to create. They are in a way anathema to her philosophy of the free soul—present even from the beginning ("So now there was nothing that one could not say, that one could not do, at 46 Gordon Square"; MB, 174), being moreover too heavily dependent on the other person to make readily available the lightness of unartificed touch sensed in the journal. Carrington's exclamation to Gerald Brenan about letter-writing goes in the same sense: "Oh if only one could write nakedly. In complete intimacy" (February 26, 1923). She does not, as Virginia does not, think it possible, in spite of the extreme sensuality of the brain thus passing over into the writing hand. Carrington to Brenan: "I like to enjoy very slowly the sensation of writing to you, making sentences which only you will read . . . What might not one say?" (February 18, 1913). Nor can that kind of happiness both Virginia and Carrington take in the trivial always pass easily into letter form: the private here is somehow not sharable with even one other: "We privately are so content. Bliss day after day. So happy cooking dinner, reading, playing bowls" (August 28, 1939; VWD: V, 231). Something so simple set down is there for the self and not for the other. Patriotism in time of war seems difficult to reconcile, as she says explicitly, with this light touch, these inessential and heart-filling occupations. But we remember: "Thinking is my fighting" (May 15, 1940; VWD: V, 285), after all.

Yet that very lightness of thought and almost transparent expression is in some intimate sense often and deeply joined to a sweep of instantaneous feeling that is able to, apt to convey vitality itself. Her imagined gait allies the energies of walking to the intensities of writing, the love of which she so frequently exults in. In the following lamentation (by the writer "chained," she says, "to her rock"), the powers of language and those of sensation are so aptly met that they break, at the end of the passionately visual outpouring—an outpouring nevertheless coolly careful of each of its words—into a bouquet of brilliantly contrasting colors:

> No one in the whole of Sussex is so miserable as I am; or so conscious of an infinite capacity of enjoyment horded in me, could I use it. The sun streams (no: never streams floods rather) down upon all the yellow fields & the long

low barns; & what wouldn't I give to be coming through
Firle woods, dusty & hot, with my nose turned home,
every muscle tired, & the brain laid up in sweet lavender,
so sane & cool, & ripe for the morrow task. How I should
notice everything—the phrase for it coming the moment
after & fitting like a glove; & then on the dusty road, as I
ground my pedals, so my story would begin telling itself;
& then the sun would be down, & home, & some bout of
poetry after dinner, half read, half lived, as if the flesh
were dissolved & through it the flowers burst red & white.
(August 18, 1921; VWD: II, 133)

This conditional telling of mood goes far past the realm of
the explicit literal narration of fact to reach the imagination,
circulating objects and reactions, letting the emotion break
through, into bloom.

The diary also photographs the sense of scene, as well
as the scene itself, maximizing details: for example, from a
dinner at Herbert Read's we note the decor etched in high
clarity and the moment etched there with them: "Steel chairs,
clear pale colors: talk of pots; brainy talk, specialists talk"
(February 20, 135; VWD: IV, 281). In the journals, the force
of such scenes set in relief provides a steady anchoring point
against the easy flow of anecdotes in an abbreviated version,
for the memory, whereas in Virginia's letters they often serve
as links between the correspondents, moments offered to be
looked at together. In one letter, Stella Benson's drawing
room full of a "light faded grey" has a purely descriptive and
aesthetic value, but sets the tone of the letter, as opposed to
the extraordinary picture in Virginia's journal of Vita as she
reappears, grown fat and with heavy lipstick and bright nail
polish, a picture held up to be contrasted with the earlier
picture Virginia had of her, radiant in the market in the full
flush of their mutual love. We are saddened with her, as if
we cared too about Vita; this sense of the visual enlivens
everything Virginia writes, of course, but particularly as we
feel her emotions involved: in a letter to Ethel Smyth of
November 12, 1935, the red is not just applied and cosmetic,
but colors instead the entire picture: "Then Vita came;. . . . I
can't really forgive her for growing so large: with such tomato
red cheeks and thick black moustache—surely that wasn't

necessary: and the devil is that it shuts up her eyes that were the beaming beauty I first loved her for, and altogether reduces her (to look at) to the semblance of any fox hunting turnip stalking country lady" (VWL: V, 447). The moustache stands out in the photograph so mercilessly framed in permanence—Virginia's mental hold on everyone getting the letters now includes all of us. These punctual brilliancies give us the illusion of a double presence, ours to the scene and Virginia's to us.

The scenes are set pictorially, at an angle. Virginia writing to Stephen Spender (June, 1935; VWL: V, 407), takes up the idea of perspective in relation to his present point of view on D.H. Lawrence, which has value for him now, but less for her, as she is in a past relation to that author. The notion of angling was to matter greatly to her, the slant given to anything: on December 9, 1939, she is wondering whether to begin an article "with a definition of angle, to explain my angularity?" (VWD: V, 250). Angularity, precision, exactness: never is the picture drawn with a blunt point, and rarely is it painted with sweeps of pastel colors.

But behind and around this profusion of bright-colored scenes, backing it up and giving it profundity as creative fiction is this great "pressure of meaning" (VWD: V, 282) that is its living essence. For it is not a question of "surface bloom," but rather of depth. Gathering in so much of the external, as she says, she has somehow to relate inner and outer, the self and the scene, without asking that they be united (writing to Ottoline Morrell, October 4, 1935; VWL: V, 429): "Now Leonard has turned on the wireless to listen to the news, and so I am flicked out of the world I like into the other. I wish one were allowed to live only in one world, but that's asking too much." Sensing that she writes more about herself than Leonard does about himself (VWD: IV, 174), she has somehow to make this mix work: not just the horizontal one between inwardness and outwardness, or that more vertical mix of up and downness of writing (a fact she shares with all other Virginias writing other books; VWD: IV, 262), but transitions in general, about which she was deeply concerned (VWD: IV, 281: "A very difficult problem: this transition business"). For combining the living and the writing worlds, the exigencies of life as rush and people—after each visit, that necessity to draw oneself in "from all those wide ripples & be at home, central" (VWD:V, 299)—and that other quiet writing time in which the mind can take its flight, the perfect preparation proves indeed to be the journal. Its combination of writing and mood depiction, its very mode of realization, is already pressing together events into a strongly lived texture spontaneous but nourishing, already bearing the changes at their most intense, already concerned with finding for them the shape they most intelligently require. To her original idea she has to cling, whatever anyone says, in order to complete what she envisions. As Roger Fry saw the world always benevolent, in a dispensation Virginia comments on with humor, or as full of "awfully swell" masterpieces of art, so she sees it as potentially full of great novels. And the fortunate reader of the journal sees that potentiality itself, in this case, being aware of its own gathering nature: "now I must press together; get into the mood & start again. I want to raise up the magic world all round me, & live strongly & quietly . . . The difficulty is the usual one—how to adjust the two worlds. It is no good getting violently excited: one must combine" (VWD: IV, 202).

And just this combination bestows, in her journal as well as in her life, the fullest possible intensity on the moment— the question is, always, a variety of the same issue: how to make "1 hour and 35 minutes blaze" (VWD: IV, 5). Such blazing energy is nourished exactly by the violence of alterations in emotion, of those swings in sentiment between happiness and despair that are familiar to us from her journal, whether she is looking at the present or, as in this case, the past. About Cornwall, early on, she remembers back from 1921 (VWD: II, 103); "children running in the garden. A spring day. Life so new. People so enchanting. The sound of the sea at night." To cram it all in, to savor every moment, it all has, somehow, to be written; again in August, 1921: "It goes too quick, too quick. If only one could sip slowly & relish every grain of every hour!" (VWD: II, 128). Never, she continues here and everywhere, can all the books be written, the hours be lived and fully recalled, the whole thing be captured: still in this August, people are playing a ball game, now at

Asheham, and, like the life in Cornwall, she desperately desires to keep the scene with its players, colors, light—to catch
it and hold it firm, as if the metaphor for writing were given,
once again, by the game: "I caught them at it, as I stood in
the road beneath, pink & blue & red & yellow frocks raised
above me, & nothing behind them but the vast Asheham
hills—a sight too beautiful for one pair of eyes. Instinctively
I want someone to catch my overflow of pleasure" (VWD: II,
129).

Writing in the catch mode: it is all done with texture, not
structure—thus the diary chooses, holds, preserves, like the
Proustian project. It catches as it sketches, and follows, in its
swiftness, the flight of the mind, "that old problem" (VWD:
V, 298). It is exact, rapid, ablaze. What a terrible capacity I
possess for feeling with intensity, she says, so screwed up in
a ball that I can't get in step, can't "make things dance"
(VWD: IV, 102)—the other side of this terribleness is radiant
in these pages, over these years. Not without its despair, to
be sure, often, and before the end. But what we might well
remember is the positive light: if the "thinking stuff" is like
some web in which other people's thoughts and lives are
caught, fertilizing it, the private radiance needs nourishment
only by . . . the simplest elements. The sun, say, on some
bright day in September, leaves you feeling "so pure, so good,
so high" (September 21, 1929; VWL: IV, 91), beyond anything
human, even happiness, a feeling like that in a cathedral; a
severe headache, but then "on Whit Monday the sun blazed,
making the grass semitransparent. And space & leisure
seemed to lie all about; & I said, not once in an exstasy, but
frequently & soberly, This is happiness" (May 28, 1931; VWD:
IV, 27); or on a December day, "The sun is flooding the downs.
The leaves of the plant in the window are transparent with
light. My brain will be filling," writes Virginia from London
(December 27, 1931; VWD: IV, 56). Between that plant in its
reception of the outer light and the way she wants to and
can write, with its equal blaze-catching and transmitting
transparency, there is a superbly-felt parallel. As she says
elsewhere (VWD: IV, 26, of Lytton's *Portraits in Miniature),*
"These things wont tarnish & drop & let fall their petals."

For the ups and downs, she keeps a barometer (VWD: V,

64–65), exactly what spiritual temperature she has reached, with its peaks and its lows ... Seeing a show of Duncan's, with its lightness of color, she undergoes what she describes as "a bubbly rapture in Fitzroy Street. I must ask Nessa why we are so happy" (VWD: IV, 30). That is June 23, 1931; and in November, "But oh, the happiness of this life," she writes (VWD: IV, 53), and continues: "I was thinking to myself today, few people in Cheapside can be saying 'It is too good to be true—that L. & I are going to dine alone tonight.' "

Yet quite naturally, since this is indeed a life and not just a verbal construction, dark patches come invading: "then of course, for no reason, L. is rather silent & sad at tea; Vita does not come; I cant get on with Philip Sidney; & so my perfect crystal globe has a shadow crossing it." Will dinner be good or not? Leonard is printing ... And later she adds, "But dinner was very good" (VWD: IV, 3). From tea to dinner ... from down to up to down, outer to inner and the other way. The faithful transcription of moods itself nourishes the later moods, in their own temporary despair, as in their own no less temporary elation, according to Virginia's cycle of ups and downs.

Virginia Woolf read Ruskin. Whether or not she was acquainted with the ways he had of describing sinking things, sunsets over the Alps for a striking example, her reader, following the rhythm of Ruskin's description of fading and then that of her own, may find the reading enriched by the double perception of that pathos in rapid passage:

> Now the light has left the bases, but it is far along to the left on the broad field of snow, less and less but redder and redder. Oh, glorious! It is going fast; only the middle peak has it still—fading fast—fading—gone. All is cold but the sky ... when shall I—Nay, now there is a faint red glow again on the snow fields to the left. It must have been a cloud which took it off before—When shall I see the sun set again on the lake Leman and who will be with me, or who not? All is cold now.
>
> (Ruskin, *Diary*, 201).

And Virginia's vision, so resembling Ruskin's notation of that dying of light, from blaze to lingering red, to cold, joins mood to memory unforgettably. Writing to Ethel Smyth, two months before her suicide, she describes a sunset in unmistakably Ruskinian terms and rhythm:

> Every other second I take my eyes off the page to look at the elms outside—burning orange against a deep blue. Then there the little cross of the Church against the snow. Only the snow is going. Yesterday it was a livid purple. Lord! How quickly the sun sets! Only one red slope now is left on Caburn.
>
> (January 12, 1941; VWL, VI, 460)

We become newly aware here again, reading these recalls of intensity, these shifts of mood in landscape and mindscape, of the ways in which the great impassioned writers are equally great readers of landscapes with their imprints upon the mind and its habits of passion. That very passion is enhanced, in a cycle as clear as that of the cyclo-systemic character of the Stephen family, by the self-writing of diary notation: excitement, intensity, feeling, are all allied with writing, and when one is lacking, the other is not caught.

It is not without interest to note here that just as Ruskin was forbidden the possibility—because of his mad periods—of thinking about anything that would excite him, or writing about it, and permitted only to make botanic sketches, so Virginia was required by Dr. George Savage simply to garden, and forbidden to write. But habits, like journals, die out if they are not used:

> It is a bitter windy morning, & Caburn, when I came in was white with snow. Now it is black. Shall I ever 'write' again? And what is writing? The perpetual converse I keep up. I've stopped it these 5 or 6 weeks. That excitement, which becomes a habit, is over. Why take to it again? I am dispassionate.
>
> (VWD: IV, 57)

This deficiency in excitement or this dispassion seems somehow allied with a seemingly salutary immunity to the fortunes and vicissitudes of others and the self. On July 14, 1932, she meditates on this immunity, as a "holy, calm, satisfactory flawless feeling . . . beyond the range of darts," quiet in an existence away from suffering and friction, calm and content (VWD: IV, 117)—yet it is not the same as happiness, and will not protect one from the fears of mortality and the shifts of self-evaluation writing flesh and spirit are heirs to in everyone, Virginias or not. And so, after Roger Fry's death, on September 19, 1934, she feels a fear of death: "Of course I shall lie there too before the gate, & slide in; & it frightened me. But why? I mean, I felt the vainness of this perpetual fight, with our brains & loving each other against the other thing: if Roger could die" (VWD: IV, 244). A week later, however, she can write; and with writing comes the rest, undefinable, but which she tries, once again and always, to catch: "the other thing begins to work—the exalted sense of being above time & death which comes from being again in a writing mood. And this is not an illusion, so far as I can tell." Not that it can last: that entry is from September 20th, and by October 2, "Yes, but my head will never let me glory sweepingly: always a tumble" (VWD: IV, 245). Were she to have gloried sweepingly, we would quite surely not be there with her. This journal takes us in, striking us as truth, unsentimentalized and unprettied. Unglorying, and deeply moving for that.

Later that same month in 1934 (October 17; VWD: IV, 253): "I am so sleepy. Is this age? I cant shake it off. And so gloomy." Knowing this is the end-of-the-book fate, she looks up former diaries, with their like admissions; so there is nothing to be done. But Roger is not there with his own corresponding intensity ("How he reverberated!") and no longer does his death blaze across her with all the colors of the setting sun, in her excitement and sense of loss: now just dullness and cold "and no protection . . . I can't get up any steam. I'm so ugly. So old. No one writes to me. I'm . . ." Then she catches herself, against the regret of outer glories, pulls herself up in time to get on with the modest affair of living: "Well, dont think about it, & walk all over London, & see people, & imagine their lives" (VWD: IV, 253). The inner-directed becomes the outer-directed, as it must be, for sanity, for writing and living strength.

And then a resurge: on November 2, 1934, suddenly,

"about 2 in the morning I am possessed of driving ey(e)less strength, let all praise & blame sink to the bottom or float to the top & let me go my ways indifferent. And care for people. And let fly, in life, on all sides" (VWD: IV, 260). On all sides indeed, for the radiant force of her writing, even of the diary, can best be pictured as outgoing energy, as the absolute and unrelenting encouragement in others of the resilience she repeatedly found in herself, the packed and pressed accumulation of the spiritual intensity her style urges upon its readers with its surges of emotion in both directions, its momentum building up: "How resilient I am; & how fatalistic now; & how little I mind, & how much; & how good my novel is; & how tired I am this morning; & how I like praise; & how full of ideas I am; & Tom & Stephen came to tea, & Ray & William dine; & I forgot to describe my interesting talk with Nessa about my criticising her children; & I left out—I forget what . . ." (VWD: IV, 288). Then this notation crammed and stuffed, rich in momentum, moves on to motion itself: "Where shall we go? How happy I am" (VWD: IV, 288).

The ups and downs to be shared with other Virginias are here, transcribed in what seems transparency, with its ellipses and obscurities and moments of vision and visionlessness. Were these violent swings of emotion to have been cured or flattened, the color would be missing, with the life. These are indeed the flights of the mind and soul, captured and noted in their passage, with their delays, setbacks, and profound discouragement. On November 30, 1939, "Very jaded & tired & depressed & cross" and so she has to fill her mind "with air & light & walk & blanket it in fog" (VWL: V, 248), combating the first elements, mental, with the second, natural ones: turning the pillow, taking the walk, giving the brain a larger scope, as she talks to herself about getting on with it, against the current. "Thus defeat the shrinkage of age. Always take on new things. Break the rhythm &c" (December 2, 1939; VWL: V, 248).

The breaks in rhythm, like alterations in emotional states, enable, even when they seem to impede, that very mental flight with its spiritual component intact, its energy unchallenged. In a letter to Ethel Smyth (June 6, 1936; VWL: V, 399), the question arises, never to be answered except by the life itself, with its own ambivalent response: "How can I cure my violent moods? I wish you'd tell me. Oh such despairs, and wooden hearted long droughts when the heart of an oak in which a toad sits imprisoned has more sap and green than my heart: and then d'you know walking last evening, in a rage, through Regents Park alone, I became so flooded with exstasy . . ." From that to the gloom of January, 1941, with the world in shambles and herself in depression: recounting the gloom, she attempts to be both "curt" and compressed, after a strained visit to Charleston, aware as she is of the dullness and dampness of Monk's House, the darkening days: but they will lengthen, and the despair she senses as about to engulf her, she struggles against. Because, as Virginia herself knew, the passage between moods and their writing, the shifts of self-evaluation and self-renewal, weave the very texture of the work and form into the coherent essential stuff of the sensitive soul, unshrinking and unshrunken, until it finds its "old spurt," sensitive to the external as to the internal, to all the elements of being. These various aspects, which she presented, as she said, to the sun—as we all do—are finally in anyone's self-writing, the essential. They are part of the deepest discourse answering the most urgent questions and the most urgently angled, being "the soul's changes."

Vanessa: A Tale of Two Tubs

To see her in later life, brush in hand, was to see her happy.
Angelica, of Vanessa (DK, 84)

This is a plea for our being allowed to tell our own tale, whenever we can, for through another's eyes, no matter how close that other (or, because that other may be so close), it may take on a tint foreign to our own conception of our story. No stories are told in art, said Virginia, but it may well be that one's own self-expression in that art is, in its own way, one's story of another kind. It may neither refuse or invite interpretation, but it is there and some self with it, speaking as it chooses. We onlookers read it and answer, I presume, as best we can.

Whatever the portrait or self-portrait seems to express, and however auto-destructive its mood may seem, explicitly or implicitly, any account by the other—any other—may defeat the point, detract from the chosen values, and fail to convey the particular morality the artist as speaker might have wanted to represent.

Vanessa Bell's *The Tub* of 1918, about which interpretations freely flow, brings up by its problematic character with the naked female figure standing in uneasy relation to the upended circular tub and the three flowers in the vase on the sill like some form of annunciatory signal, the specific and crucial question of self-portraiture and self-rendering, even through the figure of another. That this originally represented Mary Hutchinson, Clive's mistress, is at least a possible cause for the unease felt in the picture, as Simon Watney points out. Vanessa says to Roger Fry (September, 1917), that the figure is "rather too like Mary"; Watney comments about this remark that: "given Mrs. Hutchinson's close relationship with Clive Bell," it may begin to explain "something of the air of apprehension possessed by this picture" (SW, 146). In any case, Vanessa's reluctance to commit to any sort of print her intimate feelings, keeping no journal and remaining reserved about feelings even in her letters to her sister, lends to such expressions all the more importance: we have thus no record of her possible alterations of feeling toward her situation, only her counsels to Roger (in the same relation to her, in a sense, as herself to Duncan), and her paintings. Virginia's fascination with her sister's calm and generally closed exterior as opposed to her inner vulnerability and pain was endless; the observer's relation to such pictures as this may be no less so.

In all the radiance of the early years, when Vanessa's discoveries in art coincided with her involvement with Roger and then with Duncan, and the extraordinary mixture of work and love and dedication in its various workings out, what she would have asked to take to a desert island, says Angelica, would have been a painting by Giotto and endless quantities of black coffee: how clear the picture is, and how convincing. As the years went on, and the situation with Duncan—in which Vanessa was always the more loving, always the one wanting a completeness that the relationship was bound to deny her—found its status quo, always an uneasy one (although she had the extreme diplomacy and tact to manage to hold on to it, as none of Duncan's other lovers could have done), but particularly after the death of her son Julian in the Spanish Civil War, and then the suicide of Virginia and the outbreak of the war, Vanessa's outlook became glum indeed, and her pictures darkened. Now Angelica says of her mother, and even earlier, that she "often gave way to the temptation of self-denigration, applying it, not without reason, to her own appearance, but far more distressingly to her painting. I never heard her say she was pleased and proud of something she had done, and the effect of this attitude was demoralising" (DK, 164). This judgment passed by Vanessa on herself seems to be passed on, in its turn, to others judging her. Not without reason, says the daughter, looking at her mother's looks. And still worse, because more demoralizing (presumably, to the other-as-daughter) is her mother's viewpoint on her work. With or without reason, Angelica doesn't say this time. Vanessa's failure is here seen as a failure to encourage as she might have, to set a more cheerful example. The daughter feels deceived, and not just by the "kindness" with which she was not told she was Duncan's daughter (and thus had become at her marriage to David Garnett, the wife of her father's former lover), but also, specifically, by the judgment passed by the mother artist on herself as worth little. And again, not just in regard to Duncan as artist (whose value, says Angelica, her mother had to over-estimate in order to justify herself and her love), but in regard to her former buoyant self.

Apart from this being a definitely no-win situation, for both mother and daughter, in its terrible contrast as seen and stated with the joyous, expansive, and liberated early Vanessa, and apart also from its being, alas, a not so exceptional reaction of an aging woman to her appearance and work, justified or not, the special problem is perhaps not so wrongly stated by Angelica a few sentences later. It is about this problem that much turns, in the case both of Vanessa and of Carrington.

"In talking about her work," continues Angelica, "she was

really talking about herself, and her despairing statements about the inferiority of her painting were one interminable question addressed to Duncan who, though he may well have understood its nature, was in no position to satisfy her. She longed for recognition not so much as a painter but as a woman, and this he could not give her. . . . there must have been a strong element of masochism in her love for him, which induced her to accept a situation which did permanent harm to her self-respect" (DK, 164). Vanessa, in Angelica's eyes, had to find Duncan gifted even beyond his talent to make sense of her sacrifice of person and of personal dignity. It is upon this page that a drastically aged photograph of Vanessa in 1951 figures, and a sad photograph it is, appearing in striking contrast, for example, to her self-portrait of 1956 with a hat, in partial profile, in the Tate, expressive of an extreme intelligence. In this frontal photograph, Vanessa has hair shorn almost to the scalp, staring and tragic eyes behind thick glasses, a mouth that seems never to have smiled . . .

But more than that figures there, implicitly. Angelica does an entirely negative diagnosis of *The Tub*, wherein she describes the woman standing beside the circular shape of the tub as "stark naked and alone." Indeed she is unclothed, but the very starkness of her adjective "stark" stands out, as bare and shocking as the nude body, with which, after all, most people climb into the tubs they may be seen standing by first. (As for that, many also take baths alone.) Stark naked, says her daughter, and alone, she stands symbolizing loneliness and a moment of self-questioning, at a crisis point, like a call for help. Consequently, Vanessa put the painting, presumably too naked in its truth, away in the attic for years.

In this reading, the figure of Mary Hutchinson (clothed) has become the figure of Vanessa (unclothed, and as she says, more decent thereby), and at that point must be hidden, for what it reveals, in a sort of Dorian Gray scenario.

The War—said Vanessa later—killed Bloomsbury. But her art remains, living in spite of her self-questioning in all its spareness, like her increasing frugality ("In front of her stood the joint of cold beef from which day after day she cut a few grey slices, while at the bottom of the salad bowl there lurked some leaves of lettuce, and in the pewter dishes . . .

there were hardly enough sprouts and potatoes to satisfy our appetites . . ." DK, 165). Yet the suggested depth of that self-examination, the fullness of its potential inner state, together with the extraordinary transformation from the picture of another woman to that of the self in successive renderings encourages re-reading. The rich relation of self-portraiture and self-representation to the *act* of bathing is itself worth meditating on.

And the description given to Roger Fry in Vanessa's letter about her bathing in the presence of Duncan is worth reveling in again: "You see he wanted to shave & I wanted to have my bath (he stayed to dinner) & he didn't see why he should move & I didn't see why I should remain dirty" (VB/RF, November 23, 1911). This buoyant passage puts the whole topos of the tub in the light of a rather joyous romp, and who is to say that this later rendering of this tale of a tub does not bring back the earlier? The whole theme and imagery of bathing, of various swimmers in and out of water, proliferates vigorously in the work of Grant and Bell—like the revelation of some natural way of being both in nature and in painting, and still reflecting on both simultaneously.

The actual tubs at Monk's House and at Charleston, paid for by writing in both cases, provide an immersion in the luxury of living, as of art. A Duncan Grant *Tub* of 1913, also in the Tate, like the Bell *Tub*, shows a Matisse-like cross-hatched female standing in a tub, with her arms raised, and looking downward in a concentrated and yet cheerful position, the circle of her arms caught in the circular mirror behind her; Vanessa's rendering is indeed more withdrawn, more inner-directed than this one, and is also less curvaceous in rhythm than her Omega workshop woodcut of 1919 which it prepares, less connected also to the form of the tub. Simon Watney describes Bell's *Tub*, painted for a specific room at Charleston, as being a "strangely disquieting nude woman playing with a pig-tail of hair" (SW: 103): his disquiet and Angelica's stark shock at the unclothedness mark this picture for us, regardless of the terms in which we ourselves would express our reactions. This, it seems to me, is one of those test case pictures, about our own relation to our bodies, dressed or not, or, perhaps, our own pasts, revealed or clothed.

Bell's painting has an earlier state (1917) with a water jug resting near to the tub, with the woman on the right. Mary Hutchinson, who posed for this picture, wore a chemise, and there were some objects in the left-hand corner. Vanessa, removing this piece of clothing and these objects, speaks of this picture positively: "Also I've been working at my big bath picture and am rather excited about that; I've taken off the woman's chemise and in consequence she is quite nude and much more decent" (1918, VB/RF, n.d., no. 253). There are thus three stages to this picture in three successive years. Now I think this is an important point: Frances Spalding wonders if the "strained relationship" between the woman and the tub in the 1918 picture indicates her own sense of incompleteness, particularly at this moment, at which Duncan was more than usually unsure of his relation to her. From his diary at the time, when she and Bunny Garnett are speaking of their jealousies in relation to Duncan—a conversation he found exciting but bothersome—he writes: "I was hurt slightly by her saying she got no more from me than a brotherly affection. I was paralysed by this as I always am. I am so uncertain of my real feeling to V that I am utterly unable to feign more than I feel when called upon to feel much, with the consequence that I seem to feel less than I do." I suppose, he continues, that some passion is lacking in these feelings, because it is crushed "by a bewildering suffering expectation of it (hardly conscious) by her." And so, he says, all he can do is to build, and the word he uses is "slowly"—exactly the opposite, then, of passion—"a completely strong affection on which she can lean her weary self" (VB, 172–73). That self, expressing its loneliness here, is all the same exciting in its very expression to its author.

To be sure, then, the earlier picture has a generally more joyous atmosphere, but this one has Vanessa's attention. I believe we should take that into account, and for that reason am now dwelling upon it. In the late stage of the woodcut of 1919 called *The Nude*, the body—now on the left—is more curved and bending, more integrated with the tub. She is indeed revealing something in the change from one attitude to another. Watney explains his view of the 1918 painting: "The numerous pentimenti in this large painting seem to reinforce the significance of the act of undressing before us, a curiously apt metaphor for this further paring down of her pictorial vocabulary, allowing her to pursue that distinctive dramatisation of the qualities of related brush-marks in the context of an extremely personal iconography which abstraction could never have allowed" (SW, 103). In short, she is able to reveal her art even as she unclothes herself, disquieting the onlooker and simply playing with her own pigtail. Are solipsism and loneliness being telescoped? Is Watney's disquiet based on the separation between body and tub, or on the changes wrought in the picture to which the pentimenti bear witness? Do we tend to over-read pain and withdrawal in this mesmerizing picture? Was Vanessa so unhappy in this pictured aloneness that we are forced to picture, and *confront?* Might this not rather be an exciting experiment in the art of revelation, even, of artistic joy revealed only on the interior of that meditation?

We cannot refuse, I think, a certain connection between the two ideas of bathing and of revelation, as of presentation: the contrast of bathing and viewing in the two main protagonists of this chapter may be, in itself revealing: we could well call this: Vanessa's Version, Duncan's Version.

There is a radical difference between Duncan's calm presentation, in several copies, from 1918 (original destroyed, recopied in 1940), and 1919, of Vanessa in exactly this Omega-shaped tub—and Vanessa's 1918 version with the body standing to the side of the tub, before her 1919 version as a woodcut just mentioned, where the body, curved instead of angular, stands close to, almost mingles with the circle of the upturned tub. Duncan's destroyed 1918 version shows a richly curved yellow-green body the same color as the inner rim of the tub, where the blue water cradles the figure sensuous and slow, a hand below the left breast reaching towards the back, and the arm curves out like a pitcher handle, exactly in the shape of the tub itself, echoed by the curve of the buttocks and more strikingly still by the pitcher standing alongside the tub to the left, its handle repeating the curve. Alongside the tub, the soap in an oval form resembles precisely a sort of egg, leading to yet more reflections on the date 1918, the year Angelica was conceived, while to the right, a towel drapes over a rack in an open oval, giving the whole picture a strongly mythic sense, a kind of earth mother feeling against the rich brown of the background. The ledge behind the tub—instead of holding the vase with flowers, 2 or 3, as in Vanessa's version—gives the feeling of a yellowish-green earth, the color of the woman's body, with a clearly-marked horizon under a whitish-blue sky: again both the sense of openness and the mythic is strong.

In Duncan's 1919 woodcut of the same scene, the figure is reversed (probably due to the technique itself), with the arm curving out to the right, and the towelrack and its oval form contiguous to the tub on the left, but with the ledge transformed into a theatrical space, whose imprecise forms surround the woman's head and torso. The head is framed perfectly and dramatically by overhanging curtains that emphasize the dramatic presentational sense of the woman bathing, in a circular form, giving the gesture a sense of the beginning of the world. These pictures should be read along with Vanessa's tubs, as Duncan's version of the story . . . unsurprisingly, more about a kind of primitive unity and less about self-reflection.

As I have meditated on other bathing scenes by Vanessa and by Duncan, a certain cohesion of image has seemed to me detectable: in many of Duncan's—*Swimmers,* for example, and *The Red Sea*—what is remarkable is the rhythm of the bodies as they reply to each other and stand out against the highly marked and abstracted backdrop of waves. They resemble, more than anything else, figures in various renderings of a Matisse *Dance*—*Dance I* (Museum of Modern Art, 1909), *Dance II* (Barnes Collection, 1932–33), *The Dance* (Hermitage,1912)—none of them individualized in the slightest, but there all together and all at once in musical response and harmony.

On the other hand, the figures in Vanessa Bell's haunting *Studland Beach* are all—to the contrary of the Tub figure in her frontal stance—turned away from the observer, in their long dresses and, in the case of the two in the background, their hats. The two behind watch the group next to the water, consisting of three figures huddled on the right, two in black robes surrounding one in white, and one huddled figure on the left, again in black. Between them, hieratic in her pose and looking like a combination of goddess and sacrificial victim, stands a tall woman, in front of a dressing cabin, standing in a dark two-piece dress outlined against the whiteness of the cabin, itself against the darker blue of the water. The severe contrast between the standing figure and those huddled, the great distance, filled by nothing, between the two watching figures and the other group, the very strangeness of the scene and its almost religious high solemnity is reminiscent of the *Rückenfigur*, that figure whose back is always turned towards us in the paintings of the German Romantic Caspar David Friedrich, for example. A sadness and melancholy pervade such paintings, and yet we are taken inextricably into the scene, precisely by the watching figures in the background, who become our vicarious onlookers, inlookers almost, into the scene.

On a 1913 screen for the Omega workshop painted by Vanessa, there are once more *Bathers in a Landscape*, nude this time but again turned away, amid the strange mountainous lines with which they—like Duncan's bathers—enter into harmony. Sadness is less in evidence here than mystery. And mystery is, in my reading, the central element in the earlier *Tub* by Vanessa also, the tradition she had already proved her interest in by her other bathers. Whether this particular one represents her or not, the importance of the relation between water and the self is undeniable; the relation is more about depth than about surface, more about the self as opened to itself in this relation, and to observation of a meditative tradition than about a personal and specific sadness.

Finally, as for Vanessa's own opinion of herself, Quentin Bell points out that she and Virginia both said of their works completed, at a certain point, "this is a complete failure." In part, he says, "this was a kind of insurance against disaster, and in part it may have been an appeal for reassurance. But mainly it was due to the fact that they loved the first hours, the initial drawing and then, as the inevitable complications arose despaired. Vanessa Bell in fact was very severe on those painters who avoided those later horrors and were content with a sketch." All three of these women knew of these horrors, intimately.

I read the self and the art here as an open and yet closed figure, the tub standing also, as it were, open and yet also symbolic of closure and completion, that tub like some circle sufficient unto itself. Wait to be filled, some would still now say of woman; you are enough alone, say others: the lesson of the tub, as I read it, is simply a meditation on how to represent the reminiscence of a full past, and an openness to some deeply sensed future. The tub has to be read at once in association with the bare female figure, gathered unto itself and yet not closed off from us, whom it faces, nor from the world of nature, manifest in the background, in those flowers, nor from the world of intellect and art upon which—for all we know—it may be mediating, and in touch with which it is supposed to be seen. The figure is likely to be felt as disquieting only on the terms of others, not on its own; some figures, after all, call out not for help, but to be taken—with their clothes on or off, but their choices intact and unjudged—on their own bare terms. We should take them neither, I think as models nor as sounding-boards for our own work, self-evaluation, self-doubt, gladness or despair.

This tale might lead us, if we so permit, to some reflection about the preservation of the self as its own best interior interpreter, and judge. Might we not also conclude that the viewing of the other and the whole problematics of an artist, in life as in art, is bound to involve a necessary reviewing of the self, crucially centered in all judgments from within or without?

Carrington: Lytton Strachey Reading

But I should like only to offer to you the most worthy telling. Since you deserve the very best.
Carrington to Lytton, August 12, 1917 (DC/LS)

. . . & have I ever told you before—your appearance. I love it so much.
Carrington to Lytton, May 11, 1919 (DC/LS)

In view of the diverse readings of Vanessa Bell's *The Tub*, the question of self-portraiture as read by others takes on a peculiar significance for the woman artist. How, we might wonder, does one legitimate the picture of oneself ("yes, this is really me"), and how, the picture of another as that other? An attendant issue arises, especially pertinent in the case of Carrington. It may be possible, in a few special situations, to read through the artist's portrait done so intimately of another, greatly loved, to a potential portrait imaginable and makeable, of the loving self.

Now the fascination of Carrington's personality, of her bisexual nature and her unique appeal certainly matched the appeal of her art, exhibited or not. But in fact she had so strongly vectored her whole being towards that of Lytton Strachey that I would read, in particular, her most celebrated portrait of him as a special case of the sort I am suggesting. Many, if not most of the portraits of Lytton are done with him reading, as he is here, but usually sitting upright or with his legs outstretched, sometimes reclining a bit; never, except in this case, is he lying down. The portrait has both a strangeness about it and a strange history. It was offered at one point to the Tate Gallery as a gift, and rejected by the Tate as not one of the artist's best pieces: they would have liked a Carrington, but not that one; it will eventually go to the National Portrait Gallery, where, no doubt, it belongs.

The proliferation of portraits of Lytton reading and writing, that is, absorbed in something, has an interesting sidelight thrown on it by a letter he wrote to Carrington about staying with Roger Fry at Durbins (July 22, 1917) in the year when she completes this portrait of hers we are considering. Roger, says Lytton, is "very agreeable and alarmingly intelligent. I have just given way and agreed to be painted, but it's to be done while I write." The most frequent portrait pose we associate with Lytton is in fact that with a book, his head slightly bent, and covered, in many of the outdoors portraits, by a hat, and his beard coming well down on his chest. In every case, Lytton-with-book is what we retain a picture of. It serves to shut out the viewer from the scene.

But Carrington's portrait of late 1916 has an entirely other feeling. Everything about it tends towards the hagiographic: the pose and the angle are reminiscent of nothing so much as a saint or noble figure in a great recline: the representation of a dead body, or a *gisant* lying down on a tomb, but here holding high the text or at least the volume. The marked continuities in it all act towards the general uninterrupted celebration of the figure: the dark hair with its few separated locks over the forehead makes a visual rhyme with the black jacket, as does the russet beard with the dull orange of the book's right-hand edge and the comforter pulled up as far as the beard. Between the beard and the fabric, the extraordinarily lengthened right hand with the delicate and tapered fingers reaches up the side of the volume and out from the dark jacket cuff to contrast with the curve of the left hand; it makes a vertical divide and focus balancing the horizontal recline of the body steeply angled on its light pillow, of the same color as the wall behind the head. Whether accident or intention, the result of the crossing of the horizontal and vertical lines makes just as noble an impression as the evident eulogizing of the face—this painting is that of a saintly figure, the book held up almost as the suggestion of a cross.

When we examine the studies for the painting, we see the hands were originally pictured as together, and crossed over in a rather intricate fashion upon the right-hand page of an open book, rather than separated and contrasted in their pose, with the startling elongation of the right one. The appropriate question here is surely not: how long were Lytton's fingers?, but rather what effect does this elongation produce? Upon these fingers the reading concentrates—they are the focus of stress, and their distortion—like the elongations of El Greco, like the elongated legs of the standing figure in *The Tub*—should not be blotted out. The obsessional hands can be seen as part of some mannerist or early baroque painting (the term *mannerist* is particularly fitting in view of the *hands*—"manus," the origin of *manner* and mannered, thus, the individual style of the hand, here impressively overdetermined). That the body should be truncated in this way, with nothing below the torso appearing, accentuates still more the baroque character of the scene—the statuesque form will never get up from that position, and will never allow himself more contact with the world or his adorers than this. He is forever to lie there, book in hand, looking fixedly at the text.

More interesting still, the head was originally pictured as nearer to an upright position, by about thirty degrees, thus, far less conducive to the saintly effect. The final picture is imposing largely because of the extreme patterning of recline against upright, as well as the impression of high asceticism playing against the richness of color and fabric, where the green of the wall against the red-orange stuff brings in, as if by a further hint, the colors of Christmas. The painting is done at Christmas-time, and says both evidently and subtly what I am suggesting: this is quite definitely the picture of an idol, done by a believer. It is an icon. It is Carrington's Lytton.

Now the point I want to make is not so much a point about Lytton, bookish, witty, bizarre Lytton, as about Carrington who so loved him. Carrington starts her diary of January 1st in the new year with her reflections on that picture and, by an appropriate if minor footnote, dates the first day of the year 1917 still as 1916. To a large extent, this rendering of Lytton by Carrington sets the model for their lives, and for her death. When he died, sixteen years after this, she made a laurel wreath for his head and tried it out on hers first ("it was a little large. I went in and put it round Lytton's head. He looked so beautiful. The olive green leaves against his ivory skin. I kissed his eyes, and his ice cold lips. The sun shone through the open window," and later, when she was urged out for a drive, "I knew while we were away men would come with the coffin and take Lytton away. That was what I could not bear . . . All the time I thought of Lytton with his pale face lying on the white pillow with the green leaves," HB).

This picture, then, could be read as a trial for a death portrait, a rehearsal of a death scene, in which human love mingles with a more worshipful attitude of looking up to the beloved figure, pictured in a noble and lasting form. My reading of it, as the truest picture of Carrington's love, seeing herself so often through Lytton and in relation to him, stresses the problematics of our own attitude toward her attitude toward him. That Carrington should have wanted nothing more, after his death, than to huddle herself in his jacket, to enmesh herself in his relics, as she says, these longings are in

all probability marked as reprehensible by most readers—
we want her to get herself together, start painting, be, well,
herself—and there she is, forever, in her diary and her soon-
to-be-ended life, refusing still. She is condemned not only by
many of us, for whom she never would have cared, but by
him, whose judgment she so hung on, and mostly by herself.
We cannot, however we care for her and for what she represents as artist and as woman, change her text, reassure her
that patriarchal disapproval is to be disapproved of, even as
it is projected on to the self:

> That craving for death which I know he disapproved of
> and would have disliked. If I could sit here alone just
> holding his clothes in my arms on the sofa with that
> handkerchief over my face I feel I would get comfort, but
> I know these feelings are bad. And if I become bad then I
> should feel he would disapprove and all would be worse.
> So I must and cannot go backwards to his grave. . . . What
> can I do. . . . What does anything mean to me now without
> you. I see my paints and think it is no use, for Lytton will
> never see my pictures now, and I cry.
>
> (February 1932; HB)

When she took her life, six weeks later, it was not that
she had not tried to live without Lytton, just that she saw no
point in it. It is, again, around this point that readings of
Carrington tend to turn; so powerful is the story of the end—
that it takes over our own story and demands to be repeated:
she borrows the gun to kill rabbits, she says, is left alone
because it seems safe, fixes a rug so it will look like an accident, misaims the trigger and does not die immediately, worries that the doctor who rushes to the scene will be upset, and
sends him to have a glass of sherry. She tries to reassure
Ralph her husband that she will recover and that it was a
mistake, and says quietly that she has bungled it all, her life
and her death. So powerful a story is it that even Michael
Holroyd's massive and authoritative biography of Lytton
ends with the story of Carrington, quoting Gerald Brenan as
saying: "No one could understand it." I wonder, first, why
not; and second, what the story itself, partly about the despair

of living through the other, might also be about, in relation
to an artist who is—and it may matter—a woman.

To take it as a warning tale is all too easy: we have, as
we know and she knew, to lead our own lives. Otherwise,
the long fingers of Lytton and others, perhaps even our own
fingers, long or stubby, might find themselves pointing to
some living figure, so intimately related to another's dying,
as "bad." I'd like to think of it as, to present it as, somehow
more complex and challenging to the mind, and maybe the
soul, than just that. Going back to the portrait of Lytton in
recline that I am presenting in some sense as proleptic, we
read Carrington's reflections on it, and find the presentation
of the verbal text no less complicated than the visual one.

It is an entry written in her diary, then, on the first day
of the new year, but written to Lytton as if diary and letter
were inseparable, as if he, even here, were present through
and to herself; the very intensity of this conviction renders
possible the opposite scenario I am trying out here: that by
an extreme reversibility, the true Carrington self-portrait is
her portrait of her love of him. In any case, the identification
is strong:

> I wonder what you will think of it when you see it. I sit
> here, almost every night—it sometimes seems—looking
> at your picture, now tonight it looks wonderfully good,
> and I am happy. But then I dread showing it. I should like
> to go on always painting you every week, wasting the
> afternoon loitering, and never never showing you what I
> paint. It's marvelous having it all to oneself. No agony of
> the soul. Is it vanity? No, because I don't care for what
> they say. I hate only the indecency of showing them what
> I have loved.
>
> (January 1, 1917; ["1916"] DG, 52)

What is it to be an artist and not to wish to show? We
know, I presume, what it is to be in love and want that not
to show—but art has often seemed to be about something
else. And yet in a sense, it should be about interior forces of
creation, instead of spilling forth: it might well be that the
step toward exhibition is less psychologically fulfilling than

the initial steps of conception and realization. We have perhaps made too much of a matter of the difference between
private and public, between the silent and the manifest. Carrington's case is, visibly and textually, a case in which the
private and the public are accorded different situations from
whatever the regular ones have been supposed to be. Just as,
here, the diary and letter are confused, the one included in
the other, the receiver made part of the writer; just as, in the
portrait, as I read it, the artist is made part of the subject
reading, revealing herself and her love so terribly, or so wonderfully, that she longs not to expose it. Not, as if they were
to be equivalent, to send the letter the diary includes, or the
message the portrait conveys.

But there is yet a further complication: "never never
showing you what I paint" and "the indecency of showing
them what I have loved." Surely the beloved "you" of the
address to Lytton is as far as humanly possible from the
other "them," who are un-Lyttons at large, and the "dread" of
showing Lytton what she has wrought should be different
from the "indecency" of showing the public at large whom
or, as she says, "what" she has loved. The very confusion of
all the terms of intimate and public, on the level of writing
(letters and diaries) and on the level of exhibition (that of love
and portraits) makes the further identification or confusion
of person and portrait, of beloved other and loving self less
impossible to grasp. Again, I wonder how we can fail to
understand it. I have no portrait of Carrington; I see her very
clearly.

It may take a revision of our point of view about self and
other, and call for less of a moralistic pointing the finger at
the choice Carrington finally made, after having tried a six-
weeks conformity with the will of others, the pull-up-your-
socks and get-on-with-it mode of thought. Perhaps the multiple sorts of experience and of affection associated with art
could help us redefine other sorts of anguish than those relating to the whole bundle of sadism/masochism complexities
and simplicities, and the proliferation of documents and
speculations of the *Smart Women who Love too Much*, or the
Intelligent Women, Stupid Choices school. I do not believe
Carrington's life should be seen as exceptionally tragic either

because her love was of an extraordinary sort, or because she died by her own hand at its absence; I see it, in fact, as more exceptional than tragic. I have wanted to invoke and yet shift the time-honored formula of great-art-from-great-suffering, that is, the art of pain, by seeing it here as a choice enabling Carrington's passionate discovery of the self, that selving that goes past pain to art.

For I do not think one can claim that Carrington did not find herself, not finding her art her whole story. That in the end she should have made her own choice is surely not to be discounted as unworthy because it does not enter our own moral framework. It does not, in fact, enter mine, and I have no longing to defend either self-sacrifice or suicide as ways into art or out of pain. But I do want to defend, on whatever terms I can muster, the choice made by anyone—the woman artist in particular—to find the terms of her own art and life, and to make, albeit not along the lines considered more normal, the portrait of her own most passionate involvement, whenever and however she can, leaving it up to others to try, or not to try to understand.

It may come about that one day, as we read along in her diaries and pictures, in those letters and other texts that we peruse, following our own lines, we shall find ourselves no longer part of a "them" before whose eyes the exhibition of an unusual love or an unusually couched self-portrait will seem indecent. We might somehow—by some readerly miracle of perception—find ourselves becoming part of the "you" in the self, to whom, in the long run, the greatest and most intimate diaries and portraits are addressed. That may well be the way the right address or self-address is finally to be found.

Notes

1   Personal Criticism

The initial quotation is from *Moments of Being: Unpublished Autobiographical Writings* (ed. Jeanne Schulkind [New York: Harcourt Brace, 1976]): I would hope above all to be capturing a sense of what these women were like, as well as how I think of them. The relation between their early lives and their later ones is discussed at some length, in the case of the Stephen sisters, by Louise de Salvo, and Thomas C. Caramagno in particular: see the chapter on Virginia's life for more details.

This is, of course, a question of linking, and the quotation from Virginia Woolf about the way in which female texts "continue" each other in their reading and writing is exemplified by Nancy Miller's recent "Writing Feminist Criticism," included in her *Subject to Change: Reading Feminist Writing* (New York: Columbia University Press, 1988), p. 6. Virginia Woolf is here speaking—as often—says Miller, commenting on that "web" of citing and rewriting that we are all part of, of the universal from the point of view of the woman writer. This is not just a privilege for a few female writers, but, in all probability, a felt necessity for feminist critics. Just so, I would add, the going against expectations practiced by all these women, voluntarily or not, finds itself in some remarkable continuity and might be so seen.

As for the continuity between teller and told, the difficulties are immense, and the inspiration multiple. I am invoking here especially Carolyn Heilbrun's persuasive *Writing a Woman's Life* (New York: Norton, 1988). Examining what it is to write that life, she urges us to call upon the collective consciousness that will empower us to create, by our narratives, fresh lives for women.

They will have to be lived with courage, but will never be—as she narrates them—devoid of the humor that courage would seem to bestow. The person whom Heilbrun would have us bring into being is, as she boldly puts it, "woman herself," at whatever age. (Wherever, or rather whenever we are now, it may not be until later that we can see our way to delight in her, and in her—and our—power of telling.)

Heilbrun makes the case for the recognition of power and control necessary to a lucid feminist self-consciousness; it must hold up against that "rhetoric of uncertainty" which Patricia Meyer Spacks detected in so much self-writing by enormously accomplished women, where they somehow wrote about inadequacy instead of ambition, turning a tradition-honored face of modesty toward the universe (Heilbrun quotes from her *Imagining a Self* [Cambridge, Mass.: Harvard University Press, 1976]). Only in that way can the "woman's quest for her own story" (Heilbrun, p. 18) described by Sandra Gilbert and Susan Gubar finally exert its own potential efficacity over the plots of closure and safety and domesticity that impede woman's becoming herself, in youth or age.

Miller's warning about women's lives being particularly vulnerable in their "relation to the culture's central notions of plausibility" and her pithy statement: "To justify an unorthodox life by writing about it is to reinscribe the original violation, to reviolate masculine turf," both of which are taken up by Heilbrun, are particularly appropriate in relation to these three women, whose choices were unusual. Finding "the courage to be an 'ambiguous' woman" Heilbrun puts in first place: that term comes from Deborah Cameron's discussion of certain male attitudes *(Feminism and Linguistic Theory* [London: Macmillan, 1985]), as she observes that according to these (alas) not altogether extinct ways of seeing, "Sex differentiation must be rigidly upheld by whatever means are available, for men can be men only if women are unambiguously women" (pp. 155–56). It may well be, as is certainly the case with both Virginia and Carrington, that the ambiguous woman has more difficult a time, and is more at risk in meeting with the "clear sense of self" Spacks speaks of (p. 23).

In the evaluation of the remarkable marriage of Virginia and Leonard, a woman of genius and a man of talent, Heilbrun calls upon the very moving description given by Nigel Nicolson: "She deeply respected his judgement on what meant most to her, her writing; and he, lacking the flight of soaring imagination and recognizing that she possessed it, shielded her, watched her fluctuating health, nurtured her genius, and with instinctive understanding left her alone in a room of her own, while he remained always available in the common room between them" ("Introduction" to *The Letters of Virginia Woolf*, ed. Nigel Nicolson and Joanne Trautmann [New York and London: Harcourt Brace, 1976–1980]: Vol. II, 1912–22, pp. xii–xiv).

The courage to be: what Paul Tillich taught, by that title, so many of us to care about has now found a different focus. It is surely reinforced by that saving sense of laughter in common, that freeing impulse Heilbrun calls upon. Shared texts and shared attitudes are part of this community I invoke in my acknowledgments, and among the texts shared are those that Virginia left as traces. The traces Quentin Bell speaks of in his biography of his aunt *(Virginia Woolf: A Biography* [New York: Harcourt Brace, 1972], Vol. I, p. 138) are what we would most profitably follow: we can in any case be glad she left them.

2   These Working Women

About Bloomsbury, Nigel Nicolson's "Bloomsbury, the Myth and the Reality" (NFE) is enlightening, and our collective reinterpretation of that very myth as well as that reality has accumulated its own myth. The more memorable parts of it tend to spin about in our own heads in much the same way Virginia describes Duncan's canvases: like so much white wine—thus the colorful atmosphere in the Strachey household, described by Douglas Turnbaugh in his *Duncan Grant and the Bloomsbury Group,* and various descriptions of them all by each other: one of the more delightful accounts is that of Forster, commenting on the painting Roger is doing of him in December, 1911, hilariously indicative of the general reception of Roger's paintings: "It is too like me at present, but he is confident he will be able to alter that. Post-Impressionism is at present confined to my lower lip which is reduced thus . . . and to my chin on which soup has apparently dribbled. For the rest you have a bright, healthy young man, without one hand it is true, and very queer legs, perhaps the result of an aeroplane accident, as he seems to have fallen from an immense height on to a sofa." (Quoted in *The Omega Workshops: Alliance and Enmity in English Art, 1911–1920,* ed. Anthony d'Offay, foreword by Pamela Diamand (London: Anthony d'Offay Gallery, 1984), n.p.

And again, take Lytton's comments: neither he nor, any of the Bloomsbury group rated Roger's painting very highly—nor alas, did Roger generally, as his letters to Vanessa witness. Lytton writes for Carrington a wittily dreadful and yet affectionate rendering of the atmosphere at Durbins on July 22, 1917 (LS/DC): "Roger is very agreeable and alarmingly intelligent. I have just given way and agreed to be painted, but it's to be done while I write. There's a frightful arrangement of Nina Hammet, just done by him—full length in blue check, most carefully disposed red and yellow still-life, and a still-life face. Le pauvre homme!. . . . Roger is extremely active—but over what it's difficult to say." This statement bears out Vanessa's rather more affectionate alarm over Roger's always rushing at something: it would be hard to imagine a starker contrast in personalities than that between Roger and Lytton himself.

But Roger himself was not so depressed always about his art: in some of his letters, he comments on the favorable reception of his own painting in France, in comparison to that of Duncan; about the latter, he makes the point that he does not think it is just envy and jealousy on his part that inspires him to say this. "The strange thing is the universal verdict against Duncan and very much in favour of Vanessa and me. Vanessa's a revelation to them, but on the whole they seem to like me best as far as I can judge. You won't cry all this aloud on the housetops: I know it would look too like jealousy of D. which I really haven't" (RFL: II, 447; April 12, 1920, to Margery Fry). And, again to his sister, about the opinion of the Polish artist Landau, "He thinks that Duncan and Vanessa are not at all in the same rank as I am—that in Paris their sort is too common to count. I don't attach much importance to this except as a general indication of where the younger men in Paris are but at least it helps me not to suffer from Vanessa's tacit assumption that nothing I do is any good. I do feel now that I've got somewhere where no one else in England has but I don't think that that'll help me in England" (RFL: II, 516; November 1, 1921). These comments shed some light on the England-France controversy, taken up again in the chapter on Vanessa's art.

Roger impulsively rushing about, as Vanessa describes him, figures large in the picture composed for us by many details in the various letters: the teeth-knocked out episode is recounted in a letter from Vanessa to Virginia, and it includes his breaking a few ribs beside; Virginia then re-counts it more drolly still. The tragic outcome of Roger's involvement with Josette Coatmellec may be seen as the result of two such intense personalities rubbing against each other: Josette, feeling criticized and unloved, has already shot herself when Roger sends her a letter on March 31, 1924, expressing his tenderness for her and regretting her "fantastic explanations of what I say and write"—you can't believe, he says, "how simple, innocent and naive I am" (RFL: II, 552). He seems indeed to be right about his qualities, which are endearing at their best.

In a sense, all these three women had about their work that sort of simplicity and rushing-at-ness that Roger had in his life: in a letter to me of 1988, Quentin Bell, discussing the art of Vanessa and Virginia, points out how greatly they preferred sketches to completion. This quality Carrington certainly had; her conception was, like theirs, more interesting to her than any carrying through of it.

About Carrington, see Gretchen Gerzina's careful biography *(Carrington: A Life of Dora Carrington.* London: John Murray; New York: Norton, 1989); an extraordinary portrait of her ("Carrington, a Modern Witch") by Julia Strachey is to be found in *Julia: A Portrait of Julia Strachey,* by herself and Frances Partridge (Boston: Little Brown, 1983), p. 120. I have wanted some of this sunlight to communicate itself to my text. About the refusal of honors by Duncan, Turnbaugh's is the supposition I take up here (p. 75). Virginia's wondering about herself as the Grand Old Woman of English letters is quoted in Lyndall Gordon's *Virginia Woolf, A Writer's Life* (Oxford: Oxford University Press, 1984), p. 252, and her description of Vanessa's Tate picture done by Duncan is just right: she sits there in the posture of a watcher, in her "layers and folds of formality" with her narrow fingers and black-pointed shoes, her "charms pared away . . . this consequential Victorian character." Gordon quotes, in this context, Sidney Waklow's comment in 1910 about Vanessa's iciness and cynical artistic temperament as opposed to the far more emotional Virginia, who was "interested in life rather than beauty." From Virginia's demonstrativeness, Vanessa always, as she was the first to say, shrank away (pp. 130–31).

3 *Virginia*

The vexed problem of the relation of Virginia and Vanessa's young life to their lives later has its most explosive chapter chronicled in Louise De Salvo's *Virginia Woolf: The Impact of Childhood Sexual Abuse On her Life and Work* (Boston: Beacon, 1989). She details the young lives of Virginia and Vanessa from the point of the view of their molestation by their half-brothers Gerald and George Duckworth; "George," says Quentin Bell in his biography of Virginia, "had spoilt her life before it had fairly begun" (Quentin Bell, *Virginia Woolf: A Biography,* p. 44). The story of Vanessa and

Virginia subjected to George's "violent gusts of passion" (recounted to Clive, quoted p. 71), to the massive glooms of Leslie, and to the intense depression of their mother Julia Stephen, leads to de Salvo's conclusions that the future lives of the sisters had to repeat these patterns, and their pain. ("I still shiver with shame at the memory of my half-brother, standing me on a ledge, aged about 6 or so, exploring my private parts": so Quentin quotes Virginia as saying in his biography of her, p. 44.)

So also, in this way of telling, Vanessa's life with Duncan from 1914 to 1965 would reproduce the set of conditions she had known: "her life with Duncan repeated the pattern of perpetual mourning and profound depression" of her mother, and—since she had been so abused so young—she was set up for accommodating herself to Duncan's male lovers in the household, being Duncan's "perfect darling" as she had been, in the former household, "the Saint" (De Salvo, 74–75). In addition to comforting him when his love affairs did not go well, she was obliged to comfort him also over his guilt at hurting her. (!)

Both sisters manifested a great deal of nervous tension, thought Leonard (De Salvo, p. 83); Vanessa as well as Virginia, suffered bouts of "mental instability." Virginia's attacks of madness and her suicide are attributed, by De Salvo, directly to her early life, whence came her vision of herself encased in "cotton wool," thus incompetent to manage. Learning that she was an unwanted child was intensely harmful, and the bombing of London the final blow, but the abuse gets the main accent; because of it, and in order to distance herself, she had early on created the character for herself of "Miss Jan," writing her diary in order to build, by words, her own psyche and her sense of self, partially by the aid of this other.

Thomas C. Caramagno, in his precisely argued "Manic-Depressive Psychosis and Critical Approaches to Virginia Woolf's Life and Work," *PMLA* vol. 103, no. 1 (Jan. 1988), pp. 10–23, shows how the "neurotic-artist" model functions easily for doctors and critics and for herself in Virginia's case. The archetypal madwoman label was easy to deal with, whereas, holds the author, "biology, not psychology, is the primary mechanism of predisposition" (p. 12) in the case of her manic-depressive malady, to which she was already predisposed by the cyclothymia of her family. Her difficulties in "establishing an identifiable self-structure" (p. 13) are detailed here, together with the sudden accesses of heightened moods, intense sensual experiences, and bouts of excessive and occasionally incomprehensible volubility: her imagination, said Quentin in the biography, had no brakes then (p. 15), as she felt a kind of omnipotence, an "extravagant intensity of perception" (VWL: IV, 231). Writing was the only way to compose, to synthesize: fiction, says Caramagno, was good therapy for her. (And a little more too.)

She had to make interpretations, and so do we, but also to put up with incoherence and non-coherence. The author summarizes the findings of Edward Wolpert *(Manic-Depressive Illness: History of a Syndrome* [New York: International UP, 1977], p. 584): "Depression is a vicious cycle because it can fabricate evidence justifying itself, fulfill its own prophecy, and 'read' in the environment what it has produced. Depression is not reliable evidence of a repressed suicidal wish, and guilt, if primarily due to a temporary neurohormonal imbalance, may only be the result of a disturbance, not the cause"; he concludes that whatever "deep-seated conflict" we discover may be "as much a fabrication of hers as of ours." There may be no biographical order to this, even as we long for one. And so, avoiding a coherence in her fiction that would make things too resolvable, she invites countertransferences (p. 19), frustrating those who would fit things too easily. Her fiction, says Caramagno, "draws attention to our attempts to clarify and systematize complex texts. The author liberated herself from reductionism by creating characters out of her symptoms and allowing them room to assert their own 'truths' within ambiguous contexts" (pp. 20–21). She gave voice to her illness, he says, authorizing herself, representing without simplification, accepting not just her illness but her wellness. "Critics," he ends, "must likewise learn to suspect psychological preconceptions that reduce complexity to simplicity by eliminating the meaning of complexity. When a psychological profile makes too much sense, something has been ignored" (p. 22).

The warning about our reading of Virginia is, I think, to be taken seriously. As some counterweight, we should surely insist on her development through her reading as much as through her early life. As a notable example, essential for my topic here, take her absorption of Walter Pater's luxurious and silken celebration of the passing of moments: impressionism gone literary. What is most real for Pater, and subsequently for Virginia, reduces itself to something single and sharply felt, from among the flow of those multiple "impressions, images, sensations . . . that continual vanishing away, that strange perpetual weaving and unweaving of ourselves," in which we have, according to him, our momentary being. (From "The Conclusion" to *The Renaissance: Studies in Art and Poetry;* I am using the 1893 edition, edited by Donald L. Hill, Berkeley: University of California Press, 1980, p. 188.) This crucial passage abounds in such extensive and suggestive implications for a whole way of sensitive perception and hyperintense living (and the tinge of "anti-normal" against the staid Oxford society of the time) that Pater once removed this conclusion from this study, "as I conceived it might possibly mislead some of those young men into whose hands it might fall" (See p. 186). It is beautifully and fully expressive of that deliberate choice of conversational and critical flux, that fluidity of borders and points of view encouraging to just the aesthetics of the moment that Virginia's work and being—visible in her letters and diaries—so movingly incarnates. *Mrs. Dalloway* (London: Hogarth Press, 1968) and Virginia's memoirs justly entitled *Moments of Being* are her unspoken allusion to Pater's high, ardent, and passionately lyric intensity of the burning and flame-like instant that concludes *The Renaissance*. For he finally restored the passage, and it is justly famous, beginning: "Every moment some form grows perfect in hand or face; some tone on the hills or sea is choicer than the rest; some mood of passion or insight or intellectual excitement is irresistibly real and attractive for us,— for that moment only." Great passions, he writes (and he first wrote of "high" passions, removing the adjective as too provocative) "yield you this fruit of a quickened, multiplied consciousness" and since art best contains and conveys them, it offers "the highest quality to your moments as they pass, and simply for those moments' sake" (p. 188). The whole affair is high, the style is—to use the proper word—exciting, and its numerous progeny would be most improperly overlooked, undervalued, or orphaned. Pater's hand and thought and intense emotional involvement should not be, cannot be disavowed. (Perry Meisel's *The Absent Father* takes up the relationship at length; New Haven: Yale University Press, 1984).

Add to the fleeting and the momentary, the deliberate instability of attitude, the longing not to dwell solidly in any place: this, above all, is the feeling in *The Waves* (Harmondsworth: Penguin, 1964), to some extent accounting for what the contemporary critics referred to as "its strangeness" (for example, Gerald Bullett, in *The New Statesman*, quoted on the back cover of Harcourt Brace's 1959 edition of *The Waves*). This very instability is reminiscent of what Stevie Smith, in her *Novel on Yellow Paper* (London: Virago, 1982) establishes as the contrast between the "foot-on-the-ground" person who will be made nervous by reading this novel, for whom it will be just a "desert of weariness and exasperation," who should therefore just put it down, and the "foot-off-the-ground person" the reader might turn out to be (and if you do not know which you are, says Stevie Smith, come with me, and you will find out, pp. 38– 39). The solidly placed foot-on-the-ground person will have grave doubts about this work, says she. The cover of this edition carries Carrington's picture of her brother Noel's wife, Catherine Carrington—more interweaving.

4 Together, with Virginia

In *The Sister's Arts: The Writing and Painting of Virginia Woolf and Vanessa Bell* (Syracuse: Syracuse University Press, 1988), Diane Filby Gillespie brings a needed corrective to the usual notion of the sharp division between art and writing on the part of the sisters. Their inter-nourishment is surely at the heart of things, as is their parallel mutual envy—the most discussed testimony to this may be Virginia's ambivalence about maternity, that state of things denied her by the doctors because of her fragility: thus the interest of Vanessa's peculiar suggestion that Virginia involve herself with the writing of giving birth. Of course, Virginia's feelings about maternity were scarcely unambiguous (to understate the case): take Vanessa's letter to her sister about her having told Barbara Bagenal, who has "threatened" to return to visit Virginia, that "you objected violently to the maternal instinct & that I rather agreed with you" (VB/VW, beg. April, 1928).

Jeanne Schulkind points out the Talland House connection in her introduction to Virginia Woolf's *Moments of Being*, where the passage is found on p. 111; it seems to me that the relation with Virginia's well-loved Proust is all the more valid because of this first connection—this is exactly the network of references in which Virginia lived, within the flight of her mind. Virginia's closeness to Ruskin is commented on elsewhere in this book: with Proust between them, they make a good threesome: impassioned great souls, leaving us their great writing.

5 Vanessa

About Vanessa's choice, as about Carrington's, to live with a homosexual, we could adopt the point of view—as others have—that it was the pain of their early life that rendered the choice understandable: having experienced so much suffering, one expects it, courts it, finds it, and lives it. Thus, De Salvo comments: "Vanessa had begun to fall in love with Duncan when he was still involved in a relationship with her brother Adrian, which had been ongoing for a few years; and she decided that she wanted to have a child with Duncan when Duncan was involved with David (Bunny)

Garnett. Vanessa could not predict that she was inviting trouble and pain for herself; but she was unconsciously reproducing a set of conditions that would involve her in an emotional life very much like the one that she witnessed and also lived with in her childhood home" (p. 75).

This negative standpoint shows up also, according to the same commentator, in the most domestic of Vanessa's undertakings, those paintings of the nursery and of teas therein and the images she painted on the wall of the actual nursery room showing, in the former, the nurses with their disapproving faces, castigating a little girl, and an unsmiling little boy, or then a child pulling away from the nurse, a mother looking at her son as he looks away, and, in the latter, the beasts of prey as what Angelica called a "petrified zoo" (De Salvo, p. 79). These are not, says the author, paintings "about the sustenance and happiness and lively glow of how children are treated in the nursery," but the evocation of a place of pain, an institution of sorrow. The nurses are larger than anyone else, and the figures of the children, diminished. The entire picture seems on the negative side, of the life as of the art.

Now the question of the art of Vanessa, Duncan, and Roger has its own natural problems, relating to the importation of French canons to England, and to the question of post-Impressionism. One thing is clear, and that is the immense excitement Cézanne proved for these painters once they discovered him: see Clive Bell, "The Debt to Cézanne," in *Art* (New York: Capricorn, 1958), pp. 135–44. Roger's laments about getting to Cézanne too late are found in his "Retrospect," in *Vision and Design* (Harmondsworth: Penguin, 1937), p. 233.

Simon Watney, one of the most informed commentators on this period of English art, maintains in his *English Post-Impressionism* (London: Cassell, Studio Vista, 1980), that Vanessa's canvases of this period manifest a "startling originality" (p. 82) in her response to Post-Impressionism. But then, when showing her "retreat" into representational and less avant-garde art, he picks out those paintings with featureless figures, speaking of the loneliness of the situation, and says of her work and of Post-Impressionism, that in the time between 1914 and 1918, "the social order from which it had sprung seemed to have been shaken to its foundations" (p. 132). This situation he finds comparable to that of Virginia Woolf: "recognizing that the necessarily radical changes in social structure which she looked forward to, could only be read at the expense of the very culture within which her own writing had value and meaning . . ." According to Watney, Vanessa's previously clear "self-image as an

artist" faltered, the chance to adapt Post-Impressionism was lost—
except in the area of private decorative projects, so that Design was
once again separated from High Art—and, perhaps worst of all, she
and Duncan were, finally "misunderstood and misdirected" by the
same Roger Fry who had fought so hard for an independent English
school of painting that would be up to its times. In rejecting the
importance of subject matter, and subsequently of abstraction, he
deprived them of the feeling of relevance to any "issues of context"
(p. 134), and—by extension—of context.

Watney's judgment of Vanessa is harsh, his story of her story,
sorrowful in the extreme, but no more so than that of Angelica:
"This was particularly the case with Vanessa Bell, who, in the
darkening of her palette and generally timid approach to matters
of subject, appears to have preferred to follow Grant mutely and
uncritically into painterly reaction. Her courage failed" (SW, 134).

Her courage failed. What a masterful recall of all the nobility
of Englishness in its hope, glory, and glorious defeat: The light that
failed. Like all those myths faltering: Kipling, the colonies, and
now Bloomsbury. Because she followed, first Roger into his conception of a Frenchified avant-garde, and subsequently Duncan, when
he deserted abstraction—thus, into his misguided and influentially
sad *arrière-garde*—she lost her clarity of self-image. (Duncan's own
point of view about the shift in his work toward the representative,
in about 1916, is clearly stated in the sketch of his life he prepared,
preserved in the Tate Gallery Archives [no. 7241.1]: of his shaped
and abstract paintings, he says quite simply that "they didn't lead
anywhere.") The case is clearly stated: for Watney, Roger, the authority and the theoretical leader, had in this case, and in this
reading, equally failed her, and Duncan, and English art.

At first glance, his case is not unconvincing: so that looking at
the early and late pictures, it is tempting to see a close correlation
between her darkened palette, and her personal and privatized
despair, tellingly represented by Angelica's description of the gradual sparseness and silence of the Charleston meals, as contrasted
with the effulgence of the earlier life, full of wine and work and wit,
and by the photograph of Vanessa with cropped hair, thick glasses,
and an unsmiling face on the same page as her discussion of *The
Tub*. And yet this is perhaps to confuse, unwisely, the interior evolution with the exterior witness borne it in the world of art: they are
not necessarily identical, nor is it necessarily the case that the
excursion into color and French liveliness, upon which Vanessa
writes at such length in her letters, was the harming agent here.
Roger, an explorer, liked leading others to new things—even excur-

sions one returns from forever can have teaching power. And who is to say that this one failed?

6   Carrington

Virginia's disappointment over Pelican's rejection of Carrington's illustration for her book of stories is profound, and strikes the reader and the observer as justified; for example, Carrington's illustration of a cemetery and figures in black cloaks, eventually printed with Leonard's "Three Jews," simple and stylized, and somehow haunting, renders exactly the atmosphere needed. It is her grasp of the atmosphere that predominated in all her work, over the details. When a small printer rejected her woodcuts for Christmas cards because they seemed so odd, she refused to make the adjustments he called for, to make the figures look more "normal": she stuck, in most cases, to her original conceptions for her work.

7   How We See, How We Are

No stories in art: Virginia says this in her preface to the *Catalogue of Recent Paintings by Vanessa Bell* at the London Artists Association in 1930. In view of the relation between Roger Fry and Vanessa Bell, another sentence from this catalogue, quoted by Simon Watney in his *English Post-Impressionism*, p. 145, is wonderfully relevant on the issue of "no stories" but in things. "If portraits they are, they are pictures of flesh which happens from its texture or its modelling to be on equality with the China pot or the Chrysanthemum." And Roger Fry's 1909 "Essay on Aesthetics" claims, in a similar vein: "It is only when an object exists in our lives for no other purpose than to be seen that we really look at it, as for instance at a China ornament or a precious stone, and towards which even the most ordinary person adopts to some extent the artistic attitude of pure vision" (pp. 29–30, in *Vision and Design*, Harmondsworth: Penguin, 1937). The point of pure vision is, in general, the issue about which Fry's noted interpretation turns. This is precisely the kind of question discussed in what Virginia terms "Old Bloomsbury" (pp. 159–79 in *Moments of Being)*, and especially at 46 Gordon Square, where all four Stephens moved in 1904, after Leslie's death.

About self-telling and the narrative sense, much feminist work is being done, in addition to the sources quoted in the first chapter about finding and making do. In the initial chapter of the work she edited, *The Private Self: Theory and Practice of Women's Autobio-graphical Writings* (Chapel Hill: University of North Carolina Press, 1988), Shari Benstock takes up Georges Gusdorf's notion of autobi-ography as a re-erecting of the boundaries between self and other and treats it as male, similar to the project of Augustine or Rousseau or Jefferson or Henry Adams with their stable "I," as opposed, for example, to Virginia Woolf's "elastic" diary, able to hold odds and ends without necessary continuity, conscious arrangement, or by any censor or arranger or plasterer-over in the self. (See "Authoriz-ing the Autobiographical," pp. 10–33, especially pp. 15–21). Mem-ory plays tricks; Virginia finds it "nearly impossible" to name her-self (p. 26), calling herself "Adeline Virginia Stephen," a name she was not known by, as opposed to the many nicknames she had for herself in relation to various receivers of her letters: Mandril for Leonard, B. for Billy or herself to Vanessa (who had called her a billy goat), and Pixie or Pixy or Witcherina Maxima for Angelica. Seeing and hearing everything up too close, the flowers on her mother's dress, the lapping of the waves, and the wind blowing the blind out (p. 22). The too closeness leaves, as does the blind, a part necessarily obscure. In the discussion of the journal as narration, we might remember Frank Kermode's discussions, in *Genesis of Secrety*, of all narratives as obscure, as necessarily leaving a part in the dark—thus, the abbreviations and ellipses of the diary, and the embroideries or augmentations on the other hand, would be formal indications of the emotional strength of certain episodes, shortened or increased.

Susan Stanford Friedman emphasizes, in her "Women's Auto-biographical Selves" (pp. 10–72, in Benstock, op. cit.), the sense of collectivity and interdependent existence that women share in their community of identification with others, but which is foreign to most male conceptions of autobiography (p. 38). And Jane Marcus's "Invincible Mediocrity: The Private Selves of Public Women" (Ben-stock, pp. 114–46), stresses the double consciousness of women who are at once individualist and collective (esp. p. 124). All three writers manifest most vigorously the instability of the self, the woman as other, at the same time placing creation, even of a jour-nal, at the center of the universe, where the human artistic imagina-tion takes the place of God.

The question of Vanessa's self-representation in *The Tub* is vexed. Angelica Garnett, speaking of her mother's self-deprecation, says that the traditional "bugbear" of the Stephens, passed down by one generation to the next, was a "masochistic self-pity" (DK, 159). But in relation to Vanessa's art, Quentin Bell pointed out that when she complained to Duncan and Clive and Roger of her work, they told her she was wrong. Clive irritated her, in fact, by praising her work in public. Duncan, continues Quentin Bell,

> did pay her what seems to me the finest compliment that one painter can pay to another by getting her to work with him on equal terms in big decorative projects. I remember when I incautiously said that in the Berwick Decorations he was "in command" he protested vigorously and, so far as Vanessa Bell's work was concerned I think that he was right. Finally it is just worth noting that the public in the 'twenties and thirties frequently confused Vanessa's work with Duncan's. Vanessa Bell thought the public silly, but it was not I fancy a wholly disagreeable form of silliness.
>
> (Letter to the author of April 5, 1988)

About the version of *The Tub,* some of this information comes from Frances Spalding's *Vanessa Bell* (London: Macmillan, 1983), pp. 170–71; she points out the likeness of the figure to Matisse's original standing figure in *Le Luxe I* (that was shown at the Second Post-Impressionist Exhibition). Vanessa's picture was meant for the garden room, and the relation of the figure to the circular tub— there were no real bathtubs at Charleston in those days, so that this was exactly the kind of tub used—is what is at issue. Since Bunny Garnett is sharing a room with Duncan at this point, Vanessa feels particularly left out, and Spalding suggests that the three flowers, two red and one yellow, may reveal her jealousy and loneliness— her health was poor, she was cut off in the country from her friends, her children were being taken care of, and there are few paintings from this period perhaps for those depressing reasons.

The Conversation (*Three Women*) Courtauld Institute Galleries, Fry collection, 1913–1915, makes an interesting contrast with the 1917 *Tub.* The window opening and the flowers on the ledge behind the figures in each, framed by the stagey curtains in one and the panels or walls in the other, join them, being at once an opening on the space beyond and a reinforcement of the space within: Frances Spalding, reflecting on the window seen in many of Vanessa's paintings, comments on her need for domestic security in these years— the key ones for the correspondence examined in the present study. About the *Conversation* itself, she points out that Vanessa seems to have reworked and darkened the women's dresses to contrast them with the bright colors of the flowers and the animated chatter of the three women. Of its biting humor, Virginia remarks (VWL, II: 498–9): "I think you are a most remarkable painter. But I maintain you are into the bargain, a satirist, a conveyor of impressions about human life: a short story writer of great wit and able to bring off a situation in a way that rouses my envy. I wonder if I could write the Three Women in prose."

The strange colors of *The Tub*, with its warm orange-brown of the bather's body (Mary Hutchinson, Clive's friend, was originally clothed in a shirt: she took off the shirt, said Vanessa, to make it purer) and of the major part of the foreground, echoed by the darker brown of the wall to the right, to which the reddish terracotta of the vase responds, would seem to counter the presumed aloneness of the subject. These tones play against the greener-yellow of the tub's inside and the woman's hair, as well as the ledge beneath the red vase and its red and yellow flowers, and the whole picture finds a top closure in its strips of orange-brown and yellow-green above the elliptical curve of the window opening, where the base is perched upon a lavender strip. In the flowers, the yellow color alludes to the green elements, and the two red ones, to the warmer elements, while the heavy arch above them, greenish-blue, corresponds both to sky and grass, with its curved shape echoing the gentle curve of the bottom of the tub, and supporting the more rounded lines of the top like one large suggestion of a circle between air outside and tub inside, infinitely slow and able to contain the omega shape as well as the hint of the annunciation (the flowers on the sill behind the meditating figure). The colors work toward a surprising harmony. The extraordinary relation between figure and ground, between inside and out, flower and human figure, side wall or drapery and the ellipsis of the opening, further join this seemingly introverted picture of 1917 to Vanessa's seemingly extraverted *Conversation* of 1913. In each, the flowers are a color not in the rest, whether red plays against yellow, as in *The Tub*, or whether they are mixed with white, as in the earlier *Conversation*, where profusion of talk and color is the rule, and the elliptical curve in the opening swoops up and open, like the conversation itself, as opposed to the closing and enclosed lines of the window and the tub in the later picture.

We could read these as the two sides of these Bloomsbury women, their private creation and meditation, or their more open and socially conversant roles: opening or closing lines, the vivid colors or the more reflective ones, the socializing and localizing gossip in the heavy lines of the group of three, or the infinite chasm of the omega-tub and the delicate rendering of the lonely figure. In their opposite treatment of line and form and elements, the two paintings stand in an oddly complementary position to each other, quite like these two women themselves.

Virginia's remark about art as a world where no stories are told, made in her preface to the *Catalogue of Recent Paintings by Vanessa Bell* at the London Artists Association in 1930, often put in juxtaposition with the faceless portraits by Vanessa, stresses the side of things that Roger so strongly supports, and that he calls "pure vision." Among all her works, *The Waves* is surely the closest to this concept, with its structural and painterly intensity: it is this very textual intensity allied with its emotional force and its Proustian striving for the salvatory in the work of art that give it its particular importance, which I have tried to stress in my chapter on Woolf in *Reading Frames in Modern Fiction* (Princeton: Princeton University Press, 1986).

Pure vision and clear self-seeing would seem to have some implicit link, insofar as they are about lucidity, uninflected by emotion and by involvement. It is upon this clarity of vision and unself-pitying quality that I would like to lay the final accent. For when Carrington kills herself, she quotes, and all the biographical works requote, from Sir Henry Wotton, 1627:

> He first deceased. She for a little tried to live without him.
> Liked it not and died.

The matter-of-factness of the verse, its dreadful and unaffected simplicity, catch the imagination of readers, and writers: it is in no way a faked feeling, and has—quite casually—the ring of truth. This is simple telling, at its most essential. To use Carrington's own term, speaking of a drawing by Duncan, we might well "reverence" such telling. Her note to David Garnett on January 22, 1919 makes a good stopping place for this book, as she sends a message warm and very like her: "Give Duncan my love. Tell him I liked his drawing in the Burlington Magazine very much indeed. And reverence him for drawing it. My love to Vanessa also. Don't forget." (DG, 126)

Appendix 1:
Reading Vanessa

To read Vanessa's letters to Virginia, in particular, is to read an unforgettable diary of the love of work and life: everything comes out intense. On February 6, 1912, she recounts a discussion: "Roger was here Sunday and the air is teeming with dicussion on Art. They think they are getting further. I don't know. Roger's views of course are more mature than ours. He is at one pole & Clive at the other & I come somewhere in between on a rather shaky foothold. But none of us really agree with Leonard—whatever he may say to the contrary & Duncan tells me it is a gross libel to say that he does either. So your husband had better reconsider his position I think. We shall go on till doomsday I suppose" (VB/VW). That wonderful sense of inexhaustibility is just what informs these letters.

About each other and their friends, they can all afford to make adverse judgments, and Vanessa does so with gaiety: Mary Hutchinson appears "in about ten different dresses," but Vanessa doesn't "have much opportunity of judging how that couple is getting on"—of course the fact that the other member of that couple is her husband adds a certain irony to the letter. Lytton reads his biography of General Gordon, and Vanessa is sceptical: "I suppose it will be a great success won't it. It seems to me the Strachey mind is purely dramatic & that the result in writing biographies is to give a superficial & unreal effect. But don't say I said so. I must admit that both Duncan & I slept soundly (but he more soundly than I) through most of each reading so perhaps one can't judge" (April 9, 1918).

Vanessa's admiration of her sister, as she expresses it to Roger on January 7, 1913 ("really I am sometimes overcome by the finest qualities in her. When she chooses she can give me the most extraordinary sense of bigness of point of view. I think she has in reality amazing courage & sanity about life") is the visible backdrop for these letters, so very different from Vanessa's letters to Roger, with their necessary involvement in emotion: a typical letter after she has turned her affection to Duncan reads like the one on August, probably in 1914: "I'm not irritated by your suffering. I want you very much to give me something that I can take. Up to now—that is for the last few months—I haven't been able to take what you've wanted to give & because of your pain at that, you haven't been able to give anything else. But perhaps you will now." Serious, almost stern, her tone is the diametrical opposite of that she has in writing Virginia. The closeness of the sisters gives to the mingling of irony and teasing an inimitable warmth: on Noverber 22, 1918, after discussing her interest in the writers' feelings about peace ("of course the Stracheys are simply ashamed of having any feelings they can give a name to"), Vanessa urges Virginia for more news: "Roger said in his last letter that he did *not* write the most interesting letter he had ever written to me about his feelings as he knew I should not reply sympathetically. As you were just going to dine with him no doubt you got the benefit of them. So please write & tell me all about them." And so she did.

The correspondence is quite as fresh as when it was writtern: reading Vanessa is, in general, pure delight.

Appendix 2:
Reading Carrington

Some self-confessions, perhaps by their very nature, by their own deep seriousness, have their own most secret courage. Seen from a step back, the most intimate passions can be turned against the speaker, all the more efficaciously by herself. Now Carrington's truth-telling seems to intensify her self-deprecation, most famously expressed in her letter to Lytton, written upon her making the decision to marry Ralph, so as not to hang heavy on the man she loves, who cannot love her: such a statement is difficult to read in all its pain, without accusing it of sickness:

> I cried last night Lytton. . . . to think of a savage cynical fate which had made it impossible for my love ever to be used by you. You never knew, or never will know the very big and devastating love I had for you. . . . Say you will remember it. That it wasn't all lost, and that you'll forgive me for this outburst, and always be my friend.
> Carrington to Lytton
> (May 14, 1921)

This letter of Carrington's (about which she says, in the middle of writing it: "I am telling no one what I've told you. It will remain a confession to a priest in a box in an Italian church", G, p.177) is of a quite outspoken courage, as it does not try to take back what it says, even as it knows. The conclusion of the postscript is a promise of future undiscussion, of tactful silence, a confession that, even here, not enough has been confessed, and a heart-breaking plea, again, not just for Lytton's friendship, but for a restatement, a retelling of truth, to respond to hers. This masterpiece of confession and request, artless in its overwhelming sincerity, was of course to move Lytton, as it moves us:

> I'll always care as much, only now it will never burden you and we'll never discuss it again, as there will be nothing to discuss. I see I've told you very little of what I feel. But I keep on crying, if I stop and think about you. Outside the sun is baking, and they all chatter, and laugh. It's cynical, this world in its opposites. Once you said to me, that Wednesday afternoon in the sitting room, you loved me as a friend. Could you tell it to me again? (G, p.178)

She has begun the letter by a statement of her "incompetence" at saying the "great deal to say" that she must, and confesses she wrote many letters the preceding evening and night, until 3 in the morning, including one which "bared her soul;" but this morning, she says, she does not feel so intimate. Now this strikes the reader as rather an amazing way to begin a letter of confession, by saying one does not feel intimate, just preceding an outburst for which, then, apology must be made.

The truth told in this letter to Lytton is all the more terrible for being prefaced by Carrington's accounts of three previous truth-tellings at second-hand, in which she had been told by others of Lytton's reactions to her. For her to tell him of that triple knowledge, and in the way she does, here, in this marriage letter, is to confess a searing pain, worse by being inflicted indirectly, and then retold—like some dreadful plague-in-the-round, more deadly for its manner of spreading.

Alix Strachey has told her what Lytton told James Strachey: that Lytton was terrified of Carrington's becoming dependent on him "and a permanent limpet and other things." (G, p.175) Ralph repeats, in bed with her, what Lytton had told him, which alters everything for her, so that she never again goes to Lytton's bedroom for "terror of being physically on your nerves and revolting you." The third telling is again Ralph's, of what Lytton had said to Virginia and Leonard Woolf about not intending to come back much to Tidmarsh after Italy, and being nervous Carrington would have a claim on him if she lived with him for a long time. The awfulness of the recounted scene mounts: "Ralph was so happy," says Carrington, "he didn't hear me gasp and as it was dark he didn't see the tears run down my cheeks." The insensitivity astonishes the most hardened reader: to tell her, not to imagine her feeling in advance, not to detect her feeling once he had spoken, but to be, oneself, happy during and after inflicting such pain . . . Yet surely the culmination is Ralph's recounting of Virginia's recounting of the general opinion held in relation to Carrington's worth: "they all wondered how you could have stood me so long and how on earth we lived together alone here, as I didn't understand a word of literature and we had nothing in common intellectually or physically. That was wrong," she continues, asserting herself stubbornly, refusing to lie down under the attack, "For nobody I think could have loved the Ballades, Donne, and Macaulay's Essays and best of all, Lytton's Essays, as much as I."

And then, but reacting against her primary and excessively honest reaction, Carrington declares her future non-declaration: "So now I shall never tell *you* I do care again. It goes after today somewhere deep down inside me and I'll not resurrect it to hurt either, you, or Ralph. Never again." (G, p.176). Again she states the contrast, dreadful to hear and tell: "I cried last night Lytton, whilst he slept by my side sleeping happily." That "big and devastating" love she has for him, which he never knew or would know, is heart-rending in its detail: "How I adored every hair, every curl on your beard. How I devoured you whilst you read to me at night. How I loved the smell of your face in your sponge. Then the ivory skin on your hands, your voice, and your hat when I saw it coming along the top of the garden wall from my window." (G, p.177) This is what she asks him to remember, to assure her it won't be lost; this is also the outburst she wants forgiven, so that they will always be friends.

In particular, she doesn't want the all too perceptible pain to be thought of as his having wounded her (but how could it not be thought of as that?): "You mustn't think I was hurt by hearing what you said to Virginia and Leonard and *that* made me cry. For I'd faced that long ago with Alix in the first years of my love for you. You gave me a much longer life than I ever deserved or hoped for and I love you for it terribly" (G, p.178). I was crying, she says, at realizing that "some times I must pain you, and often bore you. You who I would have given the world to have made happier than any person could be, to give you all you wanted." What she has most longed for, she phrases as a child would, or a saddened grownup looking at the ideal longing of a child—and this woman-child's longing was to make the man she loves happy. Just that. Not a longing for herself, but for giving what she would have wanted to be able to.

This is the revelation and the confession that hurts most—that the selflessness she longed to give couldn't be accepted as what it wanted to be. The giving-retracting, telling-untelling, showing-concealing mode of Carrington's great letters such as this one is unequalled in its fervor, unsurpassable in its grief.

Yet we have, I think, not to forget the other side of Carrington, not to let it be overrun by our sense of her sadness. For she was—as it has been recounted to us by herself, in her journal and letters, and by others, in spoken and written testimony, as well as in their own letters—unique to the point of seeming extraordinary to those who knew her, and cared about her. Exasperating, childish, passionate, intuitive, mischievous, devious, deceptive, honest, generous, awkward, Carrington fascinated those around her, and those who now follow her diverse tracks. She engages of us what is, in us, most able to respond to the diverse sides of her nature. We must not let them be flattened out, or her original style reduced by a one-tone reading.

An extraordinary style: that no one denies her, in her writing or her living. "It's *no* good being anything but what you are and the great thing is never to do anything one doesn't feel genuinely inside oneself." (Carrington to Rosamond Lehmann, 1931, KCL) Her peculiar spellings as well as her strangely appealing childish drawings might well enter under this heading. (One of the books she most enjoyed reading, Daisy Ashford's *The Young Visiters*, is more oddly spelled even than her letters, and there is for the reader, the same kind of delight in the presentation.) Like a child too, her mop of golden hair and brilliant blue eyes, her brief attention span, and her general way of comporting herself, with her short white socks and her toes turned in, her little gasp, and her intense dislike of being blamed for anything. She would initiate things and then break them off or withdraw: this was the case with Mark Gertler, with Ralph, and with Gerald, Ralph's best friend, all Carrington's lovers. She took a particular delight in coming between people, and yet, with her strange diffidence, hesitated over each affair, its prolongation, its vicissitudes, its ending.

The doubleness of her nature was surely one of her most notable characteristics: Julia Strachey's portrait of her, to be found in Frances Partridge's book on her, pictures her as both angelic and devilish, pure and flirtatious, as a being of two totally opposed natures. Many are the testimonies to exactly this doubleness, in her androgynous attitude, as in her psychological and physical characteristics. For she had at once the air of a child and someone time had used. The sketch Gerald Brenan gives of her in 1924, when they were having their usual series of complicated interchanges about seeing and not seeing one another, about Carrington's—CIROD, as she wrote DORIC—caring and concealments, her happiness and disheartedness, sticks in the mind, it too with its ambivalences and its combination of the terrible and the sublime, the outer perception and the inner feeling; as she walks alongside Ralph, or rather, as was her custom, slightly behind him: they were arguing, she in a low angry voice, he in his naturally deep one, on which Lytton's "peculiar treble" had been grafted, so that it made a hoarse squeak:

> Beside him, looking short and squat and dressed in ugly yellowish cloth, came C. Her hair was a yellow mop; her face as it often does when she is alone, looked anxious and haggard. Her expression was disagreeable, her age might have been forty. As she walked, she turned her ankles inwards and she kept a pace behind him, as though she were an inferior. . . . Yet as she passed me I caught sight of her bare hand. It was the same hand on which I had so often fixed my eyes as though all the beauty in the world

and all my happiness were contained in it. Now at this
moment it seemed to me that nothing had altered, and
that this middle-aged, dull-looking married woman was
in some way another 'myself', since she carried about in
her so large a part of my life. I felt for her as one only feels
for oneself, loved her as one only loves other people, and
I knew that no alteration in this would ever be possible.
(G. pp. 308–9)

This "middle-aged, dull-looking woman," who says of
herself, when she first meets Henrietta, how "plain and aged"
she is, held enormous appeal for many, men and women. She,
in her turn, never wanted to give up anything or anyone she
had loved, and all the men who loved her continued to be—in
varying degrees—obsessed by her. She and Ralph quarrelled
interminably after their marriage, and yet when she died,
Ralph went temporarily mad with grief. In all her ambivalence and her self-concealment, as in her raw self-exposure
to Lytton, she makes a difficult case, and one worth reading
with all the understanding we can muster—thus the emphasis on that term in the preceding pages.

We have, then, to learn how to read Carrington, to read
her pain—but also her text—richly, in ambivalence, and not
reductively. Even as we have tried, so many of us, individu-
ally and collectively, over so many years, to read Virginia
Woolf, as richly as possible. Intelligent reading presupposes
that the growing process has as many participants as there
are readers for our tales, of ourselves as of others. Carrington's life was not, I think, made up of an inappropriate passion, either for painting or for the being she loved. Nothing
about the art she showed, in her telling, visual and verbal,
strikes us as irrelevant, either to us or in the short life she
did, in fact and in the long run, not bungle.

Finally, about self-undoing, and her writing of herself in
Her Book: Carrington's end raises a mammoth problem, that
of reading lives, like hers, so strongly marked by their ending.
The integrity of her being is nowhere so movingly expressed
as in the book of her four last years, Her Book indeed. As to
our own integrity of reading, the most we can do, I think, is to
celebrate the art of wholeness wherever we see it, perceptible

even amid the fragments of lives. It is up to us not to misread Carrington by a too-simple melodrama-of-the-ending, by a reading backward of the tragic into the whole of her life. It was, often, a life of gaiety, of a splendid sensitivity to detail and in depth—this study would have as its too-difficult aim just such a sensitivity.

Restrained Bibliography

Bloomsbury

Clive Bell, *Art* (New York: Capricorn, 1958).

Quentin Bell, *Bloomsbury* (London: Weidenfeld and Nicolson, 1968).

Paul Delany, *The Neo-Pagans: Rupert Brooke and the Ordeal of Youth* (New York: Macmillan, Free Press, 1987).

Leon Edel, *Bloomsbury: A House of Lions* (Philadelphia: Lippincott, 1979; New York: Avon, 1979).

Frances Partridge, *Love in Bloomsbury: Memories* (Boston: Little Brown, 1981).

Richard Shone, *Bloomsbury Portraits* (Oxford: Phaidon; New York: Dutton, 1976).

George Spater and Ian Parsons, *A Marriage of True Minds: An Intimate Portrait of Leonard and Virginia Woolf* (New York: Harcourt and Brace, 1977).

Simon Watney, *English Post-Impressionism* (London: Cassell, Studio Vista, 1980).

Vanessa Bell

Angelica Garnett, *Deceived with Kindness: A Bloomsbury Childhood* (London: Chatto and Windus/Hogarth, 1984).

Diane Filby Gillespie, *The Sisters' Arts: The Writing and Painting of Virginia Woolf and Vanessa Bell* (Syracuse: Syracuse University Press, 1988).

Frances Spalding, *Vanessa Bell* (London: Macmillan, 1983).

211

Gerald Brenan

Personal Record: 1920–1972 (New York: Knopf, 1975).

(Dora) Carrington

Carrington: Letters and Extracts from her Diaries, ed. David Garnett (London: Jonathan Cape, 1970; reprinted as paperback, Oxford: Oxford University Press, 1979).

Noel Carrington, ed., *Carrington: Paintings, Drawings and Decorations* (Oxford: Oxford Polytechnic Press, 1978).

Gretchen Gerzina, *Carrington: A Life of Dora Carrington* (London: John Murray; New York: Norton, 1989).

Michael Holroyd, *Lytton Strachey: A Biography* (Harmondsworth: Penguin, 1971).

Aldous Huxley, *Crome Yellow* (New York: Doubleday, 1922).

Julia Strachey and Frances Partridge, *Julia: A Portrait of Julia Strachey* (Boston: Little Brown, 1983) (for "Carrington: Portrait of a Modern Witch").

Roger Fry

Roger Fry, *Vision and Design* (Harmondsworth: Penguin, 1937).

Letters of Roger Fry, ed. Denys Sutton (London: Chatto and Windus, 1972).

Frances Spalding, *Roger Fry: Art and Life* (Berkeley: University of California Press, 1980).

Virginia Woolf, *Roger Fry: A Biography* (New York and London: Harcourt, 1976).

The Omega Workshops: Alliance and Enmity in English Art, 1911–1920, ed. Anthony d'Offay, preface by Pamela Diamand (London: Anthony d'Offay Gallery, 1984).

Duncan Grant

Douglas Blair Turnbaugh, *Duncan Grant and the Bloomsbury Group: An Illustrated Biography* (Secaucus, N.J.: Lyle Stuart, 1987).

Virginia Woolf

Complete Essays, ed. Andrew McNeillie (London: Chatto and Windus/Hogarth, 1988). (5 vols. projected.)

Mrs. Dalloway (London: Hogarth, 1968).

"Reading," in *The Captain's Death Bed and Other Essays* (New York: Harcourt, 1950).

The Letters of Virginia Woolf, ed. Nigel Nicolson and Joanne Trautman (New York and London: Harcourt Brace, 1975–1980). 6 vols., 1888–1941.

The Journal of Virginia Woolf, ed. Olivier Bell. (New York and London: Harcourt Brace, 1977–1984). 5 vols., 1915–1941.

Moments of Being, ed. Jeanne Schulkind (New York: Harcourt, 1976).

The Waves (Harmondsworth: Penguin, 1964).

Virginia Woolf: special issue, *Twentieth Century Literature,* vol. 1, 25, Fall/Winter 1979; especially Brenda Silver, ed., "Anon," and "The Reader."

additional letters, in *Modern Fiction Studies* (Summer 1984), col. 1, 30, no. 2, pp. 175–202.

Elizabeth Abel, *Virginia Woolf and the Fictions of Psychoanalysis* (Chicago: University of Chicago Press, 1989).

Quentin Bell, *Virginia Woolf: A Biography* (London and New York: Harcourt Brace, 1972). (2 vols. in Great Britain.)

Rachel Bowlby, *Virginia Woolf: Feminist Directions* (London: Blackwell, 1988).

Susan Dick, *Virginia Woolf* (New York: Routledge, 1989).

David Dowling, *Bloomsbury Aesthetics and the Novels of Forster and Woolf* (New York: St. Martin's Press, 1985).

Lyndall Gordon, *Virginia Woolf, A Writer's Life* (Oxford: Oxford University Press, 1984).

Patricia Laurence, *The Reading of Silence: Virginia Woolf in the English Tradition* (Stanford: Stanford University Press, 1990).

Jane Marcus, *Virginia Woolf, New Feminist Essays* (Lincoln: University of Nebraska Press, 1984).

——— *Virginia Woolf and Bloomsbury* (Bloomington: Indiana University Press, 1987).

—— *Virginia Woolf and the Languages of Patriarchy* (Bloomington: Indiana University Press, 1987).

Phyllis Rose, *Woman of Letters*. (New York: Harcourt Brace, 1978).

Louise De Salvo, *Virginia Woolf: The Impact of Childhood Sexual Abuse on her Life and Work* (Boston: Beacon, 1989).

referred to:

Roland Barthes, *La Chambre claire* (Paris: Editions de l'Etoile, Gallimard, 1980).

Shari Benstock, ed. *The Private Self: Theory and Practice of Women's Autobiographical Writings* (Chapel Hill: University of North Carolina Press, 1988). See Nancy Walker, "Wider than the Sky: Public Presence and Private Self in Dickinson, James, and Woolf."

Mary Ann Caws, *Reading Frames in Modern Fiction* (Princeton: Princeton University Press, 1986).

Carolyn Heilbrun, *Writing a Woman's Life* (New York: Norton, 1989).

Peggy Kamuf, "Penelope at Work," in *Signature Pieces: On the Institution of Authorship* (Ithaca: Cornell University Press, 1980).

Frank Kermode, *The Genesis of Secrecy: On the Interpretation of Narrative* (Cambridge, Mass: Harvard University Press, 1979).

Teresa de Lauretis, *Alice Doesn't* (Bloomington: Indiana University Press, 1983).

Perry Meisel, *The Absent Father: Virginia Woolf and Walter Pater* (New Haven: Yale University Press, 1984).

Nancy Miller, *Subject to Change: Reading Feminist Writing* (New York: Columbia University Press, 1988).

Walter Pater, *The Renaissance: Studies in Art and Poetry*, the 1893 version, ed. Donald L. Hill (Berkeley: University of California Press, 1980).

Marcel Proust, *Du côté de chez Swan* (Paris: Gallimard, ed. Folio, 1988).

John Ruskin, *The Diaries of John Ruskin*, ed. J. Evans and J. H. Whitehouse, 3 vols. (Oxford: Clarendon Press, 1956).

Stevie Smith, *Novel on Yellow Paper* (London: Virago, 1982).

Patricia Meyer Spacks, *Imagining a Self* (Cambridge, Mass: Harvard University Press, 1976).

Index